EFI

--EVERY FOOT AND INCH

One Man's Adventure Riding a Bicycle Across America

Perry

To my good friend
XC16

Enjoy the book

Champ
Walker

AuthorHouse™
1663 Liberty Drive
Bloomington, IN 47403
www.authorhouse.com
Phone: 1 (800) 839-8640

Published by AuthorHouse 02/22/2016

ISBN: 978-1-5049-6769-3 (sc)
ISBN: 978-1-5049-6770-9 (e)

Library of Congress Control Number: 2015921117

Print information available on the last page.

Any people depicted in stock imagery provided by Thinkstock are models,
and such images are being used for illustrative purposes only.
Certain stock imagery © Thinkstock.

This book is printed on acid-free paper.

authorHOUSE®

EFI --Every Foot and Inch

Acknowledgements

I would like to thank my family, wife Veronica, and sons Christopher and Eric for their love, encouragement, guidance and support in this cross country biking effort. My success would not have been possible without their help.

I would also like to thank photographers Rich Burk of Burk Photography and Kevin May of Kevin May Photography, two outstanding photographers, for the unique photo on the back cover of the book.

A special thank you goes to Pam Tomka who spent hours editing this manuscript.

In addition I would like to express my appreciation to all the people associated with the experience. From my friends, the excellent support staff, to the other riders who allowed me to use their image in this book and the many people I met along the way, a heartfelt thank you.

Contents

Midwest

The East

Introduction

EFI. This is an acronym for anyone who rides a bicycle across the United States of America without using a SAG wagon for a lift, walking any part of the trip or using means other than the bicycle to do so. Many interpretations have been applied to these letters. The most common use is Every Foot and Inch. Another would be Every Fantastic Inch and for those who overcame the many obstacles presented along the way Every F _ _ _ _ _ _ (fill in the blank) Inch.

Why would anyone write a book of this about riding a bicycle across the United States of America? For me the explanation is twofold. First, it describes the adventures of an older bicyclist who decided to undertake an adventure that would test his mental and physical abilities. Secondly, it illustrates and hopefully encourages individuals of every age to establish goals and do all in their power to accomplish them knowing that success is not always measured in completing the task, but in doing ones best to do so. From that perspective an explanation of terms used frequently through the journey needs attention. The two most used are EFI and SAG.

At first, EFI was just a vague notion as one of my goals. Figuring I would "bump", walk when necessary or take an occasional day off to recover during a seven week bike ride, I deemed it was not a primary concern. But as the ride across America progressed, it evolved from a vague idea to a possibility to a maybe and finally a near obsession. In fact, as the goals were presented, while they remained important, toward the end of the ride EFI was a compulsion. Of the 26 people who began the ride in Los Angeles, 17 contracting to ride the entire distance to Boston, only 5 were able to realize this goal.

My achieving this end does not denigrate those who were not able to do so. For many it was irrelevant to their enjoyment of the experience. Some who attempted to accomplish EFI were presented with obstacles that prevented them from doing so. In terms of the company supporting the ride, they held no great importance for those accomplishing EFI because it sometimes encouraged risky behavior.

Other terms that may need some explanation are century, peloton, route rap, and SAG. As used in the text it is assumed the reader has knowledge of these concepts but maybe not in cycling sense. A century is a one hundred mile ride. Some insist a century can be ninety five miles but for purists a century is what it is; one hundred miles.

A peloton (from the French for platoon) is usually a group of bicyclists involved in a race. For the purpose of this manuscript it refers to our riders of our group forming a two by two line riding in unison from point to point.

For our purposes, the route rap was a meeting after each ride for the group to discuss the next day's agenda. It would include the route we would follow, dangers along the way i.e. hazardous R.R. crossing, bridges, etc. and points of interest we might want to visit.

The SAG acronym refers to the concept of Support And Gear. Used often in the text, it refers to any group or individual who helps the bicyclist attain their riding intention. Usually it is a vehicle that the rider would use to "bump" ride to the end and has equipment needed to assist with mechanical problems. With this as the background, let the adventure begin.

Chapter 1

THE START

"YOU DID WHAT!!?" exclaimed Dr. Phillips, a noted orthopedic surgeon in the central Illinois specializing in knee procedures. "Let me explain it in terms you can understand. You have about 100,000 miles left on that knee. How fast do you want to use them up?"

"What are my options?" I responded

"Swimming or bicycling" Phillips exclaimed, still shaking his head somewhat bewildered that I would continue an activity that had done, and would continue to do, destruction to my newly repaired knee. I could mentally read the words "dumb ass" in the imagined thought bubble over his head. This conversation took place in the summer of 1996. I had just undergone arthroscopic knee surgery the previous week and the knee felt well enough that I ran my regular five mile route around our town. Granted, it was on concrete and asphalt, but I was proud, nevertheless, and figured Dr. Phillips would commend me for getting back to my regular exercise routine. It was obvious from his reaction he was not especially pleased.

Consequently, I felt my only viable option for continuing my aerobic exercise routine was riding a bicycle as swimming was not in the cards with no pool available year round. At the time I thought it would be a "piece of cake" but, as I was soon to learn, there is more to biking than just cruising around the neighborhood looking at the pretty flowers and fending off joggers who wander aimlessly down the bike path. That is especially true if I were to maintain the level of fitness I had attained through years of weightlifting and running. Thus began a journey that culminated when I rode a bicycle from Los Angeles, CA. (Huntington, Beach) to Boston, MA. (Revere Beach). 3,415 miles (give or take) was the official distance and the deed was

1

accomplished from May 9th to June 26, 2009. Since then, I have also completed a journey on my bicycle down the East Coast from Portland Maine to Daytona Beach Florida, for an additional 1,700 miles. As expected, both experiences turned out to be quite an adventure. However, this story is about my transcontinental journey across the Unites States.

Following Dr. Phillips advice I decided to purchase a bicycle that would meet my needs for enduring long distance cycling. Washington IL. is blessed with one of the top bicycling shops in the area; Russell's Cycle and Fitness. I realized I would need more functionality than the three gears I had on the Sears special I had ridden on occasion since the early 80's. So, I purchased a Specialized Crossroads cycle which was a cross between a touring/road vehicle and a mountain bike; commonly referred to as a hybrid. Even though I was not particular familiar with the different styles, I was sure a mountain bike was out of the question. After looking near and far in this "neck of the woods", I ascertained there were no mountains to climb and few off road trails that I had no interest in riding. With no idea of the extent to which I would become involved in the sport, I began the journey. In the interim years I progressed from a very tiring initial 10 mile traverse around Washington to an annual average of approximately 3,000-4,000 miles. This progression started at 10 miles three times per week and ending in 30-50 miles 6 days per week.

Recalling my first prolonged ride of 10 miles I was surprised my legs became very fatigued following a short 4% incline climb. At that point I began having doubts about "biking" as a source of exercise. My average speed in the inaugural phase was around 12 mph, which is considered normal for beginning bikers. Today, seventeen years later, I average around 17 mph and with a nice "tailwind", 19 or 20 mph for a 40 mile jaunt. In fact, my best training speeds before the RIDE averaged 15 mph. In addition, I do at least one "century" each year as I trek from Washington to Champaign.

During my early rides, I recall one day in particular averaging 16 mph over 25 miles and thinking that was pretty fast. Today, if I don't at least average 16 mph I feel I have had a bad day and may even be losing my MOJO. Okay, for some out there I know that is not a great speed but as you will learn, my Clydesdale body is built for the steady grind and not "horse racing" at top speeds. So speed is a relative term. I know my capabilities and admit, upon reflection, with as much riding as I had done, thinking it was adequate preparation would for riding cross country, was in fact, NOT the case!

Chapter 2

BACKGROUND

As a prequel to the actual start of the ride I will address the adjustments made through the "run up" to the cross country trip. As mentioned earlier, the first bicycle I purchased following my decision to become a "biker" was a Specialized Crossroad. It was a cross between a touring and mountain bike with panniers (metal structures attached to the vehicle used to support carrying cases) and a bag that enabled me to carry virtually everything I would need for long distance rides. Examples of items I eventually carried in this carrier included, bike tools, spare inner tubes, pry bars, knives and an assortment of odds and ends including food, that I felt appropriate for rides of considerable length. It was an excellent bicycle and is still ridden today. Eric, my youngest son, uses it to ride around his residence in Carbondale, IL. where he lives.

I also carried a bottle of water that I figured would be helpful for distance riding. Today I carry a minimum of two bottles. One of my biggest mistakes, early on, was to deprive myself of water thinking it was better for a conditioning program. That thinking came as a result of my early sports activities which promoted that kind of behavior. As I look back, it was really stupid. As a teacher and coach for 35 years, I actually knew better but thought I would revert to the "old days" where water was restricted, to develop both physical and mental conditioning. Those days have long since passed and I should have known better.

I kept my first bike for over 10 years before purchasing the newer Specialized model in 2006 as it met my particular needs during that time period. The newer bike was a beautiful vehicle as it was lighter and had newer, better components than my old one. However, it was still relatively heavy (around 30-35 pounds) with the panniers and carrier bag over the rear tire. Upon reflection I am somewhat embarrassed to admit that I did not maintain those bikes in the manner they should have been. Cleaning or oiling the chain, checking the tire pressure and rarely taking it in for a tune-up was my modus operendi.

In March of 2009, in the midst of the "great recession" I was persuaded a different, newer upgrade would make my cross country trip significantly easier. Earlier, I convinced myself the sales personnel at Russell's offered that advice in order to sell equipment. However, about a month before the big ride, I negotiated a good deal on a new bike. Let it be stated clearly. It absolutely made a difference. I purchased a Cannondale Synapse. Weighing only 19 pounds, and no panniers or kickstand it substantially reduced the load. I was amazed when I took my first ride. Exerting the same amount of effort I used on my previous bike, I was able to increase my speed by one mile per hour. That might not seem like much but over long distance it really is. After purchasing a bike of that caliber, I figured I should go "biker wild." In addition to a tire pump (something I should have had for years) a helmet (I never used to wear one. Yea, I know, not real smart, I always wore a baseball cap) biking jerseys (I had always worn a cotton t-shirt) biking shoes, (always wore tennis shoes) and an assortment of various other biking equipment completed my apparatus needs. I figured with all this "bike" stuff, I would be ready for my cross country jaunt. Ha! Not even close.

Chapter 3

PLANNING

Riding a bicycle across the United States was an idea that came to me while working on my computer researching information to enhance my lesson plans for the history classes I taught at East Peoria High School. It was in the winter of 2005. Looking at a map of the U.S., the idea just popped into my head. Knowing I rode virtually every day, and retirement was soon approaching, the thought of doing something like this became very intriguing. My first inclination was to do the trip solo. Riding around almost always "lone eagle," so it didn't seem like an unreasonable thing to do. In fact, I even mapped a route across the country from Los Angeles to Savanna, Georgia with the idea I would actually do the solo trip. The more I thought about it, and factoring in all the logistic problems, I figured I had bitten off more than I could chew. However, the idea was still attractive so I started checking into support groups that led tours across the country.

Having determined my primary goal was to bike across the country, other important goals soon developed. It was important to ride the entire distance as opposed to using other means of transportation including walking, SAG vehicles or any other mode of transportation; thus EFI. Visiting as many of the historical sites as possible to enhance my knowledge of places I had taught about for 35 years was another of my primary goals. And, engaging with the local inhabitants in the different regions of the country to get a sense of the cultural differences that exist in those regions was also vital. With these ambitions established I was ready to begin.

At this point in the planning stage, I had about three years to go before I would put my plan into practice. An abundant amount of time remained to decide whether to ride with a group or ride solo. Advantages and disadvantages to both means of riding would be weighed before the final decision was reached.

The first major advantage as a solo rider was I could determine how far I would ride each day. If it were a particularly difficult riding day, or if I were fighting a bout of illness or if the bike incurred a mechanical malfunction, I only had to rely on myself. Thus, I could stop for a few hours, or even days before continuing. With a group that would not be possible. Each day's ride from point A to B was pre-determined so, if such difficulties arose, I would have to SAG with the group losing EFI. As a solo rider, if I felt I wanted to ride 150 miles it would happen. If I wanted to do 25 miles that wouldn't be a problem. Solo riding was in character with my lifestyle. Most of my life I considered myself a "lone eagle". I rarely followed the crowd in my career or life so why start now?

A second major motivating factor favoring the solo plan was that I could spend as much time as I wanted visiting local historical sites. Doing so would fulfill one of the major reasons for doing the trip. That is, visiting the many historical places I had taught about during my 35 years as a history teacher. The idea of no time restraints was very appealing.

A third major consideration in solo riding is that it virtually eliminates the competitive factor. In a group setting it's natural for individuals, with the type of personalities conducive to attempting such a feat, to compare themselves to the other riders. I had that vision before the ride and as I discovered, that was exactly the case. Solo riding appealed to my sense of independence and freedom I felt I needed to fulfill the objectives of the ride. The solo approach would be a definite possibility if I were to do another cross country ride. But, I was smart enough to make what, for me, was the correct decision.

After thoughtful consideration, riding with a support group had an overwhelming rationale for doing it this way. Safety was the biggest and most convincing argument for the group ride. With a group, safety in numbers helps insure that the rider has a better opportunity to complete the ride. Accidents, mechanical failures, illness, and other assorted obstacles can be dealt with more successfully, as those barriers present themselves during an adventure of this nature. Knowledge of the dangers inherent in such an undertaking are more easily managed in a group setting. For example, crossing the Mohave, Senora and Painted Deserts, with no knowledge of the amount of liquid needed to overcome dehydration inherent to those conditions, could possibly result in a very dangerous and even a life threatening event. Therefore, touring with a support team in a group setting, in addition to providing the re-hydration materials needed as well as maps with proper directions, would be essential in avoiding obvious pitfalls of riding in extreme conditions.

Another advantage of the group is that virtually all riders experience a puncture at some point. (That is homage to Harry, one of the riders in our group . We normally say "flat" but Harry influenced us with his British acumen) It is almost inevitable. In addition, other mechanical problems such as broken chains, cracked wheels and gear malfunctions are quite common. Crossroads Touring, the company I chose as the group to assist my ride, provided not only a bike mechanic but carried needed bike parts to help ensure the success of the riders. With extra tires, tubes, chains, spokes, and other assorted bike parts, along with the tools needed to repair broken bikes, the group concept, at least for the first time cross country rider, was a huge advantage for a successful tour.

In terms of medical assistance, the group setting is a no brainer. Instant assistance for whatever medical emergency arises adds to the advantage of riding with a group. From minor dehydration issues, bumps, bruises, and an assortment of other ailments, the group ride was an even easier choice for me.

Also, one can still engage in a "lone eagle" experience within the group setting. So, when weighing the advantages and disadvantages of the solo versus group ride, my choice, with the encouragement and support of my wife, became very evident. From that point, I would explore the various companies escorting riders across the country and use one of them to accomplish my goals.

After months of extensive study I eliminated all but two companies and began to research them more in depth. One group virtually sailed across the country averaging 100 miles per day with the experience taking about four weeks. Even though I felt that was doable, I had a vague notion it would have been more than I was prepared to attempt.

Crossroads Cycling Adventures was the other finalist. I checked out their website. It was a very thorough and professional site. To me, that spoke volumes regarding the people involved in the company. The only drawback was the length of time it would take. Los Angles California to Boston Massachusetts was the route and the distance was 3,415 miles. Since that would be approximately 1,000 miles more than the route to Savannah it would take an additional 3 weeks to complete. Riding for seven weeks and averaging 85 miles per day was, I felt, within my riding capabilities. I knew I could do this much easier than the 100 mile group. With hotel rooms, two meals per day for most days, energy drinks and bars, fruit and mechanical support provided, it was a perfect fit for my goal of biking across the country.

Another major concern was the cost. Either method of crossing the country, solo or with a group would be an expensive proposition. My initial inspection of the costs seemed to price me out of the market. But, after choosing the best method and finally the escorting company, I started "squirreling" away funds. As it happens, I was clearly one of the poorest riders in terms of financial resources. But, as I researched the website and considered what the package entailed I reasonably determined that, even at the price quoted, it was a bargain. I figured a solo ride would cost close to the supported ride amount. Also, because it would be more than three years before I would attempt the ride, I would have an abundance of time to stash away money so it wouldn't be such a financial burden. And, if I decided to back out, I could use the cost as a semi-legitimate excuse to do so. Of course, this had to meet with the approval of the lovely Veronica; my wife.

After making the final decision to ride my bicycle across the United States, I needed to develop a plan to ensure it would not turn into an empty pledge. Now, I'm glad I did it because doubt lingered throughout the preparation process; especially the closer it got to actually paying the money and training for the trip.

Initially, my plan was to tell as many people as possible that I intended to bicycle across the United States. Because I told so many people about this goal, it would have been difficult to back out. Some people would have dismissed it as an empty declaration. The old adage comes into play here. "Some people talk the talk, while others walk the walk." Throughout my career I have been known as one who followed through on his commitments. So, the plan was launched.

Chapter 4

EARLY TRAINING

Training for my cross country ride began when I made the decision to attempt this feat. More intensive training began about a year before the event was scheduled. My usual riding distance started at around 20 miles at an average speed of 13-15 mph. I usually rode every other day and would often make excuses for not riding on a day I was scheduled to do so. My excuses included, but were not limited to:

1. Too windy-anything above 10 mph
2. Too cold-anything below 50 degrees
3. Too tired-long hard day at work and
4. Not motivated to get on the bike.

But I convinced myself that since my lifestyle had evolved into incorporating exercise into my daily routine, what was the problem with an hour or so for long term health benefits? In fact, the times I thought about NOT doing a ride, after convincing myself to do so, I was always glad I put in the time. It was similar to why a person continually bangs his head into a wall. When asked why, the response is "because it feels so good when I quit!"

The second year, following my knee surgery, I wanted to put the knee to what I thought was the ultimate challenge. Determining a ride from Washington IL. to Champaign IL. would either injure the knee to the point of replacement or strengthen it to the point of making it more secure, I decided to put the knee to the test. 100 miles was the distance I hoped to cover. Since I grew up in Champaign, with family and friends still living in the town, my destination was to brother Larry's house in Savoy, just south of Champaign. This was a good stopping point. He would provide a place I could clean up, re-hydrate with much needed liquid (usually in the form of beer) and wait for my support ride back to Washington which was usually Veronica, who I lovingly refer to as Ronni. Many people asked why I didn't just ride back. Ha! It was tough enough riding that distance at that time let alone trying to recover enough before attempting to make the ride back. Those back to back distances would come later but I certainly was in no shape to do so at that time.

My first 100 mile ride from Washington to Champaign still remains a vivid memory especially in terms of the type of roads used. It was the longest of my early distance rides because I used secondary, county roads instead of the shorter and smoother state roads. I would serpentine across central Illinois until I finally arrived in Champaign. As it turned out, my later rides were along Route 150, a more reliable state highway. This roadway was, at one time, the major arterial highway between Peoria and Champaign, long before building the interstate system. Today, it is used mainly as a secondary road that parallels Interstate 74. During the early rides on Route 150 the road was used by mostly local traffic as well as a few semi-trucks trying to avoid the weigh stations. But now, it gets quite busy at times and in certain locations. Today, that remains my main route to Champaign on all my rides over 100 miles.

As the years passed, my tolerance for distance riding increased to the point that my legs never really got fatigued. After passing that milestone, I felt I could go as long and hard as needed to accomplish any biking goal that I set. I tested that theory many times. From 25 to 50 to 80 miles per ride until ultimately back to back "centuries" I began imagining what a cross country ride would be like. I was finally ready to commit.

With the decision made to do a group ride I signed with the Crossroads Company. In addition to other valuable information, they sent out a six week training schedule with long rides combined with shorter, faster rides. While this routine was adequate and sufficient for general use, nothing in my geographical area of the country (central Illinois) prepared me for the mountains that I needed to traverse on the actual ride. Also, nothing locally prepared me for riding across deserts. So, even though I trained according to the pre ride information, the ride itself would become the training event. That is, the more I rode on the actual ride the better I became at attacking all sort of terrain and weather. As I reflect, for me, there really was no way to replicate the actual experience so I did the best with what was available.

I must confess the one major mistake I made in my training routine was dealing with the wind. As most bikers will attest, wind in the face (Okay, let's get it out early…HEADWINDS…there, I said it!!) is the worst possible condition to biking in general and long distance biking in particular. Here is how it works. Every hill one climbs, while difficult on the upslope, gives way to a down slope. Rain is only temporary. Bad roads will eventually turn into smooth ones. But, headwinds can be forever!! During my training rides, I would ascertain wind direction and usually ride with a TAILWIND (there, I now have used the two forbidden words!!) My 60-80 mile rides would be with the wind at my back and I would have someone pick me up for the trip home. Confident rides of that design were sufficient to prepare me for the cross country journey; I felt such training measures would suffice. However, little did I know, but would soon find out during the cross country ride, 80% of the time the wind was in our face making my training efforts less adequate. For example, the Dalhart Texas portion, which will be described later, was not only 20-30 mph winds into our faces, but it was a century and lasted the ENTIRE DAY. So, while I feel I trained sufficiently for the ride I soon found it to be very inadequate.

Another aspect of the training portion of the ride involved equipment. Toward the end of my training, with the advice of the good people at my local bike shop Russell's Cycling, I decided to purchase a new bike. I was told that I could do the ride on my old heavy touring Cannondale Specialized, but it would be easier with a new bike which weighed considerably less, around 20 pounds. Now, it may sound like an attempt to just sell a new bike. But, as I found out later, it was actually the best purchase I made given the nature of the trip. It wasn't until two months before the ride (March) that I decided to buy a new touring bike. It was one of the best decisions I made and glad I was convinced to do so. While the ages of the bikes in our group varied, all had touring bikes.

A Cannondale Synapse was Russell's recommendation so I proceeded to purchase a new one. It is an aluminum bike which is durable and very light. On another note, I was the only one in the group that did not use clips. Being a "masher" in the sense that I pushed down on the pedal with each stroke as opposed to those who use a spinning technique tend to pull as well as push in a stroke revolution, I chose to not place clip pedals on the new Synapse. It wasn't until much later that I found out that pedaling with clips improved cycling efficiency by about 30%. So, as it turned out I mashed across the country while everyone else in the group used the "clip and spin" technique. In retrospect, placing clips on the new bike would have given me two months to adjust to the different cycling technique. However, in that I was the only "masher", it made the ride more difficult and I was still able to achieve EFI. So, that either makes me tough or stupid. There are those who would support either theory!

Training ride in central Illinois cornfields

Another issue, relevant to the training, is the additional equipment needed for success in a venture of this magnitude. Since the road bike had no "panniers" (metal supports that attach to the bike frame which support large bags) I used a small seat bag which I attached behind the saddle and a small front carrier attached to the handle bars. Keeping the bike as light as possible was another key to a successful ride which results in a significant advantage. In each carrier were items necessary to essential bike function. In the back bag I carried my money, ID, spare tubes, tools for changing tires, CO_2 cartridges, and an assortment of small tools needed for quick repairs that could be accomplished on the road. My camera, lubricating cream, (chamois butter is an absolute must) suntan lotion, various energy gels and bars fit nicely into the front bag. Attached to the frame were three spare spokes, an extra tire and holders for two bottles of liquids; sports drink or water. Other equipment attached to various areas of the bike included a plastic map holder on the handlebars and a computer made for bikes. While many of the more affluent riders had Garmin computers on their vehicles, I used the more common version that showed distance covered, both accumulated and individual rides, calories burned, time and speed. The last, in my opinion was the most important item. Every biker, regardless of the type or manner of use, should purchase a computer because of the valuable information it communicates.

Chapter 5

Costs

Along with all the pre-ride preparations there were many other areas of concern as the ride came nearer to reality. First and foremost was the financial aspect. Many people were curious, and most have the nerve to inquire, into the cost of an expedition of this sort. Before giving a definitive response, I would describe to the inquisitors some basic information that is valuable to illustrate cost as it relates to the experience. In addition to reserving 50 nights of hotel rooms, two meals per day were provided except for rest days. On these rest days, as was indicated by participants on prior rides, they would prefer eating at a local establishment as the exception to the two day protocol. Additionally, the cost included SAG stop amenities such as power bars, sports drink, water, various assortments of fruits, sweets to replace lost calories and, on special occasions, special treats such as cookies, cakes and candies.

Another cost, and what was probably most important in terms of success of the rider, especially those who strove for EFI, was the mechanical support provided by an expert bike mechanic. To ensure each rider a reasonable chance of finishing the entire distance the mechanic was vital. Bicycle parts were available in the SAG wagons. Bike chains were broken, spokes needed replaced, gear sets needed replaced, and gear adjustments were a daily routine along with other assorted mechanical malfunctions inherit in an adventure of this magnitude. Having a mechanic was a must for success.

With all this information being provided to those inquiring about cost, I would then ask what they would estimate the value, in terms of dollar amount, of such an undertaking. Given this information, most who asked often overestimated the cost of $8,900. This does not include maintenance, gas and a reasonable profit Crossroads must charge patrons to remain viable. Compared to doing a solo event, I considered it a bargain.

The cost analysis was the basic starting point from a financial perspective. Other incidentals arose throughout the journey. Various monies were spent at stops along the way with Dairy Queen the number one recipient of fungible monies. Also, souvenir purchases added to the cost. However, with the load limit imposed by the Crossroad Company of 30 pounds minimal souvenirs were purchased.

Another consideration regarding cost was whether or not to purchase trip insurance. It was not inexpensive, $600, and a very important aspect of the cost factor. After pondering the minuses and plusses of doing so, I decided I would purchase insurance because of the uncertainty of unseen dangers and obstacles that would surely present itself along the way. So, along with the other amenities, the adventure started with an initial cost of around $10,000. There would be additional expenses along the way. As an afterthought, I would certainly recommend to anyone doing something of this nature, trip insurance is a must!

The last major cost consideration attributable to the trip was organizing the pre and post ride transportation along with rooms for the family. While Ronni would accompany me to California, our sons, Christopher and Eric would meet me in Boston. Would driving be more cost effective as opposed to flying and would we share a single room with the boys in Boston? These options increased the cost. As it turned out, we flew into LA and Ronni flew with the boys to Boston. While that increased the cost of the trip, in the final analysis, it was well worth every penny and, in my opinion, quite a bargain in the process. So, I suppose given all the expenses of the entire trip, I spent nearly $15,000 dollars.

As I have always believed you can't really put a price on experiences and adventure. I will again reiterate that of all the riders in the group, I without a doubt, was one of the poorest in terms of financial means. CEO's, CFO's, doctors, bank presidents and business owners were the norm. What in the hell was I thinking that I could afford something like this? In fact, I tried to convince Ronni, many times, we could make better use of the money. That would leave me an out and later I could blame her and use it as an excuse to back out. She would have none of that nonsense and was aware of my nefarious objectives. So, the adventure began.

Chapter 6

THE ARRIVAL

Having finished all the preparation, training and pre-ride duties, it was time to fly to California. The flight to LA and the ride to the hotel were uneventful. However, as we were flying across California, I suddenly realized how long the trans-continental journey was going to be. In fact, as I peered out the window of the plane, it stuck me that the desert and mountains that we were flying over, I would soon be attempting to bike across. I say attempt at this point because serious doubt entered my mind as I looked at the enormity of the land mass I would have to navigate. Very daunting indeed!! But, at the same time, I looked forward to the events that were about to unfold in an undertaking of this nature.

After arriving at the hotel in LA with Ronni, I observed that Tracy (the head of Crossroads Cycling) had placed a map of the United States in the lobby. I later found out this would accompany us across the country and each days progress would be charted on the map. Coupled with having just flown across half the continent, upon viewing the map of our trip, I started to believe what my friends and family said when they heard I was going to ride across the country on a bicycle. "YOU MUST BE CRAZY!!" All of these pre-ride jitters put me in awe of the situation.

Prior to the first meeting with the group who would attempt the cross country trip at, I bumped into a few of the other riders. Initial encounters with other cyclists had basically the same result. We all looked at the physical stature of each rider to see if we would be able to stay with the group. If they all looked like Lance Armstrong I knew I would be in trouble. The first individual I met was Chris. Walking through the parking lot we met, exchanged pleasantries and found out we were both doing the ride. At first I thought, and probably hoped, he was one of the support staff. As a lean and an obviously fit individual he explained he would not be surprised if he, often, were the last to check in at the end of the day. His objective was to finish the ride and enjoy the experience along the way. Ha! I should have known better. Chris was one of the best riders in the group and probably the best climber. To suggest he would check into the hotel each evening as the last rider, even though it wasn't a race, was a ludicrous proposal.

Darrell was the next person I came across. Shopping for last minute items at the local bike shop was a must. The store was close to the hotel so Ronni and I decided to purchase extra items I felt I needed for the trip. Darrell, a physician, was only going to ride to Flagstaff AZ with the group. He could not take 7 weeks away from his practice so he was going to do the ride over a number of years. He provided valuable advice and help for those who experienced medical problems in the early stages of the trip. As would be expected there were many health issues associated with what our group was about to undertake.

Oddly enough, I saw Harry (a very interesting fellow from England) a few times in the hallway of the hotel. I thought at that time, and it was later confirmed, he was indeed a unique individual.

At each of these informal encounters, I perceived that we "sized up" each other to get an idea as to how competent we were in comparison. And yes, I understand it is a somewhat primeval behavior. As I was soon to learn, initial impressions of one's physical stature really had no bearing as to their riding abilities.

To get "the lay of the land" Ronni and I went to the location where we would start the ride. It was to begin at the Huntington Beach pier. We had lunch in a quaint little restaurant near the bottom of a hill that I found out later was a 12% graded incline. For a flatlander like me it appeared daunting from the get go. I was quite intimidated by the hill and hoped I wouldn't embarrass myself at the beginning by walking my bike up these inclines. I was determined to do so even if it meant running the red light situated half way up the incline.

Because the start of the ride would begin the following day and we were several miles from the hotel, I "wussed" for the return trip. Trudging up the 12% hill, with the intent of walking back the entire distance, I could tell it was taking a toll on my knee; the same one I had surgery on in '97. "Let's stop at this place and call a cab" I pleaded with Ronni. So we took a cab back to the hotel. Wuss!!

Chapter 7

GROUP INTRODUCTIONS

The first meeting of the entire group of 26 was in a conference room at the hotel. Of that number only 17 were contracting to ride across the entire continent. Others signed up for various sections. The Southwest portion including California, Arizona, and part of New Mexico was the most popular segment of those doing the partial ride. But, one of the riders, Fred, was to journey all the way to Indianapolis. In my opinion, I thought it odd since Indy was more than three-fourths of the distance across the country. Why not finish the entire distance? But to each his own and I digress.

Our group meeting area was in the same room where our bikes were shipped and stored weeks earlier for reassembling. (Side note: the mechanics that reassembled my bicycle had a major concern. When they were finished they concluded it was a brand new bike and whomever owned it would have trouble because it takes a while to break in a new bicycle. As so happens I had ridden and trained on it over 1,000 miles since it was purchased in March. But, as a "shout out" to Russell's cycling, they did such a good job cleaning, tuning and packaging it, my Cannondale Synapse appeared to be brand new). As one would expect, at the initial meeting there was an air of nervousness, anticipation and casual observing other riders.

My first impression of others in the meeting was they all appeared to be very capable riders. I did note the divergent range in ages. The youngest appeared to be in their mid-thirties, Barbie, and the oldest was difficult to ascertain by physical appearance. The oldest rider, in fact, was Hank, who I found out in short order was my roommate. He was a vibrant 73 years old. The average age was in the mid 50's so I was glad it wasn't a group of twenty and thirty some things. Assured the entire group wouldn't ride off into the distance and leave me in their dust, my confidence grew.

Another positive impression from my initial observation was I ascertained all were very good riders because anyone who hadn't trained or prepared thoroughly probably would not have bothered signing up for such a grueling undertaking. Also, if I were the slowest rider that would be okay and I could deal with it. My intention was not to race but to enjoy the experience. While there were a few that competed to be first to the day's particular destination, most were of the same attitude as me. That is, enjoy the ride, take your time, take an abundance of photos and don't sweat the small stuff.

Tracy conducted the meeting in an efficient manner with a very positive spin. "Are you ready to bike to Boston"? was met with a resounding "hell yes." And so the adventure began.

That night at dinner I met with my roommate for the first time; Hank and his beautiful wife Carol. Ronni and I arranged to meet with them for drinks followed by the evening meal. It was here that I was relieved to find out Hank and I were cut from the same cloth in terms of personality as I will allude to later. Also, at our table, were Mark and his wife Lisa. While Lisa had no intention of riding, she was going to accompany Mark, following along with their Hummer, a large comfortable vehicle. It was a fortuitous encounter because after befriending the couple, Hank and I had the advantage of transportation when other riders needed to rely on their bikes to stray any distance from the hotels. Unfortunately, Mark had only contracted to ride to Albuquerque NM, so when they left we had to fend for ourselves. Looking fit and youthful in their early forties they owned a yacht refurbishing company. Because they couldn't leave their business for 7 weeks they were not able to do the entire distance. Nevertheless, it was a great way to start the ride. I was ecstatic.

Hank, Carol, Ronni, Me at hotel prior to ride

During the early sections of the trip, we had a great time with Mark and Lisa as we would often go to restaurants in the towns along the ride using the Hummer as a conveyance. That delayed our routine, developed later, of not straying far from our hotels after the day's journey.

Also, it didn't occur to me until later, but only 6 of the original 26 riders had roommates. Encountering the other riders at dinner following the traditional route rap meeting after each days ride, it was obvious why most roomed alone; privacy. As I alluded to earlier, in terms of finances, I was at the bottom of the ladder. It was about three thousand dollars cheaper having a roommate so for me it was a no brainer. I would give up a little privacy to save a few dollars.

After a fine meal and excellent companionship the stage was set for the beginning of what was to be a fabulous adventure riding a bicycle across, or should I say diagonally, across the United States of America.

The Far West

Chapter 1

La to Riverside

"It was the best of times; it was the worst of times!" Hey, I think that's been used in some book somewhere, sometime in the past. I wonder if the copyright has run out on that particular phrase. It certainly is apropos for this journey. It is not just a Tale of Two Cities, rather a tale of many cities. And, it certainly contained a few "worst" riding days and a whole lot more "best" riding days. So, I think I will keep the phrase knowing many will attack me as being plagiarists!! Wouldn't be the first time!

I have divided the book into sections of the country. Oddly enough these sections are very distinct and yet those geographical areas developed from the preceding ones. Each was unique in terms of land forms, weather and road conditions. The mountainous, desert Southwest gave way to the fertile rolling lands of the Prairies into the farming communities of the Midwest and eventually mixing with mountains in the East. It is from this perspective that the adventure begins.

The first day of the ride was a ceremonial 5 mile jaunt from the hotel to Huntington Beach pier accompanied with and escorted by the support vans. For this passage we had two SAG wagons and a small Ryder moving van that carried our gear and all the amenities mention earlier. We rode in a 2 by 2 peloton. I rode beside Hank. We had become, in a short period of time, good friends.

Oddly enough, just before we departed Carol, his wife, took me aside and requested that I "take care of Hank". As I found out shortly, he was one of our strongest riders and could definitely take care of himself. I may have been the one who needed attention!

Peloton formation to Huntington Beach

After arriving at the Huntington Beach Pier, we were encouraged by the support team to carry our bikes across the sandy beach and dip the rear tire into the Pacific Ocean. Stupidity was a designation ascribed to anyone who would attempt to ride across the sand. A few actually removed their rear tire and carried them as it was much easier than carrying the entire bike. I lugged my bike on my shoulder and determined I made an excellent decision to purchase a new one as it only weighed 20 pounds thus making the trek by foot across the sand fairly easy.

Dipping rear tire in Pacific-Huntington Beach CA.

Group picture at Huntington Beach

After another 20 minutes of pictures and saying goodbyes to family members, the actual riding began. To avoid the embarrassment if possibly not being able to negotiate the 4 block 12% climb, I got a good "running" start. Peddling fast and furious on the flat approach, not actually running with my bike, I was doing great in "granny gear" and was determined to get to the top. Ha! As luck would have it, after the second block, I had to make a stop at a red light, thus losing any momentum I had gained. But, I wasn't about to walk so when the light changed I was off in "granny gear" humpin' and pumpin' all the way. After reaching the top, I saw Hank in the distance and was able to catch him. I should reiterate here, when I realized Hank was 73 years old, from the information available before the ride started, I felt he would be one I could easily stay with. Hank even mentioned, as we began, that he hoped I didn't get to the hotel that night too soon and if I did could I wait for him. Ha! As it turns out, Hank proved to be quite the cyclist. I did find out later that he had engaged the services of a professional trainer who prepared him by biking about 5,000 miles in the training period prior to the ride.

12% grade across from Huntington Beach. A bit blurry but you get the idea.

During the ride from LA to Riverside, CA I was mildly surprised that the route was mostly urban with virtually no open roads. 80 miles of stop lights with relatively heavy traffic introduced me to riding techniques for which I was unaccustomed. Cruising through intense traffic, in addition to riding with other bikers in close proximity, was unique to my riding experience but I soon adapted and realized that particular pattern would be repeated often along our trip.

One of the tendencies I observed, early on, was how cyclists in the group developed relationships with others according to riding abilities. After determining those abilities, each matriculated into more formal riding groups. As for myself, I was determined to do the "lone eagle" when convenient knowing I would not enjoy the experience if my competitive juices were to engage.

Labeling them according to these groups, but in no way placing any value judgment on them, occurred to me early in the experience. It was just their riding styles that determined which classification I placed them into….no better, no worse.

From my brief experience as a forensic sociologist, I divided the riders into three groups. Those who felt the need to lead the pack I referred to as "Race Horses". They were interested in getting from point A to point B as quickly as possible. Often, I imagined, they missed many of the sites and stops that, in my view, negated the reason for riding a bicycle across the country. Maybe it was I felt I couldn't keep up with them so I can use this as an excuse for my lack of riding ability. Naw, don't think so. As I read in some of their blogs they would race to see who would be first to the night's stop. Again, this is in no way a criticism of their style, rather, an observation that played out as the journey progressed.

"Plow horses" was the nomenclature assigned to the next group according to my unprofessional observations. They were in no particular hurry and enjoyed the journey at a leisurely pace. However, as I discovered along the trip, when challenged by the terrain or negative weather conditions, they kept pace and were still successful in achieving their goals. A nice way to do the trip I suspect.

And finally, there were the Clydesdales. I considered myself in this group. Our physical stature is somewhat larger than the race horses. Often, we would plod along at an even pace but could occasionally pick up the speed if the situation called for it. Jim likened me to a quarter-horse; fast for a short distance but not over the long haul. We Clydesdales were very welcomed in windy conditions as our size was a desirable trait when pushing into the wind. In a pace line, we blocked much of the wind making it easier for other riders in the line. According to biker parlance this is called "pulling". In fact, I "pulled" Charlie, who I will discuss later, across the desert. He would often ask if he could ride my wheel and I was very accommodating.

These observations were made public in my blog with the tag line, "but someone has to pull the beer wagon." For the uninformed, Budweiser advertisements use Clydesdale horses to haul the old time beer wagons. This was obviously a metaphor that illustrated the difference in riding styles showing each style had merit and none were superior to the other. Who would want a race horse plowing your field? Who would want a plow horse at Churchill Downs?

Yet, this phrase came back to haunt me. During the rest day in Champaign, IL which I will describe later, I was interviewed by a journalist representing the local newspaper; the News Gazette. Since I am a native of that town, a graduate of the University of Illinois located in nearby Urbana, and raising money for the Central Illinois Alzheimer's Association, the newspaper thought an article would be appropriate. I couldn't disagree. They also interview my brother Larry, and Hank, my room-mate. It was an excellent article depicting the journey up to that point. However, the headline at the top of the page stated "Walker Pulling Beer Wagon Across America". Indeed!!

I received many negative comments from friends and relatives who live in the area relating to this heading. It implied, and they immediately assumed, I was on a beer drinking extravaganza across the United States. So, many didn't actually read the article and assumed the headline said it all. Obviously, nothing could be further from the truth. In fact, most of us on the ride, Harry excluded, consumed alcohol only on evenings before rest days. However, the headline implied something completely different. This falls into one of my life experiences. But, I digress.

Near the end of the first days ride coming into Riverside, CA I could feel my legs beginning to cramp. That was not a good sign since this was only the first day. It certainly was not the longest ride and not even close to being the most difficult. Prior to the ride I was diligent in consuming a supplement that was supposed to help in the rapid recovery from engaging in a distance event but had no effect on cramping during the ride. Fortunately, the good news was that both Jim and George knew enough chemistry and had expertise in endurance riding. They both suggested I add magnesium to the supplement and it would help alleviate leg cramping. Hank also experienced cramps so we both began taking the recommended supplement the following day and it indeed helped. Learn something new every day.

Another favorable amenity that helped relieve muscle cramping was that the hotel had a whirlpool. I am very cognizant of the healing powers of heat massage so I would always take advantage of this modality offered at the hotels. I was mildly surprised that all of the riders did not engage in this form of recuperative treatment. Being ignorant of the maladies that are inherit in public heated whirlpools I looked forward to them. Later I was informed of the a problem that could result in their use like spreading infections. But, I suppose the old adage applies here; ignorance is bliss.

As previously remarked, because we became friends with Mark and Lisa and they had their Hummer, both Hank and I were offered invitations to join them on days when the tour company did not offer meals. That turned out to be quite an advantage for us.

Mark and Lisa-owners of Hummer and good friends

Ironically an incident, that would be a foretelling of things to come, occurred on our ride to Riverside. One of our group, Barbie, was struck by a car. While she was not seriously injured it did brush against her and knocked her off the bike. She was lucky in that she only had superficial abrasions. Apparently a car was making a right turn into her path and didn't see her. I find that totally amazing. To suggest cars could not see the riders seemed very implausible because we all had bright orange flags flying from our rear wheel. This was the first of many road incidents that occurred during the journey.

The following day was a template of what we would replicate for the next several days. Like clockwork, at 5:30 a.m. both Hank and I were up and doing our morning routine. 7:30 a.m. was our departure time so that gave us two hours to eat, pack, check our bikes and generally prepare for the day's ride. Our trek to Indio, CA began with a comfortable, cool temperature of 60 degrees. But, because we began riding through the desert, the temperature quickly soared to a high of 102 degrees.

Again, as a routine we would follow in the foreseeable future, the day's journey began with a three mile climb of 6% grade. Now, that may not seem steep compared to topography that was yet to come, but for me, a flatlander, it was difficult and I rode mostly in "granny gear."

While I know there is no award for this dubious feat, I was the first of our entire group to get a flat tire and, of course, it was the rear tire. After leaving the hotel and making a sharp left turn I shifted down to granny gear in preparation for the mornings climb. Exerting more energy than what was normal for this grade, it wasn't long before I realized I had lost air in my rear tire. In terms of flat tires, the rear tire is the hardest to change and, for some odd reason, most of my punctures were to the rear tire. My first mistake was trying to turn the bike over onto the saddle as I was accustomed. Because the safety flag was placed on the bikes rear tire, it prevented me from using this technique. Therefore, I needed to release the wheel while the bike was in an upright position. Universally speaking, bicyclists find the rear tire the most difficult tire to change because of problems the chain presents. Removing the tire in an upright position was very awkward for me. I thought I was fairly adapt at changing tubes but felt a little pressure to get it changed as quickly as possible in order to not get too far behind the main group. As I struggled with the process, a group of riders stopped to assist. They included, Harry, Alec and Karen. Both Harry and Alec took charge and had the tire changed in a matter of minutes. Another bit of good fortune. The SAG wagon came along and I was able to properly inflate the tires. For more good news, I now knew how to find the source of the flat or more precisely the puncture. It is the puncture that causes the flat. Without finding the cause, it is useless to put on another tube because it will flatten almost immediately.

Harry, Alec, Karen, helping fix flat (puncture)

Now, what I will refer to from time to time, the Karma effect, takes over. Karma is reflected in both positive and negative behavior. After my flat, the four of us rode together as a group with Harry leading the way followed by Karen, who navigated, then Alec and finally me. I felt compelled to ride last in the pace line since I knew I was the weakest link in that chain of riders. By the end of the day, every one in our little informal group had a punctured tire. Bad Karma!

The rest of the day was relatively uneventful. After an 8-9% grade climb of six miles, we enjoyed a nice tailwind that blew at a brisk 45 mph. Fortunately, on this particular day, it was at our backs (ha, as most tailwinds tend to be). I could not imagine riding into a wind that vigorous this early in the journey. It pushed us along to the extent we averaged approximately 30 mph for over 20 miles. Look out Lance Armstrong! As we streamed along, we passed a wind farm in the valley into which we were riding and it looked like there were over 500 windmills going full blast. Imagine how much energy they were creating. What an ideal place to put windmills because, I am told, the wind usually blows every day at that speed in that particular area of California. It is a culmination of the winds coming from the ocean, crossing the mountain tops and following the valley below. In fact, there was a junction where we were warned to be very cautious because of crosswinds that would literally have blown us off our bikes. Passing the aforementioned crossroads, we did indeed encounter a severe crosswind. I was glad I was warned because bracing against the wind made it easier to cross the intersection. I can't envision what would have happened if I had not been forewarned.

The route into Indio, CA meant we would pass through the infamous Palm Springs. Having been aware of this town all my life through various movies and movie star references, I was excited to experience Palm Springs up close and personal. Wealthy individuals lived here in addition to movie stars so I looked forward to seeing it first-hand.

Passing through on my bike I observed the houses were beautiful and the city was everything I imagined it would be. However, because of the intense heat and apparent lack of a large supply of water, I tried to figure out how and why this part of the Mojave Desert had a town of such opulence built in this particular location. I mean, it is literally in the middle of the desert and in the middle of nowhere. Often, it boggles the mind as to why certain cities are built in certain areas. Nevertheless, it was quite impressive with palm tree lining the streets and luxurious, opulent homes. It was everything I thought it would be but in the middle of the desert. Now really!

Continuing to ride as a group of four, Alec, Harry, Karen and I decided to take a lunch break at a local Subway in Palm Springs. We still had over twenty miles to ride before we came to Indio and I never consume large amounts of food while riding long distances. After ordering a soft drink I noticed Alec had ordered a "foot long" sub with all the trimmings. I can't envision myself consuming that amount of food and continuing with any biking proficiency. Mostly, I would have preferred to take a nap following ingesting such an enormous amount of food. But, Alec ate the entire sandwich along with chips and drinks and continued biking the rest of the way with absolutely no negative effects. I gave him kudos and was mightily impressed.

As it turned out, we rode over three hours in 105 degree temperature. While we thought that was extremely hot, little did we know that would be the COOLEST we would experience for the next two days. Hot, sweaty, and tired the four of us lumbered into Indio. But, after a whirlpool, shower, and nutritious meal I was ready for the next day's adventure.

Karen, Alec, Harry, me, with fingers indicating the order we all had flats

Chapter 2

RIVERSIDE TO BLYTH, CA

The next morning started as one of those postcard picture perfect days. With mountains on the horizon and Mojave Desert sand all around, we were ready to begin the days trek from Indio CA to Blyth CA. After the morning hours passed with relatively comfortable 70 degree weather, the temperature quickly climbed to 110 degrees by the afternoon. In addition, this day's ride would be 100 miles with another preview of what we should expect in the coming days; the wind came from the ESE at between 15 and 20 mph. That meant we would be riding into the wind for 100 miles in over 100 degree temperature. Now the challenge really began!

Under these conditions, the evaporation factor became problematic. That is, we would be losing body fluids more rapidly than we realized, so it was crucial all riders consume massive amounts of liquid. Jack, the rider from Israel, was going to attempt the desert crossing without a camelback. Camelbacks are packs worn on the back that are capable of holding at least 70 oz. of liquid. At the evening Route Rap prior to the Blythe ride, Tracy informed everyone camelbacks would be required. At this particular Route Rap Tracy realized Jack planned to ride across the desert without wearing a camelback. She was adamant that if he did not have one, he could not ride with the Crossroad group. Jack would have no support, and basically he would be on his own. It was at this point I realized Tracy was not to be toyed with. She knew her business and no one was going to jeopardize the group. Also, I'm sure her insurance provider would have found it very disturbing if she allowed this dangerous behavior, especially if something happened to Jack under her care. I totally supported Tracy on this decision. It was comforting to realize that, as a leader, she would stand her ground when the situation called for it; an admirable characteristic indeed.

Needless to say, Jack ventured to the nearest Wal-Mart and purchased the required equipment. In Jack's defense though, I could understand why he felt compelled to ride without one. First, it is somewhat cumbersome. Secondly, it added weight to the bike. Thirdly, and most importantly from Jack's perspective, he lived in the desert in Israel which presumes he was acclimated to that particular environment.

My fluid of choice in the camelback was Gatorade. This is certainly not an endorsement, and any fluid would have been sufficient, but it contains valuable electrolytes vital in distance biking which are lost through normal perspiration. In fact, virtually all the riders took electrolyte supplements to counter the effects of losing this vital nutrient during these trying conditions. (Parenthetically, as I was exploring my options on the method for doing this ride, it did not include knowledge of the danger of trying to ride unassisted in the deserts of the Southwest. A very perilous undertaking at best!)

One instance of a negative condition commonly associated with the use of the supplement, occurred when Chris ingested an overabundance of electrolytes and needed to be rushed to the emergency room following the days ride to receive an intravenous injection of liquids. Indeed the passage across the desert on this particular day was so brutal that two other riders needed emergency room assistance to be treated for dehydration. And, these hospitalizations occurred even though the riders had a camelback, two water bottles holding 16 oz. on the bikes in addition to three SAG stops designed to cool down, and re-hydrate. This illustrates some of the conditions we endured during the early stages of the trip.

I must compliment the Crossroads personnel at this point, and will do so on many occasions, due to their professionalism, attention to detail and concern for the riders. And yes, this is an endorsement for that company. They did an outstanding job in their attempts to prevent riders from dehydration. Another very effective method they used to help keep riders cool was to pour a gallon of cold water through the top of our helmets while they were still on our heads. It drenched the entire body in water and had a very interesting effect as we resumed riding. As the wind blew across the water that saturated our riding clothes, it acted like a crude air conditioning system as it cooled off the body; quite an exhilarating experience.

One of the odd situations during the early part of the journey happened because of the lack of roads in remote areas of Arizona and New Mexico. We were allowed to ride on the interstate highways in those two states. My first experience riding interstate roads began on Interstate 10 in Arizona. Prior to the ride, my personal belief was that Interstate riding would be as safe as, and in many cases, safer than less traveled roads with little or no shoulders. While this might be true, there were other issues which became problematic that had not occurred to me to be addressed later in more detail.

Pedaling toward Blyth, enjoying the heat, (and yes! I actually enjoy riding in the heat) keeping hydrated, engaging in my usual "lone eagle" mode, I welcomed the first SAG stop of the day. After resting in the shade, consuming vast quantities of fluids and rejuvenating my body I set off. Upon entering the interstate, I noticed another rider was behind me attempting to catch up. Viewing him in my rear view mirror, I slowed enough to determine that it was Charlie, another of our groups riders. While I had not officially met him I knew who he was. He began riding my wheel. This is common practice among bikers. Mostly, I preferred to ride alone at this time. Pragmatic reasoning prevailed in this case. Since I began having multiple punctures I did not want to hold back other riders who would stop to assist, especially in that extreme heat. Another reason I preferred riding alone is because of the long, long stretches of the same scenery, I would intentionally violate one of the Crossroads rules. "Firing up" my I-pod I would begin listening to my favorite tunes. This practice was implemented on all of my rides in Illinois except when riding with friends. Doing so at this time would diminish the monotony of mile after mile of desert terrain.

Using electronic devices was discouraged by Tracy and the support crew for obvious safety reasons. It makes sense that a trip with as much inherent hazards as this, one should take as many precautions as possible to avoid danger. However, I felt I only partially broke the rule because I would place only one ear bud into my ear and have one ear free. (Now, is it really possible to half break a rule? Something philosophical to ponder!!) But, as Charlie joined me after the first SAG, I took out the I-pod so neither of us would be uncomfortable about breaking one of the rules of biking. I should mention there were enough riders who went out of their way to adhere to safety rules that those of us who would have preferred to break them were influenced to NOT do so. Since I was in "Clydesdale" mode, I pulled Charlie that day and also pulled him the next day all the way into Wittenberg N.M.

Another factor involved in riding through the desert on the interstate highway system is that I had 8 flat tires caused by the litter that was very common along the shoulders of the road. There was every imaginable piece of junk scattered along the shoulder. In terms of garbage on the shoulders of the interstates, debris from the road is varied and plentiful. Screws, a variety of tools, bungee cords, toys of every imaginable type, batteries, metal parts and the inevitable "piss" bottles that truck drivers discard, litter the shoulders. Trash of this magnitude and variety makes riding these roads less desirable than riding on state or county roads. That was one of the misconceptions I had before the ride. Now I know better.

The most common source of punctures along the shoulders was small shards of metal that gets thrown from tires of semi-trucks after they themselves get a flat. These small wires work their way into the bicycle tube and ultimately cause problems. I later learned (better late than never) it is possible to avoid as many flat as I got by following two basic procedures. First, after every stop, check thoroughly for any junk that might have become imbedded into the tire. Those objects could easily be found by lightly rubbing the finger around the tire. Doing this makes it possible to detect many objects the naked eye might miss. Small pebbles, glass, and the aforementioned wire, are just a few of the items than can work their way through the outer layer of the tire and cause it to flatten. Trust me, I learned the hard way.

A second method for avoiding as many punctures as I endured is to purchase tires that have Kevlar coating or liners. I figured the tires that came with the bike would be sufficient protection against punctures. They obviously were not. Now, Kevlar will not totally eliminate flats but it cuts them down considerably. In fact, Rick, one on the mechanics who often rode with us, claimed he has accomplished the cross country trip without a getting a single flat tire. That would be some trick but I suppose it can be done.

Biking snobs informed me that tires with Kevlar do not roll as quickly as those tires without it. I suppose highly trained, professional racers, maybe, can detect "roll" resistance but, come on, can anyone really tell the difference or is it all mental? And yet, when I replaced my original ones with VonTragers coated with the Kevlar liner, I felt I couldn't bike as fast as I did using my old tires. But, I suspect it was just a mental block because I wasn't that fast to begin with. Researchers that take the time and make an effort to explore this kind of thing might disagree with me; but, there it is!

Another point regarding riding through the desert is that I was not totally familiar with actual desert geography. My only references were pictures and oral accounts from those familiar with this particular environment. Neither did justice to the beauty inherit to this part of the country. While I'm not given to esthetic hyperbole, my impressions of this terrain remain vivid and inspiring. From the flats of the desert, views into the distance revealed mountains, which added to the diversity of the topography. I found this fascinating and it was a joy riding through these areas. Mile after mile passed without much scenic diversity and, often, my mind wandered into issues associated with this area.

In the vast wilderness through which I rode, desert critters and other assorted vermin inhabiting this region need to survive in these extreme conditions. Their existence depends on what the environment provides. Spiders, snakes and various other dangerous animals take refuge from the heat by seeking shaded areas. Rocks and other desert plants provide minimum shade and liquid opportunities. However, the advent of the interstate system allowed additional cover in the form of bridges and overpasses for the various insects and animals. Indeed, these were areas we riders could take refuge from the burning heat of the day and perform other necessary "business."

Having been warned by the support team of this fact, when deciding to take refuge in the only shade for miles, bridges and overpasses, we were careful to avoid cracks and crevices that could possibly harbor desert life that could be injurious to us. In this environment, the real danger would be seeking privacy to do one's "business"; a vital necessity when biking over long distance. As rest areas with toilet facilities were few and far between, the only place to engage in relieving oneself was in conjunction with the natural inhabitants of the area. Being bitten in certain areas not only would have been embarrassing but obviously painful and perhaps even fatal. These were factors one does not contemplate in planning for the trip. But, the good news is no one was attacked and everyone made a safe desert crossing.

Barbie, Mark, Willie taking refuge from the sun under viaduct

After enjoying another interesting day of biking in the desert we arrived in Blythe CA. The temperature was still in the 100's so we scurried immediately into the air conditioned rooms and refreshing nearby pool, not unlike the desert critters we assiduously avoided during the day. That assessment was not lost on me at the time.

All in all the long days ride ended successfully and after a refreshing shower, replenishing 4,500 to 5,000 calories, ingesting abundant fluids and sharing the days adventure with other riders I was ready for a good siesta. The routine of going to bed at 9:00 pm was beginning to take effect. I was looking forward to the following days ride through the desert into Wittenberg AZ. located at the foothills of the Rocky Mountains. That ride would include our first state line crossing to be followed by 14 additional ones.

Chapter 3

BLYTH TO WITTENBERG, AZ

Wittenberg AZ. was the day's destination and would be the last day of the Mojave Desert ride in California. It was a 115 mile endurance effort into a mild headwind which, at this juncture, provided a bit of relief from the intense heat.

Shortly after leaving Blythe we crossed into Arizona. Our group was supposed to stop and take a picture of the state logo. However, we were told there were two signs; one more opulent that the other. It was explained in detail that the second sign would be preferable since it was much more photogenic. Riding with Hank, and following the first group to depart that morning, a sign appeared that we deemed to be rather plain. While looking for the more photogenic of the two signs, we actually passed the better of the two signs. The first was just a little placard that indicated we had entered Arizona. Most of us missed it. As we came to the second sign we were not impressed so we continued without taking the time to take photos. As it turned out, we actually missed the best sign and had to "borrow" pictures from others who took the time to take a proper snapshot. This "borrowing" was necessary in order to place it on my blog and make a complete photographic record of the trip.

First state crossing-Arizona

Vials of "magic" sand used to spread onto the ground or even toss into the air after crossing a state line were provided to each rider at the outset of the journey. It was a superstition that, if believed, would ensure favorable winds and good Karma for the ride. But, of course, not only did we not stop at the proper sign, we failed to spread sand so the positive Karma abandoned us----if one believes is such things; flat tires, headwinds, rain etc. notwithstanding.

Conditions on the ride into Wittenberg were similar to previous days except the distance increased as well as the temperature. 110 degree air temperature was a little higher than the day before and the distance increased by 5 miles. This day's route was a combination of Interstate 40 and old Route 66. I really enjoyed the Route 66 thoroughfare as there remained many iconic relics from the past.

Apparently, the interstate system through Arizona and New Mexico rendered Route 66 a low priority in terms of repair and maintenance and therefore was an alternative route. That was unfortunate as there were many places we were not able to ride because the road was in need of massive reconstruction, thus the need to use the interstate roads.

Prior to the beginning of the trip, as I looked into the first weeks riding schedule, I had made a decision to bike the first 85 miles to Wittenberg then SAG the remaining miles. Knowing the following day's ride would be the first distance that included mountains, I felt this approach would save valuable energy. After nearly 40 miles on Route 66, we encountered a section that was under repair. Workers had just poured new asphalt along a 15 mile stretch of the road and, as luck would have it, they allowed the bikers to use it. So, in addition to heat from the air, the temperature from the asphalt reached at least 125 degrees. It was another of the many challenges which presented itself during the journey that the group needed to overcome in order to be successful. That, in fact, obviously made the ride much harder so I felt I had made an insightful decision to bump after the final SAG.

Entering the last SAG at mile 85 I was still seriously considering "bumping" the last 25 miles into town. Many riders had already decided to do the same and I pondered the possibility of whether or not I could do another 25 miles. After refreshing and replenishing my body with copious amounts of power bars, gels, water and Gatorade I still contemplated riding the SAG van into Wittenberg.

Sitting under a shade tree (perhaps a Bode tree because I suddenly became enlightened, well, not really. I don't think they grow in a desert) feeling rested and rejuvenated I had a revelation. (Wow, now that sounds familiar…can you say Buddha? But I digress)

George, with whom I had not ridden up to this point and deemed a plow horse, persuaded me to join him for the final leg. Also, Mack, one of the members of the support team, indicated that most of the rest of the ride into town was downhill. Ha! I actually believed him. Not so as it turned out! So, I decided to ride the last leg with George. It was a delightful ride. Later I was grateful I was persuaded to do so. First, I got to know George and discovered what a unique individual he was. We conversed most of the way as there was virtually no auto traffic thereby making it possible to ride side by side and engage in dialogue.

The second reason I was grateful for the decision to continue was one I had not seriously considered at the start of the trip. Before the ride I was almost certain that at some point I would SAG or bump to the day's stop. I had confidence the EFI concept, as a viable option, was somewhat remote, even though it was a stated goal. Many of the stronger riders started the journey with the idea they would do EVERY FOOT AND INCH. I was just determined to complete as much of the trip as I was capable of doing. But, by the end of the journey I was glad I decided to ride with George into Wittenberg. Oddly enough, another omen along the way helped in my decision. As we entered the tiny berg of Hope, AZ, I knew there was a reason I continued. Hope in the middle of the desert. Now really! There's that Karma thing working again.

Hope Az. After passing this sign, you are beyond hope!

As stated earlier, members of the support team indicated the last 15-20 miles were basically downhill. What I discovered at that time, and would later confirm, was some of support team would not always give completely accurate information about the terrain. Whether it was intentional or not, I'm still not sure, but I think it was intended to always put a positive spin on things. Also, their interpretation of what was "downhill" may be different than mine; either way, not a bad idea at all.

Chapter 4

WITTENBERG TO PRESCOTT, AZ EARLY RIDE

November, 2008, six months before the cross country ride, was my first bike trek from Wittenberg AZ to Flagstaff. In order to convince myself I could ride across the country, I needed to ride in that region in an attempt to climb the highest mountains I would encounter. While I had trained on the hills of southern Illinois, their grade and height couldn't compare with what I had to endure riding up the 10-15% inclines of the Rockies. So, Ronni and I traveled to Arizona where I rented a bike and pedaled up Yarnell Pass, over the top, through the "false flats" of the Prescott Valley over another mountain range into the town of Prescott.

Yarnell Pass precedes climb to Yarnell

Riding that first day, I gained knowledge which would help me prepare for the actual cross country endeavor. First, I would attempt to engage with the local populace establishing a rapport, creating a common bond of communication. I viewed this as a test to see if I were capable of meaningful dialog with those living in the areas I rode. This was one of my stated goals, and here would be a good place to practice. Secondly, Yarnell Pass was the first real test of my mountain climbing abilities. I will admit it was difficult, especially for a flatlander like me.

When the actual climb began, I put the bike in the lowest "granny gear" and started pedaling. My fastest speed was between 5 and 6 mph. Wind was not a factor. When it came to a time that I was tired and my heart was beating out of my chest, I stopped to take pictures, recoup some energy and hopped on the bike again. Conceding defeat was not a consideration. I convinced myself I would be able to do it. I knew Yarnell pass would not be the steepest or longest climb through the mountainous part of the trip. So I continued to climb.

Because it was a Sunday I was passed by a group of motorcyclists in full motorcycle regalia engaging in a weekend recreational ride up the mountain. When I finally arrived at the top of the pass, there they were. The town of Yarnell consisted mostly of a gas station, grocery and bar. Ronni was waiting for me and shared the following story.

"When I arrived in the support wagon,(actually a rented van) at the town of Yarnell and encountered the bikers, I asked if they had seen a bicyclist coming up the mountain."

"Indeed, we saw someone biking up the mountain" one of the bikers responded.

He continued, "We stopped to see if he needed assistance."

Champ's supposed response was "fuck no; I don't need any fucking help".

"I believed it to be true because I felt it was something he would have replied to any inquiry of that nature so I waited patiently until he arrived."

It's her story and she is sticking to it.

Finally, I entered Yarnell and she told me the story as the bikers milled within hearing distance. They all had a big laugh because they knew the yarn was made up. We then became fast friends and I had a great time talking with them.

Their first observation was they thought I was crazy to ride up such a demanding path. Then, even the youngest, about 25 years old, admitted they could never accomplish something that difficult. Those were two of the three most common comments I heard from people I met along the cross country ride; you're crazy and I could never do that.

Another experience, that helped prepare me for the cross country adventure happened as I came through Prescott Valley between the mountains of Yarnell and those bordering the town of Prescott. I ran out of water. A small town loomed in the distance so I figured I would stop and replenish my supplies at a gas station or grocery. I discovered, as I entered the town, there was neither gas station nor grocery store. By this time I had no water left and knew I couldn't make it over the next mountain range without it. At the eastern edge of town was a small café. They had no bottled water. I also had no money or credit card. Aha, I still had my cell phone. I would just call Ronni, who had already gone ahead to Prescott, and wait at the café until she came along with the needed supplies. Yea, right!! After turning on my phone, it never occurred to me; I had no cell phone reception. That meant I couldn't contact Ronni so basically I was stranded. I even tried using the pay phone on the side of the building using the collect call feature. This did not work either since Ronni wasn't getting any reception. I felt my only choices were to wait until she realized I wasn't in Prescott or try to make it without water. That, of course, was not really an option. Suddenly it occurred to me, DUH, that I could just fill my water bottles from the water supply at the café. After asking for and getting permission, I found an outside water spicket and filled my bottles. While I was somewhat concerned about the quality of water from the building, I really had no choice. So, after refilling, off I went. This experience taught me a valuable lesson. Be sure to carry enough liquids, money, credit card, ID and full battery power on the cell phone. Even today, on distance rides I carry these vital items. These were lessons well learned from painful experiences but they proved helpful for my cross country trip.

The climb over the mountains that sheltered Prescott on its western border was not as difficult as Yarnell. I finally came into the town only to see Ronni sitting in the car on the outskirts awaiting my arrival. Fortunately, she didn't have to worry and attempt to find my stranded ass somewhere along the road.

After enjoying our stay at an Indian reservation hotel in Prescott I was off the next day over Mingus Mountain to Cottonwood AZ. This would be the steepest and longest climb of the ride. While I thought the Yarnell climb was arduous, it paled in comparison to the climb over Mingus. It was steep, long and contained 158 five to ten mph switchbacks. These are hairpin turns with signs warning motorist the speed limit needed to safely navigate these turns. I stopped many times to recover and take pictures.

While the climbing was difficult, the descent down Mingus into Cottonwood was fast and dangerous. Reaching a speed of 50 mph on the downhill side indicated the high level of danger. Feathering the brakes is the preferred method of traversing the quick drop down the mountainside. Hard braking could be hazardous and perhaps fatal. If the brakes overheat, the rim could warp and create quite a hazard. In addition, there were no guard rails so any mistake could be troubling. Making it into Cottonwood without disaster was a relief and I was secure in the knowledge I would be able to handle mountain climbs.

Chapter 5

WITTENBERG TO FLAGSTAFF, AZ

Continuing with the cross country ride, Wittenberg to Prescott presented several problems and awe inspiring scenery. At a relatively short distance, 60 miles, we had the good fortune of a west wind (tailwind) blowing at a constant 15 mph. I say this because according to my calculations it would make the climb up Yarnell Pass a bit less difficult than the first time I accomplished this feat. Not so fast!! My mistake, during this section, was before we started the actual Mingus Mountain ascent, most of the riders including myself, stopped at a store and enjoyed some chocolate milk. We had discovered early in the adventure that chocolate milk was a fabulous recovery drink, but, as I was too soon discover, it is not a quick energy source. Unfortunately, I discovered this at the wrong time. The climb up Yarnell pass was more difficult than when I accomplished it in November, as described earlier. Some of the riders suggested it was because we had already ridden four consecutive days which included two centuries, enduring extreme heat and desert conditions which had taken its toll on the body. I felt it was the milk that slowed me down but after more consideration, it was probably a combination of both. Taking more breaks and not progressing as fast as I had planned caused concern by Tracy. A couple miles from the top of Yarnell, she happened to drive by as I was stopped taking a break. Pulling the van to the side of the road, she inquired if I would like a ride to the top. Believe me I was very tempted to do so. But, after considerable thought, I decided to continue regardless of how much time it took or how slowly I progressed.

So, let me be clear. As a climber of mountains I was a plow horse. But, when it came to the descent, look out race horses and move over. I loved the speed factor. Along other sections of mountains we crossed that had severe declines, several riders actually rode DOWN the mountains in the SAG van because of the dangers from going so fast. These dangers include, but are not limited to, reaching speeds of 40 to 50 mph, rough roads that send shuddering vibrations through the body and bike, in addition to having no guard rails separating bikers from a potential fatal disaster. So if a mistake is made here the results can be catastrophic. My thinking is that it is a reward for the rigors of the climb so take advantage of it.

Switchbacks with no guard rails

And, that was, by far, not the most dangerous adventure of the trip. During my earlier ride through this same territory, I developed a style of controlling my speed without endangering myself. Speed was not a factor but slowing down enough to manage the 15 mph switchbacks was the tricky part.

After a brief stop at Yarnell pass, and having descended the back side, we encountered what is commonly called "false flats." Traversing the Prescott Valley, it appeared to be flat or somewhat downhill, maybe even a slight climb. But, it was an uphill climb through the entire valley and the mind was tricked into thinking it was level ground. I still remember wondering why I needed to put the bike in a lower gear in what seemed to be relatively flat ground. Weariness was the only thing that came to mind so I just figured that was the reason. Then, after several miles of the "false flats" another range of mountains loomed ahead. They were not as steep as the climb into Yarnell and the descent into Prescott was fast and welcomed.

Prescott, AZ still remains one of my favorite towns on the trip. Nestled between the mountains of central Arizona it reminded me of an old west town. In fact, the Palace Tavern is said to be the oldest of its kind west of the Mississippi.

Mark and Lisa were still with the group and they invited Hank and me to join them for dinner in a local restaurant. We had a wonderful time with them as a distraction from the "chain" restaurants we were becoming used to. The meal was great and the wine even better. But, knowing we had much more climbing the next day, we spent little time at the historical establishments located on the town square. Many iconic western structures in and around the town would have been interesting to visit. And, of course, there was the Indian Reservation gambling casino. While lack of time did not permit us to peruse these sites, they were placed on my list of places to visit sometime in the future.

Palace Tavern-Prescott AZ

The following day's ride was very similar to the trip through Yarnell Pass. On this day, our journey took us from Prescott to Cottonwood AZ over what would be our highest climb; Mt Mingus. While it covered only a distance of 50 miles, the climbs were very steep with 10-12% inclines over 4-5 miles and the same percent coming down. Jerome, AZ was the highlight of that particular part of the ride.

Jerome started as an old copper mining town that was literally built into the side of Mt. Mingus. In fact, on the descent from the Mingus apex, it was necessary to brake hard to keep from flying through the town. Today, it is has been transformed into a unique tourist destination. With an array of restaurants, shops, and businesses, it was a welcome stop on the downward side of the mountain; a must stop for bikers and other tourists alike.

Road climbing Mt. Mingus

Recovering and refreshing at the top of Mingus, I encountered one of the most interesting characters of the trip. As stated before and will illustrate throughout this exposé, one of the highlights of such an adventure was to engage people and initiate a dialog. I introduce Spencer.

Coming up Mt. Mingus I observed a biker hauling a carrier with a sign on the back indicating "baby on board." Apparently there was no "baby" in the carrier; rather, he carried all the gear he needed for his particular riding experience.

Admittedly he violated most of the biking protocols of experienced distance bikers. He was wearing red high top Converse tennis shoes, obviously no clips, mashing all the way. While I mashed, I at least wore biking shoes. His riding outfit consisted of a t-shirt and shorts unlike the spandex and biking jersey of more experienced riders. His vehicle was a 20 year old Schwinn 10 speed bike. I was somewhat fascinated by this style.

When he arrived at the top of the mountain I initiated a conversation and found him to be a very unique character. He was going to ride from Prescott, where he was a college student, although he couldn't tell me much about his major or his year in school, to Glacier National Park in Montana. This route consisted primarily of riding up and down the mountain passes between those two points. Flat parts of this route are virtually non-existent.

With nothing more than those necessities he deemed essential packed into his carrier, he assured me he would make Montana in time to attend the wedding of one of his friends. He figured it would take him about a month.

Fortunately for him we crossed paths. Because of the age and condition of his bicycle, he was having difficulty with the brakes. Now, that might not be much of a problem on the climb but there was no way he could safely descend with dysfunctional brakes. As he was tinkering with them, I asked our mechanic, Rick, if he would be willing to assist Spencer. Knowing he violated one of the group ride rules, but also aware of the danger ahead by not helping a fellow bicyclist, Rick replaced the brake pads and adjusted his braking system. Spencer was now able to safely continue his adventure.

He reminded me of so many of the people I knew during the 1960's who just piled into their vehicles and took off on a whim with a devil may care attitude. We became instant "brothers in spirit" and after a pleasant conservation as well as my providing him "goodies" from our SAG van, I wished him good luck, God speed, safe biking and I began my descent down the mountain at break neck speed.

While the ride to the top of Mt. Mingus was one of the longest and steepest of the mountainous rides, the descent was at least as dangerous in terms of speed control. Because of the dangers present, three riders gave up EFI status. All were capable of climbing at a 9%-12% grade, but, coming down at those gradients was intimidating. High speeds, rough roads and no guard rails made the descent into Cottonwood quite treacherous. Speeds of between 45-50 mph were not uncommon. Switchbacks were the norm with posted speed limits at 15 mph so my technique involved coasting until hitting the curve, breaking hard into the turn, and begin coasting again.

Proper technique for this kind of terrain which ensured safety, as I learned later through more experience, was to "feather" the brakes the entire descent. A totally unacceptable and even more dangerous technique would have been to ride the brakes the entire distance. The problem here, as mentioned previously, is that it would have done two things. First, the brakes would heat up and possible warp the rim. Secondly, it would wear the brakes down so they would have to be replaced at some point along the trip. The biggest problem I had with moving at such a high speed was that my hands became very fatigued and began cramping. So Jerome was a welcomed respite.

Jerome, an old mining town carved out of the eastern side of Mt. Mingus about half way down, provided an opportunity to lunch with members of the group I had little or no contact with during the prior week's ride. I shared a table with Jack and we had a very interesting discussion of his occupation and his children's interests. This again illustrated one of the positives of the ride; meeting interesting people associated with the group as well as people we encountered along the way.

Another group of locals with whom I started a conversation in this quaint little town were local firefighters. Inquiring as to the burnt out sections of the trees and shrubbery that were noticeable around Jerome, they informed me that fires were quite common. Lack of rain, conservation measures that would not allow loggers to clear the undergrowth and not being allowed to use controlled fires to reduce the fire danger, resulted in many small fires. Their biggest worry was that sooner or later there would be a huge fire that would cause much property destruction and even human fatalities; very prophetic at this time.

Following an enjoyable lunch, Cottonwood was clearly visible in the valley at the bottom of the mountain. The road was carved into long, looping curves unlike the earlier tight switchbacks. It was at this point, as I made my way down the mountain, that my bike computer actually recorded 50 mph. Now, I'm sure that was entirely too fast but, as stated earlier, I felt it was a reward for the difficult climbing I accomplished two days in a row.

The night was spent in Cottonwood which turned out to be a town that was just a stop in the road; nothing remarkable or noteworthy. However, it was soon to change.

Road to Cottonwood

I should mention at this time that prior to the cross country trip, I had little experience in laundromat protocol and had no working knowledge of the cycles of washing machines, drying time, costs of doing each and use of tables for folding laundry. By the time we arrived in Cottonwood, seven days into the ride, I had become quite proficient in all aspects laundry. That may sound somewhat sexist, perhaps elitist, but it was what it was. And, I now happily launder my own biking attire; much to the delight of the lovely Veronica.

After an uneventful evening in Cottonwood, the following day's destination was Flagstaff Az a mere 46 mile trek. However, as we would experience in future jaunts with a trip of that length, the expectation was there would be quite a bit of climbing. Indeed that was the case. With all the majestic mountains juxtaposed to the serene valleys, I would personally rate that area of the country as one of the most scenic of the entire ride. Our route was State Road 89a. It went through Sedona, the red rock area of Arizona. It is, indeed, one of the most popular tourist towns in that state with small shops, restaurants and souvenir stands.

One of the more popular folklore aspects of this vicinity is the "vortex" areas that attract a multitude of people. Supposedly, these are the areas where "aliens" have come to visit our planet. Apparently these aliens are aesthetic enjoying creatures because they picked one of the most attractive locations in the entire country.

While contemplating such matters and without spending much time in town doing the "tourist" thing, I was eager to continue the trek to Flagstaff.

Sedona with red rocks in the background

For the most part the route to Flagstaff, 89a is a secondary road but well-traveled; especially on a Sunday. It follows a beautiful trail, with red rock and woods lining each side of the road followed by a mountainous entry into Flagstaff. Flowing through Oak Creek Canyon with a 10-12 % ten mile climb it would eventually descend into Flagstaff. The scenery along the route is stunning and the road is particularly busy prior to entering Sedona.

With a small stream flowing just a few feet from the road, wild animals, deer, rabbits, squirrels etc. could be heard and often seen. Exiting Sedona, the road became much less traveled since a few miles to the East was an interstate highway. So, after their visit, motorists would take the interstate to Flagstaff, leaving 89a to those who were in no hurry. By this time, I was riding "lone eagle" and enjoying communing with nature. A few miles into this serene experience I could hear behind me, in the distance, a thundering noise but paid little attention to it.

Observing, pedaling and absorbed in the experience, the tranquility was suddenly violated by the sound of a loud, roaring, obnoxious sounding motorcycle. As it approached me it destroyed the effect of what nature offered. When it finally passed me, the moron driving it began yelling loud enough to be heard from the booming noise his cycle made. He said, "Hey, that bike doesn't belong on this road." And, to emphasize his displeasure at my presence in his personal domain, he continued "get that fuckin bike off the road." Ha! I was actually mildly amused and not the least bit "pissed off." (Well maybe a little). I began to wonder if he knew how absurd his outburst was. He was either ignorant or stupid! If he didn't realize the negative impact his motorcycle had on the environment in terms of noise and polluting the air, he was ignorant. If he did, then he was obviously stupid. Either way, because of the ludicrous nature of the statement, it had no impact on my Karma. After he passed I was back into tranquility mode. So there, dumb ass!!

As the mountains loomed in the distance, I was looking forward to the final climb of the week and I stopped for a well-deserved rest on a bridge ledge that crossed a small stream of water. It was here I decided to ingest some power gel to give me that final boost. Those gels always seemed to provide extra energy I needed to climb steeply graded roads. While sitting on the side of a bridge before the last climb, I heard noise in the creek bed that ran alongside the road. Peering into an opening in the brush that protected the stream I saw SPENCER! Yes, the same young man I encountered two days ago at the top of Mt. Mingus.

He was frolicking in the riverbed having a great time communing with nature. I then noticed his bike with the carrier attached to it. The "baby on board" sign was still on the back. After yelling at him to indicate my presence, he waded out of the stream to greet me. I noticed he was not wearing the red high top Converse tennis shoes I had observed two days prior. He was now wearing a pair of, now get these…flip-flops. Yes, he was actually riding with flip-flops and took the time to play in the water before climbing the 12% incline into Flagstaff. So much for the need for exotic biking equipment "required" for distance riding. I suppose the need for what most riders use to ride distances is nothing more than a reflection of the "bike snob" mentality. Spencer certainly paid no attention to how he appeared as he rode. I suspect his comfort level, also, was not adversely affected.

After a brief conversation, I offered Spencer some power gel and a few power bars. He gratefully accepted and I set out for Flagstaff. Reflecting back, I often wondered why I didn't join him in the water. I probably thought I was too "cool" to engage in that type of activity. Boy was that a mistake!

The final 15 miles into Flagstaff were continual switch backs. I had determined by this time that carving tight curves into the road ensured travelers would use extreme caution in order to avoid dangers naturally associated with driving in this type of terrain. Oddly enough, the climb did not seem particularly difficult. This perhaps was not that abnormal because I had been climbing all week and I suspect had conditioned me so that it seemed easier. Nevertheless, at the top of the mountain was a park with awe inspiring views of the valley and mountain road I had just climbed. In addition, it was the last SAG stop of the day so before continuing into Flagstaff I took my time and just enjoyed the experience.

View of Mountain riding to Flagstaff

Flagstaff was a well needed rest day and the entire group looked forward to it. After a week of desert, with extreme record heat, followed by the highest mountains our little party would encounter the entire trip, we could finally sleep in, rest our aches and pains and work on our bikes. What the staff stated before the ride was accurate. Before the ride began, veteran staff members declared emphatically the first week would be the most difficult. If you survive the first week, the rest of the journey will be a piece of cake. While this was encouraging, it was not necessarily true. The good news was that at least we all survived. That would not be the case for the entire journey!

Of all the rest days scheduled for the entire trip, this was probably the one we all looked forward to the most. Doubts about our ability to do a cross country bike ride were put to rest for the most part. Everyone enjoyed their time in Flagstaff.

By this time, many riders needed repairs to their bikes in addition to recovery time for various injuries incurred to this point. I, for one, needed time for my injuries to heal. During the first week I had what I thought would be permanent nerve damage to my left hand. Using the second finger next to the pinkie to type my blog was problematic and even when showering I was unable to secure a bar of soap in that hand. Additionally, I drove the spiked pedal on my bike into the Achilles tendon on my right leg during the third day of the ride. Broken skin and swelling remained and it was still quite sore. The good news is that my calves were not cramping since I began taking the proper supplements.

In terms of allowing injuries recovery time, other members of the group also developed physical difficulties. These included, but were not limited to, hand numbness, butt rash from saddles, sunburn, and an assortment of other maladies. In fact, Al went to the local bike shop and had the height of his handle bars adjusted to accommodate his hand problem. Many others had their handlebars rewrapped with extra cushion for more comfort too, hopefully, avoid other hand problems.

Flagstaff, one of the major metropolises in Arizona, has many bicycle shops. Our group discovered one that was particularly efficient resulting in virtually all the bikers making a visit to it. In fact, my roommate Hank, whose chain was broken shortly before we arrived in town, queried many bike shops in the area and none had access to a chain that would accommodate his bike. Hank offered one of these establishments a $20 incentive to find one. Not only did this particular shop locate a chain, they found two, and refused to take the finder fee. I developed a tremendous amount of respect for the employees of that shop because Hank was ready to purchase a new bike if they couldn't locate a chain. Workers at the shop stated that with the new chain his bike would make it across the country thus dismissing the sale of a $2,000-$3000 bicycle deal. Good honest employees indeed. However, they were not entirely correct. When we reached Champaign, even though the chains held up, Hank's rims were cracked and he needed to purchase two new ones before he could continue his ride. And, as the trip continued, he developed more problems with his bike but Rick, our excellent mechanic, was good at temporary fixes allowing Hank to continue riding.

I reiterate, our time in Flagstaff was quite enjoyable. Although we arrived on a Sunday most of the shops, restaurants and business' were open and close to where we were staying. This enabled our group the opportunity to patronize these establishments.

Many of the riders, who I suggested earlier, had significant more wealth than me, used the "down time" to hire professional message therapists to reinvigorate tired and tight muscles. Others attended local movies. As for me, I spent time in the aforementioned bicycle shop, in addition to a delightful lunch at the Beaver Street Brewery with friends.

Harry, Ira, and Nancy enjoying time at the Beaver Street Brewery

But, for the most part, I used the time to relax, clean and tune-up my bike and mentally prepare for the next part of the journey. In addition I was able to wander about and discover other unique places of interest.

Chapter 6

FLAGSTAFF TO HOLBROOK, AZ

Monday was "get away" day as we began the subsequent part of the trek across Arizona. Knowing the "hardest" week was behind us, the group was eager to begin the next portion of the journey. As previously stated, for someone who spent most of his life in central Illinois, the roads and landscape provided a constant change of scenery even though we continued biking in desert conditions. The geography now consisted of the Sonora and Painted Desert segment of the trip. Well rested, we engaged in a 96, officially a century, mile ride to Holbrook AZ. The highlight of that ride was the city of Winslow. If not for the Eagles hit song, "Take It Easy" Winslow is a very nondescript burg. The temperature during the morning hit a high of 84 degrees and, for one of the few times on the ride, we had a tailwind, (there I said it again….bad Karma), at 10-15 mph. However, as the mid-day hour approached, the wind had shifted and began blowing from a southerly direction. As a result, we encountered a crosswind and it eventually increased to about 45 mph. One might ask how I was able to get this specific information. Again, those of wealth used Garmin's that give a full readout on such things.

Interstate 40, which ran parallel to old Route 66, was our primary road when we were unable to ride Route 66. Being in such disrepair, iconic Route 66 was the route of choice for the group but in many places it was not available for vehicle traffic. So, yes, we were allowed to ride on the interstates in both Arizona and New Mexico. Even with multiple county and state roads, in addition to a mixture of lesser roads (sparse at best in these states) the interstate was the most direct route across Arizona. Prior to the ride, I always believed using the interstates for bicycle riding was perhaps the safest and best place to travel over long distances. Wide shoulders with "rumble strips" seemed to make them safe and the only worry would be the speed of the traffic. However, little did I realize the problems of interstate biking. First, the amount of junk that people deposited was phenomenal.

Secondly, many of these items were responsible for me having two flat tires between Flagstaff and Holbrook. As noted earlier, tiny metal shards that "blow outs" from semi-truck tires had spewed across the shoulder tended to penetrate the thin rubber exterior of my tires. Those posed the biggest problem. Since my tires were not Kevlar coated, they were extremely vulnerable to punctures. And, by the time we crossed New Mexico, my tires were flattened 8 times by the road trash. I was by far the leader in this dubious category.

As mentioned earlier, the interstate system in the Southwest was built parallel to and made obsolete the great highway-Route 66. Without going into an extensive history lesson, Route 66 was built in the 1950's as a connecting point between Chicago, IL and Los Angles, CA. Because it was such an iconic highway, television moguls developed a series in the 1960's centered on it called, can you imagine? Route 66. It was one of my all-time favorite television shows during my childhood. But, I digress. Because of the construction of the interstates, as previously indicated, parts of Route 66 were impassable. Even given that exemption, parts of Route 66 were not totally unusable so when convenient our group was detoured onto it. I took particular delight in viewing the buildings that still remain as a reminder of the rich history of that roadway. Riding past these remnants gave me a sense of history associated with that time period which one cannot get from textbooks.

An old relic left on route 66 falling into disrepair

Winslow AZ is not on Interstate 40 so we were able to use Route 66 as it wandered through that portion of the country. Riding into town in this desolated part of Arizona, I couldn't help but wonder, as I did in Palm Springs, why in the world anyone would build a town in this part of the desert. Prior to my arrival, I anticipated it being a vibrant, exciting Arizona city. Nothing could have been further from the truth. It was, in fact, inhabited initially (like many of the towns along Route 66) as a stop on the railroad system leading to California. It was named for Edward Winslow, president of the St Louis and San Francisco railroad. Unknowingly anticipating a thriving community, it turned out to be, for me, nothing more than a short stop in the road. I often wondered what made the city a viable entity as it is located in the middle of Navajo country and has no obvious major business or manufacturing attractions.

However, the corner that was made famous by the Eagles song is on the main road that runs through the middle of town. It is, obviously, a tourist attraction with a statue of Don Henley, writer of the hit song, on the corner and a picture of a flatbed Ford painted on the wall of a nearby business. That particular business burned down in 2004. All that remained, as we observed while riding through, was the wall with a mural of the Ford. Of course, Hank and I had to take advantage of the opportunity to have a picture with the statue, so all in all it was a worthwhile stop.

Other than the photo op one particular episode in Winslow still remains fresh in my mind. It involved a stop at the local Dairy Queen. Dairy Queens were very desirable stops because they provided ice cream in multiple flavors that provided a quick energy source. Also, other products from DQ's are quite tasty and particularly desired by our group of riders, including but not limited to hamburgers, cheeseburgers, chili dogs and an assortment of other goodies. This particular DQ was one of the earlier models containing no inside seating. While the serving windows were covered with awnings it was a "walk up" venue, much like the one located near where I lived as a child.

Hank and I stopped, and after ordering milk shakes, I asked if we could use the rest rooms in their establishment. There were no other public facilities nearby and by this time I really needed to relieve myself, if you know what I mean…..number 1. I politely asked the two young females who were working behind the counter if it would be possible to use their restroom. Not only did they refuse to allow access to the rest room, they became quite rude and belligerent. I wished I had not already purchased one of their products. Nevertheless, I needed to relieve myself so I went to the side of the building where the drinking fountains were located and took a leak on the side of the building. Realizing committing such an abhorrent act was somewhat immature; nevertheless, I had to go really bad. I noted that it was incredibly hot and a great relief when I had finished. I'm sure everyone on the planet can identify with that scenario and as one of my many motto's goes…"if you gotta go, you gotta go". Therefore, to Winslow, I say goodbye, good riddance, and piss on you! I often wonder why in the world the Eagles exalt through song this particular town. It is located in never, never land and a very unimpressive place.

For the rest of the day Hank and I rode together and arrived in Holbrook with no further adventurous episodes of note. By this time our routine was fairly set; shower, rest, route rap, evening meal, casual conversation with other riders to learn of their experiences of that day's ride and off to snooze land. Hank was usually the first to "hit the sack" around 8:00 pm and I would use this time to keep the followers of my blog up to date. My bed time was usually around 9:00 PM, give or takes a few minutes. Knowing 5:30 AM came early and another long ride was waiting that was a reasonable bedtime.

Chapter 7

HOLBROOK TO ALBUQUERQUE, NM

After Holbrook, the rest of the towns we meandered through ending at Albuquerque New Mexico were relatively uneventful. The terrain remained desert, Sonora and Painted, so my impressions of that part of the country are very positive…Winslow notwithstanding. I especially enjoyed the scenery of black volcanic rock that is layered between the granite rocks that made up the nearby cliffs. It reminded me of my childhood days watching those old western movies.

As the miles dragged on and on I imagined I might stop, hide behind the rocks, and attack those bikers who followed with shouts of Indian war chants that would send chills up their spines. What a great re-creation of the movie scenes of my youth. But, alas, I felt a need to continue and missed out on an opportunity to create an experience. Big mistake!!

Other nondescript towns where we made nightly stops were, Gallup and Grants, New Mexico. During these stretches, I adapted my riding technique to the conditions that existed, much to the chagrin of Ira, one of the race horses who also blogged his experiences on the ride. Those of us who blogged would often read other biker's blogs to compare the day's events. As a "lone eagle", the road waste caused me to experience many flat tires as I have already mentioned. Therefore, I decided to follow other riders in what I referred to as a "sweep technique". That is, the riders in the front of the pack would sweep the debris and cause me fewer flats.

I was to learn, much too late, that my tires needed a Kevlar coating to help reduce punctures, but I had no knowledge of that during the early stages of the ride. After posting this technique on my blog, Ira read it and commented to me in a rather negative manner that that would be inappropriate. Well, maybe it was true, and at some level I would agree with him, but at this time I saw no other alternative to avoiding flat tires caused by all the road debris. If it were a contest to see who could have the most punctures during this section of the country, I was clearly the winner…. hands down. By the time we reached Santa Fe NM I endured 8 flats and my tires were cut, potted and nicked to the point they needed to be replaced. Not even half way across the country and I already needed new tires.

One major event occurred near Grants NM. Crossing the Continental Divide was quite memorable. Having sufficient knowledge about how the North American continent separates between the Eastern and Western parts, I eagerly looked forward to this geographic location. Flowing rivers run toward the west from the western precipice of the Divide and flow toward the east on the eastern side. At least that is what I have been told by the science teachers I have known for years. Testing this hypothesis was a possibility using a rather crude technique the reader can imagine, but I had neither the inclination nor desire to do so. I suppose I could have looked at the direction of my stream while urinating on the Dairy Queen wall in Winslow but it didn't occur to me at that time so the opportunity was missed. Again, I am a history guy, not a geologist so I enjoyed my stay and was off to Albuquerque.

Continental Divide-Meeting of the continental plate

Since Santa Fe would be our second rest day and since it was the next stop after Albuquerque I felt I could wait to replace my tires since I would have ample time to do so. Rich, one of the bikers who would leave us in Albuquerque, and lived in the area, did me a huge favor by finding quality Von Taeger tires that had the needed Kevlar coating. After replacing my old tires, I did not have another flat until we reached Pennsylvania. And, in fact, I didn't have to change the Von Taegar until I finished the ride and returned home.

Chapter 8

ALBUQUERQUE TO SANTA FE, NM

As a 10-11 year old child, our family took a vacation to visit relatives in Albuquerque NM. Riding toward the city I tried to evoke memories of the area. But, alas, it was so long ago that my memory recalled the visit with only a vague recollection of my kinfolk, the heat and the mountains on the distant horizon. It also offered no recollection of the tourist areas we may have visited or any of the amenities it had to offer. My assumption is that there was really nothing for a young kid to get excited about. So, while I was looking forward to riding through Albuquerque it did not stir any memorable event from my earlier visit. After all the climbing and riding across New Mexico I was quite pleased to see a 2-3 mile descent into Albuquerque.

However, I should have realized a downhill ride of that magnitude meant only one thing…leaving would be an equally long ride uphill…..the yin and yang of the universe as it applied to biking. And, as it turned out, that was absolutely the case.

Arriving in Albuquerque I was impressed with the Rio Grande river flowing through it but, again, had no recall of it during my childhood visit. The Rio Grande had no significance to me at that time or, I assume, it would have stuck in my memory bank.

Rio Grande from bridge in Albuquerque

Touring through the city, I noticed a section referred to as "Old Albuquerque." We stayed in the newer section and I had thoughts of riding back to the old part of town. However, time and fatigue prevented me from doing this. So, I continued the routine of bike cleaning, eating and readying myself for a good night sleep hitting the bed at around 9:00 PM. As it turned out, I needed as much rest as possible to complete the next day's adventure.

Ranking rides in terms of difficulty, the trek from Albuquerque to Santa Fe was, for me, the second toughest of the entire journey. Santa Fe is located in the Ortiz mountain range with climbs totaling 7,800 feet from Albuquerque along what is called the Turquoise Trail. Adding to the difficulty, the wind blew directly into our path at a 15-20 mph rate. Plus, it rained most of the day. While it was not a particularly hard rain, it made the ride rather unpleasant, nevertheless. To illustrate this point, many of us had to keep our gears engaged in "granny" gear while going DOWN HILL.

Picture of road leaving Albuquerque toward Santa Fe… Ominous

That is unheard of, and man, how discouraging was this? However, I must admit that since we were still in the high desert region of New Mexico, those of us who are visitors should not complain. Rain in the desert is a very welcomed event to the locals.

These are words seldom spoken in this part of the country. Imagine this scenario. Two cowboys are sitting around a campfire. "Ehh…Ehh" well Zeke I wish this damn rain would quit. It rains too friggin' much around here!" Now pass me another biscuit!" And yes, that was from my Hudson and Landry album.

Even though it was a difficult ride, one particular "highlight" I enjoyed was a stop at the quaint little town of Madrid (pronounced MA drid) NM. It caters to tourists and has a popular restaurant, the Mine Shaft Tavern, known for its tasty food and beverages. Madrid has recovered from "ghost town" status by building small shops and businesses that cater to the artist crowd. Upon entering town until its exit, artsy touristy establishments line the main street.

The good news is that it provided a respite from the climbing. Also, Madrid, NM became well known for, among other things, the movie Wild Hogs. Located south of Santa Fe it was a welcomed break from the drudgery of the ride.

Hank, Harry, Bob and me refreshing at the Mine Shaft Tavern

Prior to our arrival at Madrid, the SAG stop was stationed a few miles south of town. Normally Hank rides with the racehorses but at the SAG, I found him "slumming." Rain had begun to fall in torrents so he planned on waiting it out under the shelter provided by the SAG station. Combined with the rain and relatively low temperature, low 50's, this resulted in uncomfortably cold weather. It was so cold that Margaret, one of the staffers, started the engine on the SAG vehicle and turned on the heater to warm Hank's hands. Hank then inquired of Margaret if she would give him some of the latex gloves she kept in the van to keep his hands warm and dry. While my hands were able to tolerate the cold, my feet were drenched. So, drawing upon my previous experience of having wet feet during skiing vacations, I also asked for a pair of latex gloves. I then proceeded to place them on my feet between the sock and skin. It proved to be a valuable lesson in my attempt to keep my feet relatively dry. Knowing these conditions would occur later in the trip, I used this technique whenever I faced "all day" rains. Rain events which we would endure later in the ride saturated my shoes, socks and skin to an extent I had never experienced before. And, this technique of putting latex gloves on my feet actually worked in reducing the discomfort associated with constantly wet feet.

Now, on a more somber note, at the start of the ride to Santa Fe, Charlie, who rode my wheel across most of the Mohave Desert, asked if he could ride my wheel to Santa Fe. Again, it is a technique where the lead rider "pulls" the riders behind in a pace line by blocking headwinds. It is used to help relieve the fatigue of biking alone against strong headwinds. As a Clydesdale, I, who block a significant amount of wind, gladly accommodated Charlie's request. So, as we began, Charlie was on my wheel. After a few short miles into an extremely robust headwind, Charlie yelled for me to stop. His camelback, which he always wore, was convoluted and he needed to stop and straighten it. Finishing his adjustment, as luck would have it, Harry and his group, in a pace line, passed us. I mentioned to Charlie, "Let's join them so we can all share the work load." I then sprinted ahead and took a position at the end of their four person line.

Unfortunately, and at the time unbeknownst to me, Charlie never made the sprint. I assumed he felt he could not keep up as he fell behind our little group. After a while, he was no longer in my field of vision and, as I was told later, he joined George. George, the same individual I rode with into Wittenberg, is a steady rider but was in no particular hurry to complete the ride to Santa Fe.

At the SAG stop where Hank and I joined forces and obtained the aforementioned latex gloves, I felt confident Charlie would come rolling in as it was a prolonged stop for us. Since the rain continued and we were waiting for it to cease, I lingered longer than I normally would have. After an appropriate amount of time, Hank and I began riding assuming Charlie and George were taking their time with no interest in joining anyone in a pace line. After another grueling 30 mile uphill, windy, rainy jaunt we finally arrived at the day's destination.

Santa Fe, as mentioned earlier, was our second rest day of the journey. Busy recovering and making my bike ready for when we resumed in two days, I did not have the opportunity to see Charlie and inquire about how or why he dropped behind.

That night Peter invited anyone interested to accompany him to the Cowgirl Hall of Fame restaurant. It was a Mexican style venue owned by a friend of his who formerly lived in New York City.

By this time, Mark and Lisa, our "chauffeurs" left the group (he had contracted to only to Albuquerque) so Hank and I needed to resort to other means of getting to the local sites in the towns. We decided to join a group of about 12 other riders at the restaurant so we used the local taxi service to get there. The restaurant was located about five miles from where we were staying. By this time my body knew what nourishment it needed to sustain adequate energy levels for distance riding. I ordered a salmon dish. Now, I suspect salmon is probably not the best item to get in a Mexican restaurant but I am not a real fan of Mexican food. Also, since it was a rest day I was not averse to drinking a Margarita or two.

Jim was my seating companion and I noticed he needed to put his eating utensils in a precise order. Can you say anal? Wondering how he would react, I intentionally mussed up the order turning them in all directions. Can you say asshole! Jim didn't appear to be upset but I had a feeling he was mildly annoyed even though he appeared to laugh it off.

After a delightful meal and conversation it was time to leave. Hank and I took the first available cab back to the hotel. That turned out to be a huge mistake. Remember, one of my objectives during the trip was to interact with the locals and get a sense of their life experience. After we made our way back to the hotel, we frittered away the evening. If I had stayed at the bar, a local band provided musical entertainment. They played everything from oldies to blues. That would have been a great way to end the evening. Harry and his group stayed and told me later they had quite an enjoyable time. I wish I had stayed and vowed to never let this happen again. I can be quite the party animal when forced......or not!

Since we arrived on a Friday, with Saturday being a rest day, I spent time getting my bike prepared for the next day. Not only did I do the regular cleaning, oiling chain and other necessary chores, I finally managed to change to new tires with the Kevlar coating. Both Hank and I used the day to rest and recuperate with no added adventurous activities. Oddly enough, I still had not seen Charlie to inquire of him how his ride to Santa Fe progressed. While an apology was not necessary, I wanted to query his thoughts about me joining the pace line and abandoning him. It is not unusual for riders to just keep to themselves on rest days so I did not think much of it.

Sunday began the continuance of the journey with the familiar starting routine beginning at 6:45 am. Hank and I usually awoke long before then, around 5:30, and made our way to breakfast by 6:00 am. As I traversed the stairs to the hotel lobby I noticed something unusual at the door to the room where one of our riders was staying. I saw EMT's enter along with members of the CrossRoads support crew, including Tracy and Rick. Something was amiss and as I approached the scene I was politely asked to not stop but continue with my business. At breakfast, everyone speculated as to the cause of the commotion. Most knew it was Charlie's room. We figured it was some sort of health problem; probably from the extreme conditions of the ride from Albuquerque. Seeing an ambulance gave rise to wild speculation relating to Charlie's situation. At 7:30 a.m. we were ready to depart and I observed the ambulance leave the hotel. Noting they were not running any emergency sirens or lights I concluded the worst for Charlie. At the first SAG stop, I inquired of Mack, another one of our excellent staff members, about information relevant to Charlie's health. Since he could give me no good news, I again concluded the worst....Charlie was DEAD. That information was confirmed at route rap that evening. We were told he did not die from heart attack or stroke, rather "lack of oxygen". This would not be entirely uncommon because of the strain of the ascent, the height we climbed and the oxygen at that level. Afterward we found out Charlie, in his will, donated one million dollars to his home state of Vermont to build bike trails; a good man Charlie.

Chapter 9

SANTA FE TO TUCUMCARI, NM

Riding from Santa Fe, our day's destination would be Las Vegas. And no, we did not take a severe left turn north into Nevada. And yes! There is another Las Vegas not associated with the gambling city of Las Vegas Nevada. This Las Vegas is actually in New Mexico. Now, don't make fun of my ignorance of U.S. geography, most of the riders were not aware of this fact as well.

I thoroughly enjoyed biking alone during this leg of the trip. Following the Santa Fe Trail and parts of old Route 66 was definitely a thrill. There were several severe climbs but since we had a tailwind it wasn't nearly as bad as the ride to Santa Fe. Yin/Yang again. The scenery was right out of the old west and as I traversed the territory, it brought back memories of the Lone Ranger and other "B" cowboy movies of the sixties and seventies. Again, the idea of getting off my bike, hiding behind the rocks and "attack" unsuspecting riders that came along behind me was quickly dismissed as immature and juvenile. And, I was certainly above this type of activity.....or maybe not. Nevertheless, I continued. But, looking back I would probably engage in this activity if I had to do it all over again.

Picture opportunities were plentiful in this region and I took full advantage of these occasions. Of course, I needed one with me in the foreground sitting on one of the rock formations, a typical cowboy pose, so at the first SAG stop I had Mack photograph me.

Sitting on Old Western Rock…..notice garbage under rock

Since we were leaving low desert terrain and transferring to high desert, the scenery was changing from mostly brown scrub brush to green, lush trees and bushes.

Slow change to high desert region

At route rap that evening we were informed that Charlie had died and we would be doing a three mile silent peloton, in order to honor him; An excellent call by the CrossRoads team. This day's ride was from Las Vegas, NM. to Tucumcari, NM. Since most of us had never been involved in a ceremonial peloton, the staff informed us of the process. In two by two, side by side, formation we rode silently. Oddly enough a group of wild horses in the field to our left mirrored the riders. It was a spectacular site as they kept pace for the entire three miles. I often wish I had taken a picture of them but was told, at the time, that during a peloton for a fallen rider it would have dishonored Charlie's memory. After the requisite distance we again were on our own and I set off alone to enjoy the remainder of the day's journey.

Two memorial events occurred on the ride to from Las Vegas to Tucumcari. 100 miles is the distance between those two cities. Having left the mountainous areas of Arizona and western New Mexico, I erroneously, assumed there would be little climbing involved. Boy was I wrong! While the scenery continued to be amazing with a combination of mountains contrasting with the scenery of the high desert, the last 50 miles of the day consisted of continual climbing and then descending "hills" of 9-10% grade.

On either side of the road, at considerable distance, mountains stretched as far as the eye could see, even though they appeared to be quite far away. I wasn't sure if I would eventually have to go over, around or through them. It never really crossed my mind. As I got closer, it became clear this range of mountains would need to be traversed. Riding through them I noticed that the difference from prior climbs was there were no "switchbacks" requiring hard braking and instant acceleration. Great, I thought, no arduous climbing and all downhill. It would be a delightful downhill experience.

During many of the descents in this region I attained a top speed of 45-50 mph. And, after conferring with companions, some revealed they went even faster. Hank, on the other hand, did not feel comfortable with this kind of speed and elected to SAG the downhill sections. Now, one of the "givens" I learned from this experience is that regardless, for EVERY downhill there will be an UPHILL and vice versa. Yin and yang, "maat" (balance in the universe from ancient Egypt), and other equalization concepts, must prevail. That's the way of the world!

Nearing mile 60, a previous traveler with a bizarre sense of humor, (no one from our group), had written on the surface of the road, "Beware of the Wall". Looking down the road I could see miles ahead and noticed the road seemed to go straight up.....at a ninety degree angle. Impossible I thought. Because it was desert, I thought the image was like one of those mirages of pools of water thirsty a traveler frequently sees. And, the nearer one gets, of course, it disappears. Then, another thought crossed my mind. Maybe it was one of those roads we often see that are carved into the mountainside used for communication lines; usually phone or electric wires. Upon first glance, it looked far too steep to be an actual road for vehicle use.

As I got nearer, more warnings were inscribed on the road surface; "Beware of the wall" and "turn back now!" Since I was then, and still am to a large extent, not very proficient at climbing, the warnings were indeed intimidating. I suspect, at this time, it was more mental fatigue rather than any new degree of ascent we had not already physically conquered.

At mile 66 I met "the wall." While those with Garmins claimed it to be only a 9-10% grade, it seemed to me to be double that. Recalling the experience "THE WALL" remains one of the most memorable of all the climbs. It seemed to be the most difficult of the entire 100,000 feet of climbing accomplished on the entire cross country experience.

During the ascent there were more writings on the road surface, but by now they became more positive. "You can do it" "Almost there" and "Keep up the good work" are examples. Afterward, I wondered why I found this climb particularly difficult. My conclusion was it occurred after 66 miles of riding plus the fact it is always fun to play "mind games" on the cyclists.

Later, upon further reflection, I found out something most everyone involved in these types of adventures already knows or would eventually realize. The negative mindset of "can't do" can be overcome with the positive mindset "can and will do!"

Yet, at this time, all I could think of was how hard the climb seemed but vowed to not get off the bike and walk. Toppling over due to lack of progress would be the only way for the wall to defeat me. Grinding steadily in "granny gear" like Thomas the Train lugging logs, at a rate of only 4 mph, the thought actually crossed my mind that it would be much easier to get off and walk the bike to the top. But again, that would be admitting defeat and I would lose EFI. Yet, if I did, no one would know. Ha!! Yea right. I would know, so it was not an option. As I neared the summit, my heart was pounding angrily in my chest. 200 beats per minute would not be an overestimation, but I was determined to continue. And, as the old saying goes, "a watched pot never boils." When I looked up at the summit it never seemed to get any closer. So, I dropped my head and continued grinding.

At last, when I finally reached the top, my lungs were screaming, my legs were toast, and I was ready for a welcomed rest. As luck would have it, Nancy was sitting alongside the road at the top with a punctured tire. She had been riding with Hank and, as I joked with Hank later, he had abandoned her after the climb. Way to go Hank you un-chivalrous male pig!

Nancy was not especially proficient at changing a flat so I was glad to offer a hand. It provided a chance for me to rest and engage in doing a good deed as well. In fact, it was common practice at this time for members of the riding group to engage in this helpful activity. Ha, Mr. Nice Guy. As it turned out it was a good thing I stopped. She has a very expensive bike with expensive tires. The odd configuration of the tire on the wheel made it very difficult to separate them. But, after a very laborious and difficult effort, I had the tire changed and placed it back on her bike. Another bit of good fortune transpired just as I replaced Nancy's wheel. One of the SAG vans appeared at the top of the hill over "THE WALL."

That was extremely fortuitous because Nancy used CO_2 cartridges to inflate her tires and had no pressure gage to determine the amount of air displaced into the tube. The van carries tire pumps that accurately measure the amount of air and are much easier to use than the CO_2. Also, CO_2 needs to be replaced at the first opportunity because it tends to leach from the tubes so they are not a permanent solution but a temporary fix. After getting Nancy's bike back into riding shape, I resumed my quest, thankful I had conquered the dreaded "wall" and happy knowing Tucumcari was a relatively short distance down the road.

1,000 mile mark. That was the second significant event of the ride to Tucumcari. It was hard to believe we were approximately one third of the way across the continent of North America. CrossRoads staff members made signs to mark the passing of each thousand miles we covered. Those signs depicting the one, two and three thousand miles of riding were coveted mementos of the cross country adventure because they documented each level of that accomplishment.

The rest of that day's ride was relatively uneventful and I looked forward to similar conditions the following day. All in all, the journey from Las Vegas to Tucumcari was one of the more delightful rides, the "wall" notwithstanding.

Dalhart Texas would be our next destination and we would actually cross two state lines in one day. Informed at route rap the Dalhart ride would be a 96 (officially a "century) mile distance and it would involve small "hills" but nothing like the "wall." I anticipated what I believed to be an easy effort. In fact, that night I blogged "I look forward to only having a ride of 96 miles the next day." Perhaps the "bike snob" attitude was rearing its ugly head. JINXED!! I should have known better. Little did I realize what the next day had in store. It actually turned out to be, far and away, the most difficult riding day of the entire experience and many riders lost EFI during this part of the trip.

The Plains

Chapter 1

Tumcumcari To Dalhart, Tx

Dalhart Texas!! What can I say about the ride to that municipality? First a little background. Dalhart has the largest cattle "processing" plant in North America. I emphasize processing because, for all intent and purposes, (and I'm not against eating meat), cowboys working at the plant kill the cows and transport the product to various markets across the U.S. for we humans to consume. Who doesn't like a well prepared T-bone steak? But I digress once again.

Called the XIT plant, this facility can hold up to 400,000 cows nestled into pens on a several hundred acre plot of land. At the time of my ride past the plant, there were only 80,000 cattle waiting for their ultimate fate. As I approached, I noted the cattle were visible in their pens as far as the eye could see. However, the odor emanating from the area could be detected miles from the actual processing site.

While I was never a great meat eater, as stated earlier, I am not opposed to an occasional steak or roast. But, because of the length and difficulty of the ride to Dalhart, I made frequent stops; one of which was outside the pens of the XIT plant. Relying on my vast photographic experience, (ha! Yea, right) I decided that particular scenario would make a fantastic picture. The image of mile after mile of a cattle herd would be quite impressive. After leaving my bike by the road, I approached the barbed wire fence separating me from the bovines. Several cattle moseyed up and gave me a big, brown eyed, sad, forlorn gaze. It seemed as if they knew their ultimate fate and for some reason I felt they looked to me as their savior. Alas, all I could do was give a sympathetic moooo as a way of acknowledging their plight. It seemed to me at that time their attitude would be the same as someone waiting to be executed in our prison system even though they had committed no crime other that being born a cow. I actually did not eat beef the rest of the trip.

XIT cattle "processing" plant-Dalhart Texas

Without question, the momentous aspect of the Dalhart ride is that it ranks number one in terms of difficulty. That morning started on a rather ominous note; an exceedingly strong headwind. Our riding direction to Dalhart was in a northeasterly direction. And, of course, that was the direction from which the wind was coming. This meant we would be beginning the day riding into a headwind with the major portion of the day's ride continuing into it. Not to worry since by this time we were encountering headwinds on a daily basis. Usually this is not a particularly new or difficult event with wind speeds at a steady 10-15 mph. That was relatively doable but within the first five miles or so, it increased to 15-20 with gusts to 25-30 mph. I reiterate, it was howling directly into us. I was not a happy biker.

Small, unassuming hills seemed like mountains in terms of ascent yet with no relief associated with a normal descent. Unique to wind is that if you are going in only one direction with the current of air in your face, unlike mountains where there is a down after a climb, it is entirely possible for the wind to be pushing into you all day long. This was the case as we struggled toward Dalhart TX. It got to the point where I was actually verbally, not mentally, cursing the wind. And yes, I understand that was foolish but as I said I wasn't too happy about riding into a 20 mile per hour wind for 100 miles; a definite roadblock and another test of my resolve to be EFI. Don't be offended but shouting common vulgarities like "you Mo...fu...wind" "you s...head wind, and other epitaphs of that nature erupted from my vocal cords from time to time. I know, I know, readers will be shocked, but it was what it was.

Then, realizing it was indeed foolish to continue in this manner I had, for me, what was an earth shattering epiphany. A man to man talk with myself ensued; mentally at this point. The conversation went something like this. "If you continue this nonsensical tirade against something you can do absolutely nothing about, get your ass off the bike and take the SAG wagon into town. Hell, if this thing were easy everyone would do it." "Otherwise, recognize it for what it is and continue the best you can, one pedal at a time." "Change your horseshit negative mental attitude or quit!"

I don't know if other people talk to themselves in this manner but from time to time a good chastising from within is often needed, usually, at least in my case, with a positive outcome.

My cerebral response, "Okay I'll give it a try". My next verbal outburst went something like this. "Ha! Surely (I know.....don't call me Shirley) you can blow harder than that. I can barely feel the wind"... Is that the best you can do?" Oddly enough it seemed to work. While the wind blew as hard as before my mental exercise, it didn't bother me as much. Really!! There is much to be said about mind over matter. So, I continued onward with a better attitude but I was unable to observe the scenery, as was my usual technique because my head position was in a low downward tilt. Creating a smoother air flow over my body was essential to ensuring success. I was able to continue into the unruly wind with this method.

Early in the afternoon I arrived at the first SAG stop and intentionally mentioned the dreaded word "tailwind". "It looks like there is no tailwind today and I'm having fun. I could ride all day into this wind." This particular categorization was supposed to be no-no jargon as a biker superstition and was thought it would agitate the wind "gods" ensuring headwinds. At this point I didn't give a rat's patootie because I had fought them all morning. It couldn't get worse. Ha, wrong again dragon breath!! Just to test my resolve, the wind did indeed get worse. After leaving the SAG, winds from the Northeast increased to 30-35 mph with

40 mile gusts. This is not biker hyperbole. Later that evening Jim, our weather guru, confirmed it referring to his Garmin as his resource.

Entering Texas and taking a respite from the wind

Needless to say, I made many stops along the way to refuel and recover. At one of the stops I nearly stepped on a snake in the grass (no, not referring to any of my friends or bosses) sunning itself, or so I assumed. It was a rather ominous, large looking serpent. Keeping my distance, but gaining more confidence, I got close enough to photograph it. I found out later, by the Dalhart locals, getting close to that particular variety of desert snake was dangerous and sometimes fatal. If it had struck and bitten me I would have been in real trouble since it is one of the most poisonous snakes, a Southern Copperhead, in that part of Texas. Also, because I was riding lone eagle, if I had been bitten, immediate medical assistance would not have been available. It looks like I dodged a bullet, (ha! Cowboy talk) so, once again, Karma. Bad winds all day countered by good fortune of not being bitten by a snake. And so it is.

Snake (Southern Copperhead) resting in the Texas sun

With more than 25 miles to go, which meant another two and one half hours of riding, averaging only 10 mph, one of the SAG wagons appeared and three of our riders were sitting in it with their bikes loaded onto the back. "Hey Champ, hop in." "This wind is miserable and we can be at the hotel in less than 30 minutes." "We've got room for one more." Boy was that ever tempting. But, again, I was still EFI at that time and I knew it would be easier to quit in the future if I gave up at this point. After careful consideration I responded "Thanks, but no thanks" and as the van disappeared toward the horizon I wondered if I made the correct decision.

It was another two and one half hours later when I finally arrived at the hotel in Dalhart. Normally, I averaged between 16 to 18 miles per hour. Today, the best I could do was 10 mph. I started the day at 7:30 a.m. and arrived at our destination at 5:30 p.m. A ten hour ride, 96 miles at 10 mph. Harry, and his crazy crew, actually rode the remaining 4 miles to get an even 100. Now, that was really extreme.

After reading other blogs and speaking with some of the other riders, we all concurred that, so far, this was the hardest ride of the journey. Even today, when I ride and the wind picks up, I tell myself it will never be as bad as the Dalhart experience. Any riding into a headwind from that point forward would be a "piece of cake." On another note, as I relate many of the experiences in terms of Karma and the Yin/Yang of the universe, (aside from the snake of which I had no knowledge), I knew a positive event must follow.

Chapter 2

A Dalhart Experience

Her teeth were arranged in rows across her mouth in such a fashion it looked like she could eat corn cob through a picket fence. The ample rolls of adipose tissue that waved across her torso were held in place by a tight fitting sweater. She was sitting alone at a table in the middle of the tavern accompanied only by a beer and a half full bottle of Jack Daniels whiskey.

After the arduous ride into Dalhart, following route rap, a needed shower and a sumptuous evening meal, several of us decided to stop at a local drinking establishment to further replenish lost carbs. Once again, I reiterate, one of my pleasures during the trip was to interact with the local inhabitants of areas we passed in order to get a well-rounded flavor of different sections of the country. So, I eschewed the franchise establishments and a small group of us looked for a bar, restaurant, etc. patronized by locals.

One particular establishment we passed fit the description of what we deemed to be a local bar. A dingy, unattractive exterior peaked our curiosity. In the window an OPEN neon sign flashed to welcome the thirsty traveler. Upon entering the inn, real cowboys were standing along the bar rail in their dirty jeans, brow beaten hats, with a shot of whisky in one hand and a beer in the other. These were cowboys of the modern era but still resembled those of the past.

Giving us a quick glance, but not paying us any particular attention, they resumed their imbibing. Sauntering past the "lady" sitting alone, our little group found a remote location at the back of bar near the pool table area. We were going to relax, discuss the day's events and perhaps shoot a little pool.

Following a couple games of pool, the aforementioned "lady" approached our table with her bottle of Jack.

"Who would like to share a drink with the lady?" she inquired with a slight slur and a wicked smile on her face.

Suddenly the bar went silent and it was evident the cowboys were waiting to see how these "foreigners" were going to handle the situation. It was obvious, in addition to being slightly inebriated; the lady was a regular at this particular business and a favorite among the locals.

One of our group leaned over to me and asked "Are we going to get into fight?"

"Not if I can help it," I replied and noted this place did not look like a "fightin' bar," having experienced many of those in my younger days,

I quickly looked around our table and decided to take action. Knowing that to refuse her offer would be akin to an insult, I removed the bottle of Jack Daniels from her grasp, immediately gulped down a generous amount of that intoxicating liquid, chased it down from my own bottle of Bud Light, and proceeded to thank her for her generosity. With an intuitive sense born from experience, I knew if I used a shot glass I would be exhibiting a wussy attitude. I finished by raking by right arm sleeve across my mouth in true cowboy fashion.

She then placed a rather thick, heavy arm around my shoulder and declared, "You want to know something?" she inquired. "Thars are only two things that happen to me when I drink Jack." "I either go to jail or I get laid."

Responding with my usual quick wit gained from many experiences talking my way out of trouble, I replied "Well, I hope the jail cell isn't particularly cold tonight because I don't believe we can help you with that other part."

The local patrons, who were listening intently, started a laughin', a whoopin' and a hollerin. From that point, until we left the bar, we were treated like old long lost friends. When we told them of our cross country riding adventure they were in awe and implied we were crazier than the lady who offered us the drink. Who were we to argue? After playing pool and interacting until well after midnight we were ready to leave, knowing we had accomplished another positive connection with individuals native to the local area we visited.

In retrospect, I accused Harry of going back to the bar after we left and fulfilling the lady's wish by keeping her out of jail, but he still denies it to this day!

Chapter 3

DALHART TO LIBERAL, KS

After an unusually short sleep, getting in around 1:00 a.m. and engaging in the morning ritual beginning at 5:30 a.m. we left Dalhart, TX. Guymon Oklahoma was that day's targeted terminus. Our stay in Texas was brief in that we cut off the end of the panhandle as we passed through.

Dalhart to Guymon was a relatively short 79 miles with rather non-descript terrain. It was mostly flat as the topography changed from the mountain and desert areas we had endured since leaving LA three weeks prior. From the Rockies through three deserts, (Mojave, Sonora, Painted) now the terrain was relatively flat. I say relatively because there is no truly flat ground. It is just a matter of degree with undulations; some higher, some lower, but not flat; typical Texas/Oklahoma land. Mile after mile of hard pavement with wide open ranges on either side of the road that fed the cattle, alongside the occasional herd of wild horses galloping in the distance, made it an interesting and scenic ride.

Entering Oklahoma

As usual the wind was against us, which would be the rule for most of the rest of the journey, but it didn't compare to what would come to be called the "Dalhart" wind.

Since Kansas loomed further up the road, my expectation was that it would be a reasonably flat state flowing with the "amber waves of grain"; another wrong expectation that peppered the ride across America.

After the ride to Guymon a breather awaited us. I, again, must reiterate the balance of good/bad, Yin/Yang days evident in a mission of this nature. Difficult climbs, wind, and centuries were balanced by speedy downhills, the occasional tailwind interspersed with some short rides. Guymon to Liberal, Kansas was the shortest ride of the trip as it was only a thirty-seven mile trek. Because it was of such short duration, most of us could do that in about two hours. Therefore, we would have plenty of time to engage in some of the activities the town, hopefully, provided.

The highlight of the trek to Liberal was at a SAG stop in Hooker, OK. That particular town invoked plenty of interest from those who did not know its story. For myself, I assumed it was named after the famous Civil War general Joseph Hooker. January 26, 1863 saw the installation of "Fightin' Joe" as the new commander of the Army of the Potomac, and by this time, he had acquired the nick name because, unlike Union General McClain, he would actually engage the rebellious South in battle. Without going into a lengthy historical dissertation, Hooker was best known for his defeat by General Lee at the Battle of Chancellorsville.

That first assumption was Wrongo!! It got its name from a local ranch foreman John "Hooker" Threlkeld. He acquired that moniker because of his ability to "hook" a particular cow from a vast herd of cattle without disturbing the other nearby bovine.

More on the history of that part of Oklahoma is that it was originally referred to as "no man's land" where law was made and enforced by those who lived in the area. After the Chicago, Rock Island and Pacific railroads began laying tracks to Texas, it became a popular cattle collection area and that enticed Hooker to settle here.; enough of Hooker's history.

A souvenir shop greets all who pass through this small town. At the Hooker SAG stop, a store selling mementos depicted the unique aspects of the town and was deemed to be an appropriate place to take a rest; the short ride notwithstanding. Hank, not to be denied the opportunity to illustrate the Hooker image commonly associated with the expression, has a picture showing him offering an exchange of money with Nancy. Of course, it shows Nancy rejecting the offer suggesting she was not a native of the area, thus rejecting the idea she might be a "hooker".

Take it either way you want

"We're all hookers!" was the retort the female clerk, manning the souvenir stand, replied when I inquired as to how the town's people referred to themselves. It appeared that citizens of the town take great pleasure entertaining tourists with those sorts of declarations. In fact, I purchased two refrigerator magnets showing the name of the local semi-professional baseball team. They are called… are you ready for this…the Hooker Horney Toads! In addition, I bought a magnet that proclaims "support your local Hookers--Hooker OK. I always make it a stopping point in my presentations and it always offers an opportunity to evoke humor as it peaks the listeners curiosity. Hooker stands out as another of those encounters that enriched the experience and advanced my intentions of meeting the local inhabitants.

Of course, all of the riders made snide comments and remarks with the name Hooker. Mary was the clerk in the store and I immediately initiated a conversation with her. Her store sold various items that reflected the towns name and promoted its importance. As stated earlier, since I could not carry as many souvenirs as I would have liked, I was not about to let the opportunity to purchase souvenirs at this unique establishment escape my attention. So, I knew I had to procure mementos from this stop. My buying included, in addition to the refrigerator magnets with "Hooker" on them, a paper explaining a short history of the town and some newspaper items; more than enough for one stop.

While I was checking out, I delighted in asking Mary to tell me how the folks of Hooker referred to themselves using Bostonians, Chicagoans etc. as an example.

With a wry smile and an impish, innocent look on her face she replied, "We are all Hookers." Continuing her narrative she explained "I'm a Hooker, my mom is a Hooker, and everyone who lives in town was a Hooker." And, she related this barely breaking a smile. I suspect this was not the first time she described this to the clients who visited her establishment. I was mildly amused and added another persona to my list of who I consider friends I met on the journey.

After a brief stop, investing in Hooker goods, and exchanging pleasantries with the locals, we were again on the road to Liberal KS.

Entering Kansas

Hank provided an extremely comical episode upon our arrived in Liberal. As we were getting served in a local restaurant he inquired of our waitress in his usual ultra conservative manner "Since there is a Liberal, Kansas, is there a Conservative, Kansas?" Stunned by the question, the waitress stuttered that she had never heard of such a town in Kansas. Hank then retorted "Well, it looks like I'll have to call Rush and rectify the situation." We all were more that mildly amused.

Another odd instance involving Hank and Liberal is that as we entered the town there is a large sign greeting visitors with "Liberal" at its center. Hank had his picture taken beside the sign and placed it on his blog. However, later when I tried to find it, somehow, it had miraculously disappeared. I often wonder whatever happened to it, but I suspect I know.

Hank should know that Liberal is not the "dirty" word associated with that concept today. In fact the town got its name from early settler S. S. Rogers who built the first house in what would become Liberal in 1872. Rogers became famous in the region for giving water to weary travelers and settlers.

Reportedly, Liberal obtained its moniker from the common response to his acts of kindness. Ranches in this vicinity of Kansas were first being inhabited and developed by the settlers from the East. During a particularly dry season, many of his neighbors had run out of water and heard that his ranch's water well had plenty. They would come to his property and ask for help. Rogers was very "liberal" with the sharing of his water; thus the name of the town. "That's very liberal of you," was their grateful response. In 1885 Rogers built a general store and with it came an official post office. Therefore, the town of Liberal was established.

Since the ride to Liberal was so short, one of the riders who preferred to attach himself to the "racehorse" crowd, decided to mingle with the common plow and Clydesdale horses. Here was an excellent opportunity to co-mingle with a rider whom I hadn't had a chance to get to know well during the first few weeks of the ride. Willie, who worked as an executive for a large company, joined our group. As we meandered down the road at a rather leisurely pace, our conversation focused on my specialty; education.

Specifically, Willie inquired about the possibility of changing his career from being a company executive to a teacher. He indicated that early in his career he had wanted to be a teacher. But because of the nature of how life works out, his career path diverted him into the corporate world.

My first inclination was to advise against it. First and foremost, the pay differential would be enormous. As an executive in a company he would need to adjust to living on about one third of his current annual salary. Not many people are inclined to do this. Another factor we discussed was at his age, late 40's (he actually celebrated his 50th birthday during the ride) it would take many years to qualify to teach in the public school system so his best chance would be to teach in a parochial school. Many private schools do not require a specialty in education and often hire personnel whose only qualification is a college degree.

And, interacting effectively with the students of any age would involve implementing a different skill set from the corporate world. Behavioral expectations associated with various age groups are mostly pre-determined as the student advances through the normal educational process. This results in more mature teachers being less flexible in dealing with youth. For example, a first grade student would not be expected to exhibit the same behavior patterns, especially in responding to classroom management protocol, as a senior in high school. Therefore, the teacher would treat the primary grades students differently than those who teach at the high school level. While I know this to be a generalization there is a plethora of research to back it up.

After a considerable amount of discussion my best advice was that he should follow his dream if he so desired. No better way to look at it than to realize life is short and do those things you want to do before you look back over your life and say "gee I wish I would have done this or that." No regrets. Also, effective, dedicated teachers are an absolute imperative in today's educational system in this country whether it is the public school system or any of the parochial ones. I'm not sure how it affected Willie's decision but nevertheless, it was good to get to know him better. And, later, toward the end of the trip we rode together on several occasions.

Another interesting fact about Liberal, Kansas is that it is the beginning of the mythological "Yellow Brick Road" with the "Dorothy House" a major tourist attraction. One of the highlights at the house was that it still displays the glass slippers from the movie in its Wizard of Oz museum. Many of the riders took the time and made the effort to peruse this museum. But, for me it held no particular interest so I took a pass when offered the opportunity to do so.

Wizard of Oz Museum

Many riders also attended the Mid America Air Museum which displayed many vintage aircraft. So, while the ride was short, there was an abundance of activities in Liberal to occupy our time during this juncture. It also provided plenty of time to rest and recover for the next day's ride to Dodge City, a day I looked forward to for many reasons.

Chapter 4

LIBERAL TO DODGE CITY, KS

By this time during the cross country adventure I was well aware that a group of four had formed a riding group as a result of the experiences they shared early on. Mike, Ira, Karen and Alec usually started last when the day began. At some point during the crossing of the mountains in New Mexico, I became aware that they were using me as a "fox." After I started in the morning they would allow a predetermined amount of time and then set out to chase me until I was caught. I determined their objective was to reel me in and pass me with the usual "on your left" and a friendly greeting. They never told me that was their objective but one particular day traversing the mountains in New Mexico, I detected them approaching me. Just to see if they were in fact playing the hound and fox game, I increased my speed. Much to my surprise, I actually increased the distance between me and the group. Since my climbing was still limited compared with this group, it wasn't long before they finally caught me. After that day, I could tell that was their game. They would never admit that is what they were doing but I knew that as long as we were in the mountains they would always meet their objective. That, in fact, made the ride a little more interesting with the element of secrecy and challenge that would break some of the more boring rides to follow. From those actions, I would refer to the group as the "posse." That designation made them the "good" guys trying to catch the "bad" guy (me) This activity played out until we hit the flat land of the plains and mid-west making their catch more difficult.

Riding from Liberal to Dodge City, Kansas was, for me, one of the most enjoyable of the cross country journey. Getting a huge start on the posse, I was determined they would not catch me this day. Since the western part of Kansas is reasonably flat and, on this particular day, we had a wind at our backs the entire 83 mile ride, the distance passed fast and easy. In fact, the posse didn't catch me until we were on the outskirts of Dodge City. Harry confided in me they were indeed in chase mode and had to average about 25 mph to finally catch me.

The major highlight of this part of the trip was a SAG stop at the Dalton Gang hideout. This is a typical tourist stop that includes an underground tunnel between the farm house and the barn. Gang members used the tunnel to avoid and evade law enforcement officials intent on capturing their crooked asses. Most of the riders fell into the mindset that the Daltons were a modern day Robin Hood. In fact, Hank, Karen, Ira and Alec whom I still refer to as the posse, acquired the nickname Dalton Gang after this stop.

To be sure, from a historic perspective, the real Daltons were nothing more than a rag tag group of common thugs who robbed trains and banks regardless of who had ownership of the money. It should be noted that common folk would put money into banks the Daltons robbed and lost it all. There were no FDIC programs to insure savings. So, while many rich people lost money, it affected the common man more profoundly.

In addition, the gang never shared their booty with the masses and therefore should not be associated with Robin Hood from early English lore.

Me hangin' out at Dalton Gang Hideout

Chapter 5

Touring Dodge City, Ks

Rolling acres of grass and wheat blending together with mile after mile of continuous ribbons of highway was the scenic grandeur that greeted us as we made our way to Dodge City, Kansas. It exceeded my expectation of what I imagined the scenery of Kansas would be and I could understand what inspired the writer of America the Beautiful, Katharine Lee Bates. As the wheat rippled in the wind it looked like wave after wave, "amber waves of grain" a sea of grass; it was quite a site indeed.

"Amber waves of grain," Kansas

Sheriff Matt Dillon, Miss Kitty, Doc, and Chester were the iconic images from the TV show, *Gunsmoke*, I watched every week during my adolescence. Wearing cowboy clothes resplendent with a toy gun slung low on my hip and walking with a swagger than imitated the sheriff, my brothers and I often played "cowboy" with the neighborhood kids on hot summer nights. Those images were fresh in my mind as I approached Dodge City on my bike and I was eagerly anticipating my visit. The good news was that the posse who were trying to catch me couldn't do so until reaching the outskirts of the city.

Me entering Dodge City with "guns ablazin'

Upon my arrival, I went from trans-continental cyclist to every day tourist. The older part of the town was designed to replicate old Dodge City. It had the mandatory Long Branch Saloon, complete with a life size, stand-up replica of Matt Dillon and Miss Kitty. Unfortunately, the area around the old buildings was an empty grassy area which didn't blend with the original road used to enter the town. That aside, it still had the old west cowboy town flavor to it and I was "a itchin' for a gun fight."

Boot hill was somewhat disappointing but I'm not sure what my expectations were. Signs indicated the original Boot Hill cemetery had been moved several times and the graves weren't very old but it was an interesting stop regardless.

Admission into the "touristy trap" section, required visitors pay a nominal fee. However, since we were all on our bikes and in familiar biking apparel, the authorities waived the fee and allowed us free entry. Hank and I went to the ice cream parlor located on Main Street and refreshed ourselves with milkshakes. Okay, I know, not very cowboy. But, when we left we entered the Long Branch Saloon. In a somewhat gruff voice I said "gimmee a sarsaparilla." Apparently, because children were admitted, it did not serve alcohol so a sarsaparilla was the only "cowboy" drink offered. I must admit I had to go through the swinging wooden doors with a surly look on my face hankering' for a gun fight. But, clad in biking spandex I'm sure no one took me seriously and, in fact, if it were back in the old west days I suspect I would have been in for a huge ass whippin'!!

Old Dodge City--grassy street not conducive to gun fightin'

All in all the stay in Dodge City reminded me of the many trips our family made visiting tourist attractions across the country but it still was interesting and well worth the time I spent there. After the usual evening routine of route rap, dinner, casual visiting and an early bed time I looked forward to the next day's adventure.

Chapter 6

DODGE CITY TO GREAT BEND, KS

Leaving at our usual 7:30 departure time we "got the hell out of Dodge." Boy, I couldn't wait to use that old expression. Most of the riding group used it at some time during our exit from Dodge City. Great Bend, Kansas was our destination on this day. I thought this was, undoubtedly, one of the easiest 86 mile rides of the trip. The wind was from the West at 10-15 mph. Since the western part of Kansas is relatively flat, with no real climbs, I cruised at between 20-24 mph; professional bike racer speed. Our route followed the old Santa Fe Trail. It paralleled cattle trails of earlier times when "drovers" moved livestock from Texas to cattle towns like Dodge City. From these cattle towns, they would be placed on railroad cars and transported to eastern cities. Because most of the early railroads were built across the northern tier of the country, the Santa Fe, along with various other cattle trails, had to be developed. This resulted in towns and roads appearing in the cattle producing areas of the West and Southwest. It seems like short history lessons abound. As yet, I can't determine if this is a positive addition or not but I suppose it will continue.

Another interesting aspect of this part of Kansas, as mentioned previously, is the tremendous amount of wheat fields that flourish here. Being from the Midwest, wheat fields are very common, but to see mile after mile and acre after acre of blowing wheat was very impressive. Kansas is the leading wheat producing state in the Union. Since it was late May, early June, the wheat was high enough and the wind strong enough to illustrate an impressive ripple effect. It was clear to Hank and me that the "amber waves of grain" was founded on a reality based concept. And, that night I found a rendition of America the Beautiful on YouTube which I shared with Hank. The juxtaposition of having ridden through those wheat filled fields and hearing the song describing its beauty, had such a powerful effect to the extent that two tough guys, Hank and myself, if closely observed, one could perhaps see a tear on the cheek. Okay, okay maybe not so tough.

With a strong tailwind and the beauty of the wheat fields, it made for another one of the most enjoyable rides of the journey. Under these conditions many of the riders commented that if the rest of the ride were this easy, everyone would do it. But, it has been revealed to me on many occasions in many different ways, balance in the universe exists. One could easily predict these last two easy days would be followed by more challenging days of riding. Let's be clear. This is not a statement of pessimism, rather, a statement of universal truth and fact. I may not know much, but of this I am certain. Enjoy the good times and don't let the bad times defeat you. Don't allow the highs to get too high or the lows too low. Accept this and adapt it to a personal philosophy as it allows one to get through this existence in a reasonably sane manner. Engaging in such a viewpoint, obviously, is no new earthshaking approach to life, but it doesn't hurt to reiterate it every so often.

After that bit of amateur philosophizing, let's move on. With Great Bend still several miles distant, the feeling of the group I was riding with was to make the day's destination as quickly as possible. Yet, with about 20 miles to the end of the riding day, Hank and I made a stop I really enjoyed.

Pawnee Rock arises from the relatively flat plains of Kansas. It has been identified as one of the oldest rock formations on earth by expert geologists. Half of the rock is missing because remnants of it were used as building material in towns around the area. From the top, on a clear day, the view is fantastic and one can see as far as the Missouri river many miles in the distance. Also, a view of the Santa Fe Trail from which we rode and would continue to follow, can be seen for more than eighty miles in either direction making it a very worthwhile detour.

Many of the other riders passed without stopping because of their rush to finish the day. Hank and I took the time to actually bike to the top of the structure. While it was a steep incline it was well worth the effort. We spent time taking pictures and reading the placards that told the story of the area and the importance to history it provided. Interestingly enough, Kit Carson stayed on this rock and shot his mule mistaking it for one of the local Pawnee Indians, or so the story goes.

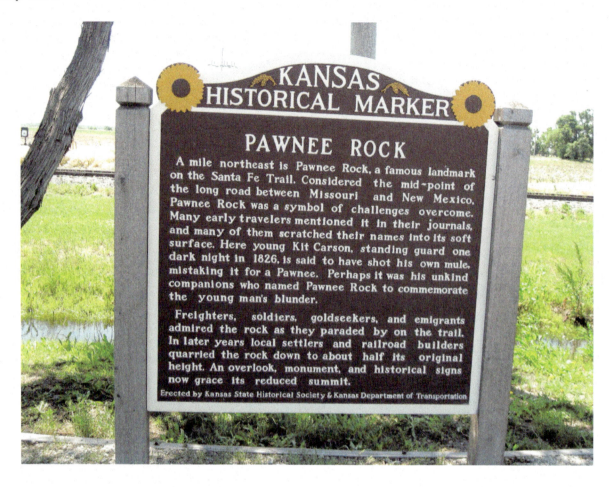

When we reached the top of the rock, two young lovers were embracing in a rather amorous display of affection. From observing their behavior, I suspect they had other intentions than reading the informational posters around the area.

Hank and I took our time looking around, taking pictures and enjoying the scenery. It appeared the couple was becoming somewhat impatient. The female was sitting on the male's lap in the pavilion located on the top of the rock. Because we were taking our time, the couple ceased their make-out session, got into their car and left. I felt somewhat guilty because this area seemed like a great place to engage in playful outdoor boy/girl activity. All in all, it was well worth the effort and a welcomed relief from mile after mile of same scenery road.

Me standing atop Pawnee rock

Our stay in Great Bend was rather routine and uneventful. So, after the usual nightly routine we retired for the evening.

Chapter 7

GREAT BEND TO MCHPERSON, KS

Great Bend to McPherson, Kansas was our next ride covering a short distance of 63 miles. By this time, a flat 60 miler was accomplished with minimal effort. While this appears to be an arrogant bike snobbery declaration, that is not the intention. Rather, it is an acknowledgement to illustrate that distances are a relative expression at this point. While the wind was from the south at 15-20 mph, it did not hinder our progress. Unbeknownst to most, McPherson was named after Civil War General James "Birdseye" McPherson. President Lincoln assigned him to take charge of the "Army of the West" during this time, thus, this area adopted his name as the town developed. There I go again, doing that history thing.

On another note, at many of the stops in Kansas I would often ask the local inhabitants certain questions about the history of Kansas as it pertained to pre-Civil War days. Specifically, if they were natives to the state, I wanted to see how they felt about the turmoil prevalent in Kansas during "bloody Kansas" activities prior to the Civil War. As a matter of history I was interested in their thoughts about the mini-war between slave owners and abolitionists, John Brown and others. Oddly enough, or maybe not so odd, most had no idea what I was talking about. While I didn't expect residents to possess an in-depth knowledge about their states history, I was somewhat disappointed in their lack of cursory information about the significance of their state pertaining to American history. Maybe that comes from being a history teacher and my expectations are too high for citizens retaining such knowledge. Nevertheless, it is disheartening that people who reside in historically significant areas of the country to have no knowledge of these matters.

It was time to add a bit of excitement to the ride. Due to the fact Great Bend to McPherson was a short ride with a non-hindering wind and mile after mile of unchanging scenery; I needed to assert myself against the posse. Looking into my rear view mirror, I could ascertain that those dastardly villains, except for Karen of course, (Harry, who had become ringleader at this time, Karen, who had become the navigator, Ira, the race horse and Alec, keeping them together by riding drag), were in hot pursuit.

Since they were always last to depart the hotel in the morning it became apparent for quite some time, they were using me as their fox. Okay I know I'm mixing my metaphors but it's my story and I'm sticking to it. They would allow me a 10-15 minute head start and slowly reel me in. While they would never acknowledge whether or not they were chasing me, I could tell that was their objective. I was determined to not let them catch me on this particular day. Maybe tomorrow or the next day but not today!

Unbeknownst to me, the hilly section of eastern Kansas loomed ahead. When I became aware of this, I was sure the posse would foil my objective so I decided to do my best to avoid being caught. As the hills approached, I increased my speed and, in fact, increased my lead. They continued in their effort to catch me and after about a 10 mile sprint averaging over 20 mph, they finally caught up. As they approached Ira shouted, "We come in peace," satisfied they had accomplished their goal and continue riding past me as they had done in the mountainous regions of the Southeast.

Ha! It was only a ruse I used to destroy their confidence. Knowing they expended a significant amount of energy catching me I kept a steady pace. When they came beside me to pass, I said my hellos to Harry and immediately started into sprint mode. Standing on my pedals, this Clydesdale was off to the races and increased the distance between us.

Startled but still determined to pass, Alec was the first to use sprint mode to try to catch me. But after about a quarter mile he faded back to the group and I was off again. This was becoming fun!! Then leader of the pack, Harry, sent the racehorse, Ira, after me. When he finally caught me his declaration "I come in peace" could be heard echoing over my shoulder. I then slowed my pace and as the posse approached I could ascertain they had determined I preformed up to their satisfaction so they allowed me to ride the final 5 miles into McPherson as part of their "posse". This was, however, a foretelling of things to come. The pursuer and pursued were now aware of each other's intentions, adding to the enjoyment and excitement to be nurtured for the rest of the ride.

Karen, Alec, Ira, Harry, in pursuit of their prey!!

Another interesting episode encountered this ride was a sign or billboard positioned in the middle of a wheat field. It stated "WELCOME to REDSKIN COUNTRY." For some reason, I had assumed outright, open racist statements like this were a thing of the past. Wrong again Redskin breath! Smack dab in the middle of a Kansas wheat field and close enough to the highway for all to see, this xenophobic attitude seemed to be tolerated in this region of the country. Indians across the country have, time and time again, been insulted by the expression REDSKIN. What other group will still accept as politically correct a term that degrades them because of the skin color? Well, sooner or later, I'm sure, they will get a clue and remove the odious, racially provocative expression.

Yes, I am aware of the first amendment free speech doctrine, but as I remind my students, no amendment is absolute!! Yet this was just another experience that added to my impressions of the nature and history of our country.

REDSKINS, really, I mean really!!

After a good meal following the established routine of cleaning bike, preparing for tomorrow's ride, route rap, relaxing and hitting the sack early, I was ready for another day and another adventure. To be sure, I was not to be disappointed.

Abilene, Kansas was our destination on this day. While many might recall from their early history that Abilene was a major "cattle head" during the early to late 1800's, today it is better known as the childhood home of President Dwight Eisenhower.

Chapter 8

MCPHERSON TO ABLINE, KS

Upon leaving McPherson, heading toward Abilene to the East the wind began as a strong crosswind from the south, but when we departed Route 54 we took a hard left turn and proceeded north onto Route 15, thereby putting the wind at our back. And, that is always good news! I rode the first part of the day's ride with Hank and we averaged around 20 mph.

The posse, not to be outdone, gave me a substantial lead. I was not really sure they would try to chase me down today so Hank and I stopped often and took many pictures. Since it was only a 62 mile ride we arrived at Abilene around noon. The scenery was basically the same since entering Kansas, flat with field after field of wheat.

After leaving the only SAG stop of the day, the posse, who arrived 10 minutes after we did, was still lounging as we departed and seemed to be in no hurry. At this time I established in my mind they had given up trying to catch me. Leaving the SAG, I was riding "lone eagle" so I made many photo stops. (Hank decided to "bump" to our hotel) Occasionally I would check to see if the posse was in hot pursuit but could not determine their intentions. Miles passed and I was certain they had given up the chase, but, about five miles from Abilene I turned and there they were; pedaling furiously to catch me. Ira's familiar "We come in peace" echoed into my ears as they passed me. Their method of chase I deemed "stealth mode." Riding single file, even after I made several checks in my rear mirror, their presence did not register in my brain. It is trained to look for motor vehicles or bikers riding abreast so the single file mode was quite effective. In addition, since I had convinced myself they were not in pursuit mode, I basically ignored my customary thorough checking method. Big mistake! From that point on, I made a vow to myself that the only way they would catch me in the future was if I choose to allow them to do so, unless a steep hill or mountain impeded my speed. As you will see later, that attitude came into play on many rides that would follow.

On this particular day we rested in the town of Abilene. "Abilene, Abilene, prettiest town I've ever seen," Women there don't treat you mean!" Well, I'm not so sure about that but it was another welcomed rest day. Hank's wife, Carol, joined him here and most of the riders spent much of their free time going through the museum exhibits that are quite plentiful in and around the area.

Since Abilene is president Dwight D. Eisenhower's home town, I, along with a few other riders visited the Eisenhower Center. It has the museum, library, home of and final resting place to our 34th president. The presentation in the museum is interesting and chronicles Ike's life from childhood through WWII, into his presidency up to his death in 1969. As something of a historian, I am always fascinated by the museums, libraries, and places of interest of famous (and in many cases infamous) Americans.

Hank and I touring the Eisenhower home in Abilene KA

After a long, productive day of touring museums, I was preparing for tomorrows 106 mile ride that included several long climbs. Part of that preparation was to take a nap. Napping is one of the training routines on days we don't ride. It does wonders for recovering and recuperating.

Chapter 9

ABILENE TO TOPEKA, KS

106 miles from Abilene to Topeka was what we had to look forward to. While this is somewhat on the lengthy side of our typical riding day, by this time it was quite doable. However, that was not the problem with the ride. Hills!! Hills!! And more Hills!! These geologic features presented the major obstacle on this section of the ride. Thinking of Kansas as hilly is inconsistent with one's perception of that state. Hey Toto, we're not in Kansas anymore. While the hills didn't compare to mountains I had previously conquered, they were surprisingly steep. Because they were not expected, it was a harder ride than I anticipated. My reaction led to me naming this part of Kansas the "Oh, Oh hills "region. Most of these climbs would come after a particularly sharp turn and, often, I did not have time to "gear down" in order to guarantee continued forward momentum. I had to mash harder than usual using far more energy that I planned on expending. What a surprise when rounding a turn and there was a 10% grade hill to be addressed. My brain immediately shouted "Oh, Oh start mashing dude or you're going to topple over;" thus the hill designation. After the hills were finally conquered I saw in my rear view mirror I was in for a very pleasant treat.

Near the town of Dover, Kansas the Somerset Café seemed to arise from nowhere. It was a very unassuming, small, intimate café located basically on the edge of a county farm road. Norma, a 78 year old lady, still made homemade pies every day for consumption by customers frequenting this establishment. As luck would have it, by the time I arrived they had already sold out of my favorite, apple pie. However, they still had a few cherry pies so I ordered one, a full quarter of the whole pie, with a scoop of ice cream. After having my picture taken with Norma, I proceeded to devour my treat in a somewhat unseemly manner. I wolfed it down like I had never eaten anything like it in my life. Trudging up and down the hills and knowing

I still had miles to go, I thoroughly enjoyed the feast. I'm not sure if it were the circumstances or the pie was unique, but I thought it was the best I have ever eaten, mom's and wife's pies notwithstanding!

Another appealing characteristic of this treat was the cost of both pie and ice cream totaled only $2.50, tax included. I fully expected to pay twice that price.

I should also mention that this was another day with a headwind approaching 20 mph. While it did not approach the Dalhart experience it was testing by any standard. And, again, if this were easy, everyone would do it.

Arriving in Topeka, the highlight, from a historical perspective, is that it is the birthplace of Amelia Earhart. Unfortunately, we had neither the time, energy nor resources to attend the museum but it is one place I will need to revisit at some point. Tomorrows ride would be to St. Joseph, MO. I was looking forward to visiting the Pony Express museum. Little did I know nor expect what tomorrows ride has had in store.

Norma and I at the Somerset Café

Chapter 10

THE WRECK

It was the second time in my life I had ever ridden in an ambulance and only the first time alone. Forty years ago I was in an automobile with Ronni and friends. Coming over an overpass on Route 45, south of Champaign, going to Sullivan, IL. to attend a Christmas play, our driver slammed into a multi-car pileup. I braced for the collision with my feet on the back of the seat and Ronni braced herself with her arms extended on the same seat. This maneuver resulted in her dislocating her elbow. When the ambulance arrived I elected to ride with Ronni to the hospital sharing it with three other people who had been injured. Since that experience I had not needed the services of any emergency vehicle.

As for my second ride in an ambulance, little did I imagine nor could have expected that a simple task like riding my bike to get a bottle of chocolate milk would result in me riding in an ambulance going to the emergency room with multiple injuries including a possible broken leg. About 10 minutes into the transport I became fully cognizant of what was going on. My left leg was exploding in pain and I began to realize what had happened. It looked like this could be the end of my cross country bicycle riding experience. It crossed my mind that if my leg wasn't broken I held out the possibility I could continue, but it certainly didn't look good. So, let me start at the beginning.

Entering Missouri

Upon my arrival in St. Joseph, MO, I planned a visit to the Pony Express museum. The fact is the pony express experience lasted only about 18 months, from April 1860 to October 1861. Nevertheless, because it became iconic to American history, I was eagerly anticipating a visit to the gallery. With its start in St. Joseph Mo. and finishing in Sacramento, CA with 157 stations along the way, it was the fastest way for mail to travel across the country from the Midwest to California during this time period. The reason it only lasted a relatively short time was because of the invention of the telegraph. I was really looking forward to my visit to the museum and I knew since Carol had joined Hank in Abilene with a car I would have easy access to it. The plan was in place.

With Carol meeting Hank in Abilene and Hank taking a couple days away from riding his bike to do the tourist thing, I began the trek from Topeka to St. Joseph MO "lone eagle". Once again, I had a suspicion the posse would be after me so I was committed to not letting them catch up. Since the scenery involved flatter landscapes like those we would enjoy throughout the Midwest, I increased my speed. Even though there was another headwind, it was only 5 mph so it would not hinder my progress. I was averaging between 18-19 mph and made it to St. Joseph in good time. Hank and Carol, driving their car, stopped and visited with me along the way. I inquired into the location of the posse and they indicated they were about 5 miles behind me. There was no way they would catch me on this day so I casually cruised into town eager to tour the museum.

It should also be noted that my intention of not allowing the posse to catch me in no way deterred me from enjoying the scenery, taking pictures and realizing my goal of enjoying the experience. Rather, it just added more excitement especially in areas of the country that droned on mile after mile with little scenic diversity.

Entering St. Joseph, having finished the 96 mile ride I decided to go from the hotel parking lot to a nearby gas station for chocolate milk which, by this time, had become my favorite recovery drink. Since the gas station was located down a small hill from the hotel, I decided to take a shortcut along a concrete drainage culvert. At the bottom of the culvert was a puddle of water. While it appeared to be an impediment, I figured with my vast biking experience (yea, right), it would not be problematic. A technique for jumping small obstructions, which I had used in the past, was all I needed to circumvent the water puddle. Using the "bunny hop" technique would be the appropriate maneuver here. Little did I know!! Approaching the water I jerked my bike into the air and the next thing I knew I was in the aforementioned ambulance with a searing pain in my left leg.

Recalling the events as best I could, after hitting an obstruction, a curb located beneath the water that I was unable to see, I found myself face down on the asphalt pavement. Flying over the front handlebars of my bike, hitting my leg and landing on my head, I crawled over to a grassy area. Lying on the grassy knoll dazed, confused, in pain and wondering what the hell just happened, I was quickly surrounded by paramedics. They arrived in a matter of minutes. As it happened, the hotel where we were staying was having an EMT conference. How fortunate for me. As they began administering first aid, I vaguely recall wanting them to just go away and leave me alone. I would be okay. They called the ambulance. A crack in my helmet convinced the EMTs I landed on my head. Additionally, visible injuries included blood pouring from my upper lip as a result of putting my front teeth through it, and I couldn't put pressure on my left leg. Because I tried to convince myself I was not that badly injured, I was later told I initially refused an ambulance ride to the emergency room. All I could think about was this would be the end of my ride across America and I was going to do anything possible to not allow that to happen. Obviously I wasn't thinking too clearly.

Members of the ambulance crew were preparing paperwork to indicate I refused their service and, just before I signed it Tracy convinced me that the best course of action on my part, to be sure I would be able to ride the next day, was to have the emergency room check me out. I'm sure she had concerns not only about my injuries but her responsibility supporting a rider who could perhaps jeopardize the group in terms of providing medical services they were not equipped to handle. I agreed and got prepared for the second ambulance ride of my life.

In the ambulance, coming down from the adrenaline rush, pain emanated through my left leg. I thought it odd that the ambulance EMT's offered no first aid in the form of placing ice on the injured leg or cleaning and dressing the blood that had coagulated around my mouth. At the emergency room, I was taken into a room, told to wait, and shortly they would take me to x-ray the leg. I informed the medical staff that if the leg were not broken, I would ride the next day. Of course, they looked at me in a mocking fashion accompanied by a few chuckles and chortles. As they were wheeling me to the x-ray room I explained to the nurse my leg was feeling better, even though it wasn't. Transitioning from the wheel chair to the x-ray table, I stood on my injured leg and performed a little jig dance to convince the technicians I was alright. They weren't buying any of this act and proceeded to x-ray the leg.

While awaiting the results, Hank and Carol appeared in my room and explained that my helmet was useless. Even if my leg were up to it I would not be able to ride again until I got a new helmet. They were kind enough to go to the nearest Kmart and purchase a new one for me. Great friends!

Soon after they left the room, a doctor entered my with the x-ray results and informed me that the leg was not broken. He indicated I had done considerable damage to the muscle and tissue surrounding the bone.

He also conceded that with that much damage he couldn't understand how the bone wasn't broken. Then, he began to outline my recovery regiment for the next week or so.

His first order was to stay off the leg for at least two days. Elevate and ice the leg 20 minutes an hour for the first two days. After that, gradually attempt to put weight on the leg and after about a week begin........ he stopped in mid-sentence. I wasn't listening to a word he was saying as I pondered how I would be able to ride tomorrow. "You're not going to do any of this are you?" he asked. I responded in the negative. "I told you if the leg isn't broken, I am going to ride tomorrow." How I later confirmed the oral instructions given to me by the doctor was because before I left the hospital he gave me written instructions describing the appropriate treatment.

Realizing his predicament the doctor then stated "Well then, Mr. Walker, let me introduce you to your two new friends, Mr. Vicodin and Mr. Motrin." Vicodin will help with the pain and Motrin will address the swelling issue". He then left with a sly smile on his face, knowing people will do what they want to regardless of good medical advice.

Good friends Hank and Carol were still waiting in the outer sanctum of the ER to take me back to the hotel. Arriving at the hotel, the group was at route rap. I must have presented quite a sight. They looked at me with astonishment on their faces. Blood on my face and clothing, bandages on both legs and walking with a noticeable limp, I must have looked like a refugee from a MASH unit. From my appearance the other bikers at route rap were convinced I would not be biking for quite some time.

After the group finished route rap and proceeded to go for their evening meal, Carol took me to a local pharmacy to fill my prescriptions. Dropping me off in my room, she and Hank proceeded to the restaurant where the other riders were eating. I was in no condition to join them as the pain pills began taking effect and I had no appetite. So, I proceeded to my room to "lick my wounds," ice my leg and begin the recovery process from the episode. Later that evening, Hank arrived at my room with food brought from the restaurant, making it possible for me to ingest fuel for the next day if I were able to ride. Talk about good friends.

Meanwhile, Tracy had taken my bike and repaired the front wheel. It was out of true and the mechanical expertise of our support team was outstanding. While they could not true it to 100% specifications it was good enough to ride if I chose to do so.

Sitting in my room contemplating my plan, I decided to attempt to ride the next morning. With the Vicodin in my system and the Motrin controlling the swelling, I would determine after a good night's sleep whether or not I was able to ride. Unbeknownst to all, even as I had ice on my left leg, and my right Achilles tendon, a huge bubble began to form on my left knee. It had gotten large enough, at least the size of a golf ball, that I considered calling Hank and Carol to take me back to the emergency room. A bag of ice and towel was placed round the knee hoping the swelling would go down. Thankfully, before I went to sleep, I saw it had shrunk enough that it was no longer a concern. There was no pain associated with the knee swelling but I attributed that to the Vicodin. As it turns out, swelling on the top of the knee was a result of the combination of the drugs I had taken, but at the time I was unaware that condition was a possibility.

With Carol joining Hank, I was able to have a room to myself. After a relatively peaceful night's sleep, I was up at 5:30 a.m. got dressed and ate a normal breakfast. I had taken another Vicodin and the leg felt better. It was not pain free but I thought I would use my bike on a test ride to see what level of pain I could tolerate.

CHAPTER 11

THE NEXT DAY

Taking the elevator to the first floor with my bike, and dressed in my biking gear, Al, who got on at the same time, realized I was going to possibly try to ride. He informed me, quite rightly, "Don't let stupidity overcome common sense."

Truer words were never spoken. In addition to the usual wrap on my right knee, I placed another wrap around my left thigh. A poster boy for elastic wraps could have been a future job possibility.

Outside on the parking lot, I tested the leg. Yes, there was pain but it wasn't intolerable. I formed a plan. I love it when a plan comes together. I would ride thirty miles to the first SAG stop and determine if I could continue. If possible I would then attempt another thirty miles and do the same.

With this strategy, I began the journey as normal. Thirty miles into the ride resulted in no increased pain. After sixty miles the pain level was about the same as when I started so I figured I might as well finish the next 35 miles thereby keeping EFI intact. The bottom line was that if I couldn't ride, I wouldn't have ridden.

Many people inquired how the Vicodin affected my riding capability. The only noticeable consequence was that I didn't sustain the 16-17 mph average I had built up to at this stage of the adventure. I was being passed by riders who usually finish the day's ride well behind me. Also, I noticed Rick, one of the best riders of the entire group and the tour's chief mechanic, riding behind me. Ha, did he think I didn't know why he was "slumming?" I even inquired of him, "Rick, what are you doing riding this far behind the main group?

" His response was that he thought he might take it easy on this day. Yea right!! I'm positive Tracy instructed him to keep an eye on me in case I ran into trouble. Good on them!!

Now, for some honesty. After I tested the leg and determined I would be able to ride, it wasn't a big deal, at least to me. As stated before and many times since, if I couldn't have ridden, I wouldn't have ridden. But, after assessing the situation I felt I could ride. I had no idea it would come under the "inspirational" category. It was just something I felt I could do. And, as it turned out, I'm glad I did.

The real "bummer" from this experience was I never did get chocolate milk for Hank and me. Also, I never did get to see the Pony Express museum and I was really looking forward to doing so. That is another one of those places I need to put on my "bucket list" to visit.

Chapter 12

St Joseph To Chillicothe MO.

As I have stated previously and will continue to illustrate; for every negative experience, there follows something equally positive. Karma, yin/yang, balance in the universe, you name it. After the disaster in St. Joe, the ride to Chillicothe Missouri, another century, was filled with one of the best experiences of the trip. While the roads began relatively smooth and flat, we were warned they would soon become quite hilly. But, after biking nearly 30 miles all the riders met two miles from the town of Maysville MO.

Traveling along in a two by two peloton, we rode into town. Arriving at the eastern entrance of the village, it looked typical of most Midwestern towns with its quaint buildings around a square. Similar to many towns in the region, a large government building was located inside the grassy square with a variety of shops and stores located across the street bordering it.

As our entire group pedaled into the cube, we were greeted by school children that were seated on a wall on the south side of the square. Wild cheering began as soon as we made our appearance and continued as we road past them.

Artist's renditions and scenes from videos which I used to play in my classes illustrating Caesar riding his chariot into Rome, with the multitudes applauding and cheering, came to mind. Quite a rush! Chillicothe's historical society provided our group with a magnificent feast of homemade sandwiches, cakes, cookies, pink lemonade and a variety of other treats. In addition, there were antique artifacts located in many of the shops that added interest and excitement for the riders.

Students, mostly elementary level, were eager to take pictures with members of the group as well as inspect the bikes. Harry's bike drew the most interest from many of the children as it was unique and very expensive--about $8,000. We discovered later in the trip that the local paper described our visit and talked to the children asking their opinion of our group. Harry's name was mentioned quite prominently in the article.

My saddle was another object of interest to the children. It was unique as saddles go and the only one of its kind among the riders in the group. The kids all wanted to sit on it to see how it felt. Even though we were having a wonderful time we all knew we had many more miles left to pedal on this day so we regretfully had to push on. The stop in Maysville Mo was the absolute highlight of the day and certainly one of the best during the ride.

Maysville Missouri with children on square

After leaving Maysville, the road started to become quite hilly with grades of up to 13%. That was a foretelling of the next day's terrain. The good news is that we had a favorable wind and it was at this time I developed a particular riding style I would employ to take me through the next several days.

Hills in the middle of Missouri were usually no more than a quarter to half mile in length. On the downhill side of the hills, I would increase my speed to about 40 mph so the inevitable uphill would not be as arduous a climb. Being a "masher" (no clips) that particular riding style was a very successful technique and I enjoyed the "roller coaster" effect.

Using that method meant I needed to continue riding "lone eagle" so the "spinners" would not hinder my progress. For some reason, I suspect to conserve energy, spinners tend to coast down the hills and use spin technique on the climb. I found by using my technique I would pass spinners on the downhill, which were often in my way, and eventually they would pass me during the climbing portion of the hill. It was better to stay out of each other's way so neither of us was impeding the other. One of the new facts I learned about Missouri is that it is anything but FLAT.

Upon my arrival into Chillicothe I engaged in my usual post ride routine except, because of my accident, I had to spend additional time icing various body parts including knee, left leg, and my Achilles tendon, that were still recovering from my previous injury episodes.

Chapter 13

CHILLICOTHE TO KIRKSVILLE, MO

Rollers!! 148 hills with 12-13% grade for 74 miles awaited us as the next day's sojourn from Chillicothe to Kirksville MO. My technique of attacking the hills, from yesterday's experience, was working quite well for me. I only needed to mash about 70% of the climb as opposed to the spinners 100%. While the wind was blowing against us at about 20-25 mph, I used the roller coaster method for most of the first six hours. But from that point on, the continuing vastness of the terrain began taking its toll.

After passing Maclede Mo. the birthplace of General Blackjack Pershing, the WWI American commander who led the AEF (American Expeditionary Force) into France, I continued my assault on the hills. A stop to visit and tour his home town may have been a good idea, but unfortunately it would have extended an already tough ride. A short history lesson here may be appropriate but, while I have done so in the past, too much historical information may render the reader into a semi-comatose lethargy.

Scenic vistas on the ride to Kirksville were rather unremarkable in that it was a continuation of the vegetation observed since entering the Midwest. Unique picture opportunities were rare so the objective was to complete the ride as quickly as possible. The occasional herd of cattle (yes, I've heard of cattle) and horse farms that littered the countryside provided a nice view but were not anything exceptional.

At the only SAG stop of the day I finally had the opportunity to take a photo worthy of presenting. It shows how the rollers continue on and on into what seemed like infinity and that was what we had to master on this part of the ride. Scenic farms intertwined with the rollers were apparent as far as the eye could see. With no other adventurous encounters, it turned out to be a rather mundane day, which, is not necessarily a bad thing. After arriving in Kirksville at the end of the day I was as exhausted as at any point of the trip including the mountains of the Southwest.

Missouri Rollers

Our location in Kirksville was not near any eating establishments so we enjoyed a catered evening meal. This was nice since it broke the routine of eating in the franchise restaurants. Another positive aspect is that we enjoyed co-mingling more with other riders. It was here that Harry acquired access to the hotel computer. He "Googled" his house in Liverpool, London. We could see it was located right next to Strawberry Fields. I always imagined Strawberry Fields as a fictional place invented by the Beatles. Now I know better. Anyway, Harry's "house" was really a mansion and he indicated he had another one in Wales. I was quite impressed with his residences. I made a mental note to be sure to visit him and he regularly asks when I am going to do so during his frequent phone calls.

As stated many times, one of the joys of this experience was the interaction with members of the local population. At the hotel in Kirksville I stumbled upon a group of individuals who were having a family reunion. Now, imagine having a reunion in such a remote location and having family actually show up. Those folks were sitting around the entrance to one of their rooms recounting family history and consuming vast quantities of alcohol. (Not necessarily a bad thing). Walking past the group, sitting in a circle around a table with many alcoholic beverages in view, I introduced myself, intruding on their conversations, and initiated a dialog with them. When informed I was riding a bicycle across the country they were amazed at the distance we had ridden and were very intrigued.

As a point of interest, when people heard we were riding across the country, most common social barriers, common between strangers, automatically seem to disappear.

Along with other topics of interest, I reminded them that when family get together at these types of functions, mixing alcoholic drinks in ample quantities, often results in a battle, often verbal but occasionally physical. Or, at least that was my experience but perhaps I was generalizing. So, when or if the "knuckle drilling" begins, I asked them to make it short and try to be quiet. I needed my beauty sleep!! All in all another excellent example of the fun I had intermingling with people I met along the way.

Another transformational event along this stretch of the bike ride was that we passed the 2,000 mile point. It was hard to believe we had come that far but realized we still had another 1,500 miles before we reached our final destination. I was looking forward to the next day because we would be entering Illinois, my home state.

Chapter 14

KIRKWOOD TO QUINCY, MO

Kirkwood MO -5:30 am. Hank and I rolled out of the sack and began another early morning routine. On this day, however, there was a severe thunderstorm outside. Checking the weather channel we could see we were in for a massive amount of rain. But, since we had ridden in the rain on earlier rides, we saw no reason to think today would be different. Indeed, one of the only weather occurrences that would delay our start is lighting. Our usual starting time was 7:30 a.m. but because of lightening in the immediate area we didn't begin our day until 10:00 AM. This meant our arrival time for the day's destination would be pushed back by two and one half hours, thus eliminating many evening activities. So, for the most part, Hank and I watched T.V. and were bored to tears.

When we finally began riding from Kirkwood Mo to Quincy IL. gusty, windy conditions were once again our challenge. It would be a 75 mile ride but, as usual, the winds were blowing directly into our faces and reached speeds of up to 30 mph. However, it was nothing compared to the Dalhart experience or, maybe, I had become a much stronger rider both physically and mentally. Nevertheless, it was a difficult ride.

One of the weirdest encounters of the entire tour happened in the small town of Ewing MO. This town is nothing more than a speck in the road with a grain elevator and gas station. Usually, by this time, Hank and I would bypass these little places and continue ahead. For some strange reason, I decided to stop and replenish my energy supply which I could tell was getting depleted.

Oddly enough, at the gas station, after peering into the freezer compartment, I discovered a "Champ" ice cream bar. Having never seen one before, purchasing one was another one of those no brainers. Of course,

I had to procure one and after consuming it, save the wrapper. (Because of my ignorance, as I would find out later, it is quite a common brand)

While standing in line waiting to pay for the "Champ" bar, a female wearing a t-shirt with EP Raider Football written across the front was noticeable in my peripheral vision. I was quite familiar with those shirts since I coached football at East Peoria High School for over 15 years and these were quite popular with the athletes. The woman wearing it was not familiar. Curiosity overcame my "natural shyness" so I decided to approach her to inquire about the shirt. As I approached, I noticed a familiar male face. I sensed he was part of my past as a teacher/coach at East Peoria High School. Sporting a great amount of facial hair, I didn't immediately recognize him but he certainly looked familiar.

It should be noted that in the 35 years I had been employed in the field of education, I had contact with approximately 10,000 students and athletes. To remember each of them individually and especially recall their names is a virtual impossibility. Nevertheless, to my credit I suppose, I recall most of the faces and can usually place a particular episode with each. During my later years in the classroom, I would remind my students that if or when I happened to bump into them in public years after they left my classroom, do not try to quiz me to guess your name. Introduce yourself, tell me your name and I will remember something from your past.

"You sure look familiar" I stated to the bearded one. He replied that he was Neil Lathrop. I instantly recognized him through all that facial hair. As a football player for EPCHS during my coaching days, I recalled he was a pretty decent player for us. Jay, his brother, was one of our managers. I recall both boys as good people from a fine family. The Lathrop family often invited the coaches to cookouts at their home and I still have pictures from those events.

This was really bizarre, I thought at the time, because I hadn't seen him since he graduated in 1988. Lo and behold, here I am in the middle of nowhere USA and I run into a former athlete. How wacky. These kinds of happenings illustrate what a small world it really is. Neil stated he was working construction in the vicinity and that was the reason he lived in the area.

After saying my goodbyes to Neal and his female friend, who hadn't introduced herself and I knew she was neither an athlete or student from my past, I joined Hank for the final 20 mile journey into Quincy.

While the route still had many hilly portions, the terrain began to become more horizontal, yet, the wind was still blowing briskly into our faces which presented difficulties.

As we approached the Mississippi River, traffic on the road began to increase. Tracy mentioned at route rap the night before the one tried and true rule to be followed for reasons of safety is, when crossing the bridge spanning the Mississippi river, there is no safety lane, so take the entire lane regardless of the traffic you might be impeding.

Crossing the bridge, I understood the reasoning and implications behind such a rule. There is no shoulder, bike or pedestrian path. If I felt compelled to pull over to let auto traffic pass I would have placed myself in grave danger. There is no safety area to bail out in the event a motorist passed to closely. One mistake by the bicyclist or driver would result in the biker being knocked over the rail of the bridge into the Mississippi. The result would have been catastrophic.

By this time Bob had joined Hank and me as we paced toward the Mississippi river. Just before the entrance to the bridge I observed in my rearview mirror a semi-trailer truck rapidly approaching. Discretion being the better part of valor and sensing danger, I pulled my bike to the side of the road, stopped and allowed the truck unfettered passage across the bridge. Hank and some of the other riders who had, by this time, gathered into a large group proceeded to cross the bridge with the eighteen wheeler behind them. I'm quite sure the truck driver was not pleased with this bike procession. Nothing was worse than having a pissed off trucker behind you with no reasonable chance of passing until the bridge was cleared, very dangerous indeed. On their best days the truckers cause massive hindrances to a biker's progress. Therefore, why take a chance, especially in these conditions. So I stopped and allowed the truck to pass.

After the truck driver passed, I began my ascent on the upward side of the bridge. About half way across, I saw Hank standing in the middle of the bridge, just to the right of traffic, taking pictures. Now, I am the first to admit I may have done some things many would consider dangerous, but to stop in the middle of the narrow two lane bridge that spanned that part of the Mississippi River to take a picture bordered on the insane. I'm not saying Hank is nuts but.........he seemed oblivious to the impending potential disaster that presented itself in that situation and continued his photography. Fortunately, it did not result in an incident but certainly the probability was enormous.

On a positive note, Hank did get some of the best pictures of everyone in the group showing the mighty Mississippi River from the bridge, the danger factor notwithstanding. All's well that ends well. But, as you will soon see, Karma needs to send a message about these things.

Coming across the bridge I was looking forward a fast downhill. After a long day of rollers, high winds and the dangerous crossing of the Mississippi I was going to put it on "cruise control" into the hotel in Quincy. Not so fast kemosabe! The entrance into the town began just over the bridge with a severe UPHILL climb. It reminded me of the climb from Manhattan Beach where we started our adventure. I suppose that was to be expected since most river valleys, by definition, are in a valley and to precede forward one must climb out of it. But, it was irritating nevertheless

Midwest

Chapter 1

THE QUINCY EXPERIENCE

Quincy Illinois! After riding over 2,000 miles and on the road for over a month, I finally reached my home state. It was hard to believe I traversed this much of the North American continent and yet…..such a long way to go. But, I was looking forward to enjoying my home state familiarity. At this point in the ride, the posse had no chance of chasing me down unless I allowed them to do so. I suspect they knew it too because it was getting harder for them to accomplish this feat even though I was still recovering from my "little" accident.

Another aspect of riding through the Midwest is that I realized I would be taking fewer pictures of the landscape since, as I reminded the followers of my blog, one could look out their own window and see the same scenery I observed as I rode through this part of America.

Several interesting events occurred upon my arrival into Illinois. First, the Central Illinois Alzheimer's Association, for whom I rode to raise awareness of and funds for, had a representative from their group meet me at the hotel. They brought a camera crew and the interviewer did a fine job of covering my ride up to this point. It was placed on the local Quincy news channel and fed to their national outlet where it was played on the NBC news program the following morning. The good news is that it reported the amount of financial support I was getting and added a promotional aspect at the same time. While watching it the next day, I was somewhat embarrassed because I still had a remnant from my accident; my upper lip was still quite swollen and it looked like I got punched in the mouth. To help the illusion, I had a picture taken with Ira throwing a fake punch and it is part of my YouTube video of the trip.

On another note, my fellow riders ridiculed me unmercifully, in a good natured way, because I was given so much attention. I suspect there was a bit of envy to some degree on their part but, at the same time, they were all honored to be acknowledged for their accomplishment.

Another positive event, after arriving in Quincy, was that one of my former student/athletes came to visit me at the hotel. Pete McMiniman (yea Pete you made the book) brought his son because he wanted him to meet someone who was attempting a feat of this magnitude. Here was the second student of mine I had come across in the last two days. We enjoyed a pleasant visit even though I was ready for a shower and some rest from a long ride. After sharing my experience with him, I inquired into how he and his family were doing and what he had been involved with since his high school days. No matter the situation I always have an interest in my former student's lives and welfare.

One of the awesome things about being a teacher is the enormous salary we receive. Ha, ha, now that is a funny one. Actually, it is quite common that teachers never know how much influence we have had on those under our tutelage. When we come across them years after they leave school it's always a genuine pleasure to talk about what they have been doing since graduating from high school. So, talking with Pete and his young son was a nice way to end the ride into Quincy.

The next item of note, upon my arrival into Quincy, was that good friend, fellow bicyclist (hey Roger, you made the book too) and his lovely bride, Lilji, came to meet me. Roger intended to ride from Quincy to Springfield with us. He had been riding approximately two years at this point and looked forward to joining our group for the "century" ride to Springfield IL. With headwinds prevailing the past few days, I was looking forward to a favorable tailwind to help during this part of the ride. Mostly, we all looked hopefully for tailwinds but for Roger's benefit it would make the 100 miles considerably easier. I didn't want to burn him out because he had taken the time and made the effort to join me. Alas, it was not to be so!

Roger and me in Quincy

Finally, and certainly the best part of the Quincy experience, is that my beautiful wife, Veronica, whom you have met earlier, joined me. She would be with the group until we left Champaign. The Quincy, Springfield, Champaign portion of the trip would be enhanced since our van was now available to the group. Among other things, our van would provide a welcome relief from the tedium of not being able to wander far from the hotels for eating enjoyment, shopping, and other excursions that our bikes had restricted us.

Usually, after all day riding, we would prefer to keep the bikes in our rooms and walk to wherever we wanted to go. From earlier descriptions, with Mark and Lisa providing transportation in the Southwest, Carol doing the same in the middle of Kansas and now Ronni, with our van it made the experience even more doable. It was greatly appreciated and made those parts of the journey a joy.

Chapter 2

QUINCY TO SPRINGFIELD, IL

"Champ, I've developed hemorrhoids. "What should I do?"

Those were words I heard after answering the phone the morning after our arrival into Quincy. All I could think was "Here we go again with this Karma thing." As things go, there were copious amounts of positive energy in the Quincy experience. But, according to the yin and yang of the universe, something negative was bound to happen. Not being negative here, just pragmatic.

Since I was rooming with my wife, this individual who at this point shall remain nameless had his own space. At 6:30 AM the room phone rang. Sid, not his real moniker, made that informative declaration. I was about to make some snide comment but quickly decided against it. It probably would have been inappropriate and he did not need sarcasm at this time.

After giving it some thought, with the implausible suggestion that he may need help pushing it back in, or something equally obscene, I suggested he get some hemorrhoid cream like Preparation H. Knowing he had no means other than his bike to go to a pharmacy to obtain needed treatment, Ronni graciously volunteered to drive to a local drug store and obtain the appropriate medical supplies for his dilemma. It occurred to me that once again Karma force was at work. After my accident in St. Joseph MO. Hank and Carol were able to drive me to get the meds I needed to continue so I wouldn't have to bike there myself. The same situation presented itself here in Quincy with Sid. Another example of the yin and yang that abides

Unfortunately, this individual had to deal with that condition for the rest of the ride. At one point, he actually needed treatment at an emergency room in Ohio. To his credit, he still rode as much as he was able until the pain was so severe he couldn't continue. There's something about the type of people who undertake adventures such as riding a bicycle across the country that makes them refuse to quit, given all the obstacles they are sure to endure.

After attending to the current crisis, many of us were sitting in the hotel dining area eating breakfast. Watching TV in the area, my infamous mug was shown on two separate segments of the local NBC broadcast. As I watched, I couldn't help but notice that they seemed to get many close-up shots of my face which still showed the effects of my accident in St. Joseph MO, thus the Ira picture. And, again, the amount of razzing was unmerciful!

At our usual departure time, with Roger joining us, he suggested if we wanted to ride off on our own he wouldn't mind. Ha, that wasn't going to happen. We were not in a race or in any particular hurry. If he could only manage a pace of 15-16 mph I would stay with him. I informed him if we were going too slow for his comfort level, to go ahead and we would catch up. As it turned out, he was able to maintain our normal riding speed of 17-18 mph which we were accustomed to at this point. And, as was common for our group with the wind blowing into our faces, no one was going to maintain an 18 mph average for a sustained period of time. So, we rode together at a reasonable rate, headwinds notwithstanding.

The distance to Springfield was supposed to be a rather enjoyable jaunt with little difficulty and stress in terms of geography and length of ride. Ha, how wrong was that. Our belief was we would bike in a NE direction since that appears to be the geographical bearing from Quincy. A strong wind was coming out of the SSE at between 15 up to 29 mph. Unfortunately, we were headed in a SSE direction so we would have a wind in our face for most of the ride. Now, how that happened I'm still not sure but it seemed no matter what direction we turned, the wind was still against us.

Another condition that might have hindered success for Roger was the ride was 107 miles. He mentioned he had not ridden a century yet and this would be his first. Actually Roger did an excellent job considering this was not a typical century because the wind conditions were more severe than expected. At one point, Roger even suggested all of these headwinds "were taking the fun out of riding." Welcome to the club Rog!!

Tracy and the support staff have a rule. Anyone who has not signed up for the ride and joins the group for a portion of it, could help themselves to all the "goodies" at the SAG stops but the company could not provide any bike maintenance or other type of support. As part of their insurance policy, supporting a large group is a rather hazardous undertaking. We all understood reasons for the policy. It was a reminder of why they would not support Jack coming across the desert without a camelback. That makes all kinds of sense. I suspected though that while non-technical support is the official policy, knowing Tracy, she would not abandon someone who needed help with their bike, regardless of the rule. As we journeyed further east, there were many riders who joined friends of the cross country group and all were subject to the rule.

The good news is that SAG stops provided nourishment needed to complete a 100 mile bike ride. So Roger would experience a small part of the experience that we all enjoyed on our trek across the country. As part of that experience, Roger also got a taste of the negative effects of an all-day headwind while biking that distance. He was also reminded that lamenting the conditions does not, and cannot, improve them so we learned early in the ride to deal with the conditions as they were.

On a positive note, our wives were driving along the route in a van and would stop to encourage us as we made our way to Springfield. However, after the second SAG stop, we didn't see them again until we reached Springfield. I guess they caught the shopping bug and they would use that time to peruse Springfield's shopping areas.

During the second SAG, Hank decided to finish the rest of the day with us. The three of us took turns riding the lead in a pace line. That helped us all as the lead rider blocked the wind and made it easier for those behind. Believe me, it actually works.

As stated earlier, it never occurred to me that Springfield was southeast of Quincy. I lived my life in Illinois and have been to both cities often. And, to add to the mystery, as we approached the city, the large coal plants with smokestacks on the east side of the city were situated to our right. That made sense. Observing them and their location I knew we were on the right road. But, strangely enough, as we approached the city, the smokestacks had appeared to move mysteriously to our left. The only explanation, obviously, was a change in the route we were following. Demolishing them and rebuilding them in a matter of minutes was the only other explanation. Ha, yea right! I thought, Oh, Oh, we are on the wrong course. All three of us checked and rechecked our route sheets and determined we, indeed, were following the correct highway. C'mon now! How could three expert male trackers get on the wrong path? Never would happen! Since I am somewhat familiar with the area, I tried to convince the group that we should take a direct path heading toward the stacks, but I was quickly overruled. How could Tracy be wrong about these things? As it turned out, we could have saved several miles if we had taken a more direct route, but then it would not have been a century.

It later became evident that many of the roads Tracy mapped out for us were not necessarily the most direct. But, that was not a decision for me to make at that time and I was certain we had ridden at least 10 miles out of our way coming into Springfield. Oh well, it was a century experience for Roger, so all's well that ends well.

When we arrived in Springfield, the girls were waiting for us in the parking lot of the hotel with fast food and milkshakes. They were thoughtful enough to purchase those goodies as a reward for our long ride. Even though the road was long and the wind was brutal, Roger still maintained he had a good time. Ronni and I tried to convince them to spend the night so they could have a whole riding day experience.

Using the van as transportation and inviting other members of the group, we ate in a very nice local Italian restaurant. Again, another reprieve from the routine of eating in the franchise restaurants. I must continually declare I had no problem eating in the franchises near the hotels but it was always nice to have a bit of variety, particularly during this part of the ride.

After a leisurely dining experience, Roger and Lilji decided to go back to Washington since it was only a little more than an hour from where we were staying. I can't really blame them but it was still nice to encounter friends and enjoy their company along the way.

Back at the hotel, conversing with other members of our troop, I assured them that the following day the wind would be blowing from the west, south, or southwest. These are the prevailing winds in central Illinois at that time of the year. I was convinced of this belief because I trained and had ridden in this environment for a long time. Through the years, I became quite knowledgeable about wind speed and direction in and around this neck of the woods, so not to worry. Tomorrow the wind will be at our backs. Springfield to Champaign is a northeasterly ride. Of that I am positive!

With a magnificent Midwestern sun rising in the east, the morning dawn found us wide awake and eager for the day's journey into my hometown of Champaign IL. With the confidence of the prodigal son, I was certain that when I opened the curtains of our room I was going to look out, stare at the smoke stacks positioned across the interstate highway with the smoke emitting from them and declare the wind was from a direction that would favor us on this beautiful day. Alas, wrong again. I was quite dismayed to see the smoke from those coal fired energy plants coming directly from the east. That was the direction we were riding on this day. How could this be? I assured the riders we would have a favorable wind today. This is my territory. I cannot be wrong!! To add insult to injury, the wind was not a gentle breeze that wafted toward the west, rather, the smoke blew in a straight stream which indicted a rather strong wind. But, at this point, I reasoned, that is what should be expected. It was like that for most of the trip anyway, so why should it be any different because it is my neighborhood? I profusely apologized to the other riders but they assured me I had absolutely nothing to do with it. In retrospect they were indeed correct. So, putting aside all my bitching we began the journey into a headwind.

Chapter 3

SPRINGFIELD TO CHAMPAIGN, IL-A DEDICATION

Often, when I do long distance biking, especially when there is mile after mile of unchanging terrain or other distractions, my mind wanders, among other things, to past experiences on the bike. The road from Springfield to Champaign fit these criteria. Conditions were similar to my first "century" from Washington to Champaign IL. Springfield to Champaign is about 86 miles and, as it turns out, the wind was only blowing from the NE at between 5-10 mph so it did not play a significant factor in the ride. As I separated from the group to travel "lone eagle" the miles seemed to drag on. My mind then drifted to that first century. A "90's flashback!!

Gary Moehle, a good friend for many years, was the individual I dedicated the Springfield to Champaign part of the cross country journey. As described earlier, after my knee surgery in l996 and after I had built what I deemed a proficient level of endurance, I decided to put the repaired knee to a true test of its ability to function normally. Because I grew up in Champaign and still had family and friends living there, I decided I would wait for a favorable day to do the 100 mile ride (actually it was 101.2 miles door to door) from Washington to Brother Larry's House in Savoy near Champaign.

For me, a favorable day was temperatures in the mid to high 80's with any wind speed from the north, west, or northwest. I wasn't about to do my first century into a wind. Gary informed me that when I decided to do this ride he would drive to Champaign with "recovery fluids" and he would drive me back to Washington. My desire to have the most favorable environment (wind and temperature) meant I wouldn't be able to plan very far in advance for the journey, certainly no more than a day or two. So, when the forecast predicted those conditions to my satisfaction, I called Gary and told him I made plans to ride the following day. Like a good friend, he informed the people at his work place he would not be coming in on this particular day in order to assist me in my trip. So, with all systems go and after checking weather conditions on all major towns along my route, I was off.

"Lone Eagle" protocol was called for as this was my first attempt at a ride of this length. My one major mistake, as I discovered on many subsequent rides, was taking all county back roads. Future rides dictated I take a straighter route with better roads. On my first attempt, I wound up zig- zagging in a serpentine manner across central Illinois to get to my destination at Brother Larry's domicile.

Gary knew which roads I planned to use and each time I took a break along the way, lo and behold, there was Gary in his trusty van. His first inquiry at each stop was to ask if I were okay and he queried as to my need for assistance. After over eight exhausting hours with at least five rest stops I finally arrived in Savoy. Pulling into Larry's driveway, there was Gary's van. When he saw me he immediately opened up the rear doors of his vehicle and, much to my delight and surprise, displayed a case of beer immersed in a cooler of ice. Man, what a welcomed site!

"Great job," he complimented me as I rode up. "That was a hell of an accomplishment," he continued. I certainly did not disagree with him and thought that would probably be the last of my endurance, long distance adventures. How wrong was that?

After cleaning up with a welcomed shower at Larry's and a fine dinner at a local restaurant we drove back to Washington. I was, indeed, grateful for his assistance and friendship. Each summer following that first ride I traversed the 100 miles to Champaign and I assured Gary I would be okay. I felt I would be imposing on him if I continued asking for his assistance each year knowing he would do it as a favor. Therefore, I began imposing on the lovely Veronica, who is from the same area, Urbana, to become the SAG for those trips. It also allowed us to stay in town, visit relatives and friends and not have to be back at any specific time. Gary was indeed a true friend.

Unfortunately, Gary passed away about three months before my cross country adventure. But, before that terrible event he continued to encourage me and was excited for me to do the cross country trip. After his passing, as the date for the cross country ride got nearer, I began having doubts, and yes, there were plenty. One Sunday afternoon in January as I was shoveling snow from my sidewalk, I observed Gary's sons, Matt and John clearing Mel's driveway. He is their grandfather and Gary's dad. I lived next to Mel since I moved into the neighborhood and he was as good a neighbor as one could hope for. Stopping my work to talk with the young men, I commented that I was considering waiting until 2010 to do my cross country bike ride. May, 2009 was rapidly approaching and I was starting to have second thoughts figuring another year's preparation would enable me to be more successful in accomplishing this task. Both boys quickly reminded me that "next year" was not guaranteed. Using their father as the example, they reminded me that if I put off the ride, what guarantee would I have that 2010 would be a better time or even if I would be around in another year? No guarantees!! They encouraged me to continue my plan of riding across the country and wished me luck. As it turns out that was excellent advice. Therefore, my ride from Springfield to Champaign was dedicated to Gary and his family for their support and encouragement.

I also need to comment on the hospitality of Brother Larry. He was always available to provide me with a destination where I could recover, clean up, ice my knee and rest until my SAG support arrived. In fact, I would make a yearly jaunt to Champaign, actually Savoy which is just south of Champaign, as my only century of the year. Through the years the riding time got shorter and the trip became easier which was one of the reasons I thought I could actually ride across the United States.

A pattern developed through those years that the night before I decided to ride I would call and let him know my plans. He always found a way to accommodate my schedule. It got to a point where, about an hour before I arrived at Larry's house, I would call to let him know my anticipated ETA. On one particular ride, in 2005, I began in a heat wave where the temperature reached 90 degrees and instead of my usual early starting time, I didn't begin until noon.

Obviously, that was the heat of the day and I'm not sure that was a particularly wise decision. But, other than that, the conditions were favorable for my yearly adventure across central Illinois. I hadn't anticipated the heat and humidity. After a very arduous 6 hours of riding in those conditions I finally arrived in Mahomet IL. That is about an hour away from the end of the ride. After a short rest, I called Larry and told him the heat and humidity had taken its toll. I was tired and asked for him to come pick me up at the rest stop in Mahomet. "Okay" he replied. "I'll be there in about 20 minutes".

"What!!" I shouted into my cell phone. "You should have told me that my goal was to ride to Champaign. So finish it! I'm not picking you up," was my smartass reply.

"Sorry, Sorry" he lamented. I'll see you when you get here"

"Hey, I was just kidding," I retorted. "I'm really tired and could you come and get me"?

"Okay," he continued, "I'll be there shortly."

Now, I suppose you have figured it out by this time as to what my response was going to be and you would be correct.

"What!!" again I shouted into the cell phone. "Wrong again kemosabe."

"Didn't I just tell you I have not finished my goal? You should have responded 'go to hell. You are zero for two."

By this time I'm sure I had him totally confused

"Alright, alright, I'll see you when you get here"

"Hey, I was just messing with you. I'm really tired. Could you come and pick me up? I'm not fooling this time"

"Fuck you!!" was his reply shortly followed by the sound of the phone being disconnected.

Ha! An hour later, I arrived at his abode, showered, iced my knee, replenished vital fluids and waited peacefully until my ride arrived.

Larry learned a lesson that day. Do not, under any circumstances, pick up Brother Champ (aha, referring to myself in the third person! How droll) regardless of his situation.

I, also, learned a valuable lesson. What if there came a time I actually needed his help? At what point would brother agree to come to my assistance? Even though I had fun joking with him on the matter of setting goals and not letting anything interfere with achieving them, I may have eliminated my safety net on my biking trips to Champaign. I suspect though, that he will be able to tell the difference. At least, that is my hope.

Chapter 4

Springfield To Champaign, IL

"Champ, hurry up and sign in," exclaimed Mac with astonishment on his face and an unbelieving look in his eye. Margaret shared his thoughts and made sure my hands were washed thoroughly before handling any of the food or paperwork. It was the first time of the entire 5 week experience that I arrived at a SAG stop first. Having not thought much about it prior to this time, I hadn't realized it was a particularly big deal, but from their reaction I could tell it was, at least, for the support crew.

Having already lamented the dreaded headwind, our group had left Springfield. Hank and I rode with the group who had, by this time, established themselves as the "racehorses," first to leave and first to arrive at the day's destination. We were averaging between 17 and 18 mph. Hank, at one point, took the lead ahead of the racehorses and was quite pleased.

"Champ, take a picture, I'm ahead of everyone!" he said.

After several miles riding with the lead group, I decided to pass them all. Familiar with the "sprint" method of biking, I put myself in gallop mode and took off. As I was passing Al, he lamented that I "shouldn't challenge Jim because he gets quite competitive and I wouldn't have a chance." I doubted that. My experience running from the posse for much of the ride and knowing these are the type of roads I trained on, complete confidence prevailed if a race was on. And, it sounded like a challenge. So, off I went. Before long I had a significant lead on the pack and as the miles whizzed by I had actually increased my lead. My average speed was between 19-20 mph. In fact, I actually got into competition technique and when I sensed the group was making up time I began what I called my "100 spin sprint." This was a training method I used preparing for the ride. I would, at various intervals, do 100 spins at top speed. This method depended on wind direction and terrain. Therefore, after checking my pursuers I employed this strategy. And, I must admit, I got encouragement from deceased friend Gary. There were times I asked Gary to keep the wind from shifting into my face. He did an excellent job of holding the wind direction and speed constant. Thanks good friend. That's my story and I'm sticking to it!!

At the 37 mile marker into the day's ride I could see the SAG stop looming in the distance. I was sure the group behind me would not be able to catch up. The amazement and look of the support crew was refreshing. The first item of business at the SAG stops was to sign in and put down the time. It helped the support crew keep tabs on the riders as a safety measure. When the group of racehorses behind me arrived, I was a full 4 minutes ahead of them. That reflected a little more than a mile separation. After finishing off replacement fluids, power bar, food and a spritzer of GU (and energy gel) I was ready to roll. Being the first into Champaign was now my goal.

All of a sudden, and I'm not quite sure what came over me, I came to my senses. This was not a competition. For me it never had been one. Taking pictures, resting when needed and riding with those tuned into the same objective was my modus operendi up to this point. Why change now? I had determined early on I was NOT in a race and had fallen victim to my competitive nature. Because of my sports and academic background, it was extremely difficult to overcome. I had avoided that temptation the entire trip. Even the chase by the posse was nothing more than an exercise in amusement to decrease the monotony of the ride, certainly not a competition. Now, here were four weeks into the adventure, and I started to get competitive. How foolish was that? Since Hank arrived with the lead group, I waited with him but still thought about heading out. I knew at this point if I wanted to be the first one into Champaign I would easily accomplish this goal. But, again, for me, it would have violated a very basic reason for doing a ride of this nature. IT WAS NOT A RACE!! And, as it turned out, it was an excellent decision to take my time and ride my own ride.

After the SAG stop, the "racehorses" galloped off while Hank and I rode together the remainder of the way to Champaign. Many of the cyclists at this time, because of the long rugged miles ridden, were encountering mechanical problems with their bikes. Hank needed to purchase two new rims as there were cracks in both of his. I knew our route would take us past one of the two major bike shops in Champaign. In fact, it was directly on our route, Route 10, located directly across from a mall on the western edge of the city.

Inevitably, because of the inherit Karma that was a large part of this experience, I somehow knew we would engage in some sort of memorable experience. And, it would soon prove to be the case. Riding into Clinton IL Hank and I decided to stop at a Dairy Queen. Those establishments were always a welcomed relief for all the riders and indeed our group in particular. After purchasing my usual chocolate shake, Hank and I proceeded into the dining area. Sitting at a table were 12 elderly women enjoying typical Dairy Queen refreshments. We found out later they had just come from their weekly workout at the local YMCA. Hummmmm. Hank being Hank proceeded to sit at their table, in the head seat, and acted like he was about to conduct a board meeting with his executives. Ogling Hank in his sexy spandex biking shorts, the women feigned mild amusement as he joined them.

"Well ladies", he began, "I'm staying at the Drury Inn in Champaign tonight. If you would like to visit me this evening, first you must do my laundry and then do my ironing." I thought of and was prepared for a massive riot in response to Hank's edict. Yet, the women began to laugh and giggle like teenagers so Hank proceeded to "hold court". He described our adventure of biking across the country and the women were mesmerized.

Impressed with how well he connected to this group of women and the enjoyment they experienced during this interaction, I realized that if I ever tried something like this, objects of destruction would have been launched in my general direction. I conceded that Hank was, indeed, THE MAN!

To illustrate how a negative can even come from a mildly amusing event, one of the bikers, nameless at this point, joined us.

"Why are these women at the Dairy Queen?" "They just finished exercising so what good did it do?" Maybe, the bike snob thing coming through.

I felt the comment was entirely derogatory and totally uncalled for. We were visiting their domain, just passing through. Judging these folks on their lifestyle choices was totally inappropriate. That being said, Hank and I finished our drinks and were once again on the road.

Anxious to get to Champaign, we headed off at a rather brisk pace. Since, as stated before, I grew up in this city, I was looking forward to arriving there as soon as possible for many reasons. First, it was one of our rest day stops which meant we would be spending more than a cursory amount of time there. I knew where to go for restaurant choices and entertainment events.

Second, my son, Christopher, drove down from Chicago to meet with me and our group. And finally, Ronni would be joining us with the van so transportation around the community was enhanced to ensure our ability to enjoy those various venues.

One of the reasons I chose CrossRoads Cycling as the company to assist my journey, was I knew they travelled through Champaign and I looked forward to the mild respite that visiting here would provide. While it is more than half way across the continent it was the perfect place to stop, relax with the family and basically recharge my batteries before the last two and one-half weeks remaining before we reached Boston. In fact, I would take the rest day to drive to Washington and have Russell's Cycling give my trusty steed a tune-up. Upon our arrival at the hotel, Christopher was there to greet me and it was great to see him.

Having graduated from Champaign High School and the University of Illinois, a reporter for the local paper, the News Gazette, inquired as to the possibility of conducting an interview with me. The focus was to promote my charity; Central Illinois Alzheimer's Assn. and look into the various aspects of doing a cross country ride from someone who grew up in the town. As stated earlier, the headline created quite a stir amongst "my people".

"PULLING THE BEER WAGON ACROSS AMERICA." This headline boomed across the News Gazette page following my interview. Wow!! After reading the article, I concluded it was an excellent journalistic effort but the headline was quite misleading. As mentioned earlier that quote was pulled from my blog where I compared the aforementioned riding styles of the cross country group. It alluded to the fact we all have different techniques for doing our ride and none were better or worse than others. As a Clydesdale my style was methodical but had worth. What farmer would want a racehorse plowing his field? What owner of a race horse would put a plow horse in the field of competition? My quote was to show value for all riding styles. The problem was the headline. Without actually reading the article, one would presume I was drinking my way across the country. Now, that might not be such a bad thing but friends and relatives in the area thought differently. Oh well, nothing one could do about it but as I have continually stated, for every positive there would be a negative. YIN/YANG...KARMA.

Activities for me, and other members of the group in Champaign, were more numerous than any of the other rest day's events. Ferrins, one of my favorite eateries at the time, was the first stop of the day. Lunch with Brother Larry, Ronni and Christopher followed. In my humble opinion as a salad expert, the strawberry, nut lettuce salad served at this particular restaurant stands alone as the best salad in the history of salads! Again, it's my story and I'm sticking to it!!

Christopher had to return to Chicago so after bidding him adieu I took several of the bikers to my favorite watering hole in Champaign, Hubers on University Avenue. Once again the van worked in our favor. We took Harry, Karen, and Chris to that fine establishment. Later Willie and others joined us. Since Ronni and I were driving back to Washington, Willie and his people could take Harry and Karen back to the hotel.

Me, Karen, Harry at Hubers in Champaign

So, what is my purpose in relating such a mundane story? As I found out later, Harry, being from England speaking with a thick, heavy Liverpool accent, impressed the work staff, mostly women, to the extent they actually stayed open past their normal 11:00 closing time. Of course, the employees were not selling alcohol past this time because it would have been illegal and perhaps they might have been fined or maybe even closed for a short period of time if discovered committing acts of this nature.

As it turns out, Harry was the center of attention and impressed those at the bar to the extent that when he returned a year later to ride with Barbie, who started with us and finished her journey over a three year period, insisted our first stop would be Hubers. And even today, when he communicates with me, he always makes an inquiry about his favorite "watering hole" in Champaign. I often mention to Harry when he calls me, the female employees, and maybe even some of the males, inquiry as to when the "Englishman" will return.

After leaving Hubers around 10:00 PM. Ronni and I returned to Washington. It is only an hour and a half from Champaign so it wasn't much of a drive. I needed to return my bike to Russell's for the aforementioned tune-up. Upon our arrival in Washington we drove past Russells and looking up at his marquee, I was utterly amazed. His bike shop is located on the main street running through Washington and in big bold letters was the greeting "Welcome, Champ Walker, transcontinental bicyclist." It was very impressive. Until that time I had always referred to the journey as "cross country" but I suddenly realized it was, indeed, a ride of that magnitude. It has a certain ring "Champ Walker..Transcontinentalist."

After taking my bike in for a tune-up the following day, I took a photograph of the entire Russells employee staff and placed it on my blog. Good advertising for the owner for doing an exceptional job helping me prepare for my journey.

Another aside to my return to Washington involved Harry's bicycle. Although an expensive vehicle costing in the $8,000 price range, through the trials and beatings it took on the road, it developed loose spokes. That wouldn't normally present a problem but most bike shops were incapable of tightening them because a special tool was needed. In fact, the two major bike shops in Champaign were unable to do the needed repair. I found that odd since they operate in a university town where many college students use that mode of transportation. With a population combination of Champaign and Urbana, together with University of Illinois students, over 100,000 people live in that area. I figured those numbers would deem it essential for these bike shops to accommodate special high end vehicles. Yet, after contacting both they indicated they could not help. The good news is that after talking to Joe Russell, he indicated they had the proper equipment to do the repairs to Harry's bike. While the cost was somewhat expensive, $30, Harry's bike was returned to "good as new "status.

As revealed earlier, many of the riders in our group at this point in the ride were in dire need of bike repairs. Even with their extreme competency and expertise, members of our support staff had reached a point where they were unable to accommodate all the needed upkeep.

Since Hank had cracks in his wheels and needed to replace both of them only Champaign Cycle shop had the equipment in stock and were able to replace them on the spot. Waiting for the bike to be fixed, I wandered around the shop looking for something I might need to make the last three weeks of the ride easier. Most of the riders use some type of seat lubricant. My choice was the popular Chamois Butter. Spread liberally across the buttocks it ensured blisters, rashes and other assortment of gluteus ailments were kept at a minimum. (Okay, now he's starting to get weird. TMI. I know.) Yet, I came across a unique lubricant that one of the employees of the shop introduced to me. It was called DZNUTS. The advantage of using that product is that it not only was an "ass cheek" lubricant but had medication mixed into it. When chaffing occurred, which happed to most of the other riders, the medication was there to begin the healing process. What a great idea. It also came with instructions for proper use, not that experienced bikers really needed it.

It should be noted at this point that, as stated earlier, most of the riders encountered saddle discomfort at some point of the ride. From the perspective of needing medicated pads to milder forms of treatment, chaffing and blisters were known to be possible side effects of a ride of the distances we covered. As for me, I never really had saddle discomfort because I buttered liberally and often. I placed extra lubricant in my front bag and often, at SAG stops, it was reapplied to possible effected areas in large quantities.

To keep chaffing at a minimum I used another tried and true method. Wearing two pair of spandex biking shorts ensured less friction being applied to a certain area; namely my ass! I know TMI. Combined with my unique saddle, which none of the other riders had or even knew about, I came through the entire ride with no discernable discomfort in that region of my anatomy.

Chapter 5

REST DAY IN CHAMPAIGN, IL

Sunday following my arrival, Ronni and I returned from Washington to Champaign with my bike restored and Harry's wheels fixed. That evening we took Hank, Bob and Tom to dinner at a nice non-franchise Italian restaurant. Again, we encountered Willie and his friends who met him there. Weird, I thought. Of all the different restaurants in the twin cities one could go to for dinner, we encountered other bikers from our group for a second time in two different places. Karma again I suppose.

Me, Tom, Bob, and Hank at Italian Village in Champaign

After a scrumptious, filling meal of pasta and wine, we headed back to the hotel to continue our rest, recuperate and recover before our ride to Crawfordsville, IN. Ronni returned to Washington and I once again was in cross country mode. While we only had two weeks to go, I reminded people who congratulated me on my accomplishment; it was premature to do so. We still had the eastern portion of the country to finish biking across and if the first four weeks were any indication, there would be many more adventures, both positive and negative to endure. Karma and balance in the universe will be maintained. I was refreshed and looked forward to the final two weeks. And, as it turned out, it was a prophecy that was to come true.

Chapter 6

Two New Riders Added To The Group

Two individuals joined our group in Champaign. Sue and Mike contracted to complete the eastern section of the cross country ride. Sue hailed from Oregon and Mike, came from Texas. Both were a welcomed addition to our group. Mike joined the racehorses and Sue eventually joined our group of four, Hank, Bob, Tom and me, which, by this time, began to ride together regularly. And, I must state emphatically, Sue is by no means a Clydesdale!

Sue's unique addition to our group was she was the only person on the ride that used a recumbent. While it looked strange compared with the other traditional bikes, she could ride with the best of the cyclists. I was amazed at how well she could maneuver the thing. A recumbent bike sits low to the ground and one pedals with their feet out in front. I'm told it is great on the back which is why many bicyclists use them. I have, in fact, tried riding this type of bicycle but, for the life of me, cannot imagine riding a great distance on one in that position.

For me, the only real downside of the recumbent is that in rainy, wet conditions, it becomes a much more hazardous ride because of the low center position of the rider to the road. As I will relate later, Sue needed to stop riding at times because of the intensity of the rain and the dangerous situation it presented. Also, cornering can be difficult and a complete stop with an immediate start is troublesome. But, all in all, Sue did a magnificent job biking from Champaign to Boston.

Sue on her recumbent. Blurry but you get the idea.

Mike, the second to join us in Champaign, and a good friend of Rick, was another of the extremely strong riders. In fact, he and Rick seemed to enjoy racing each other, especially when the roads became hilly. I found out later that Mike had back problems and usually walked with a cane. I asked him how he walked with a staff, yet, biked quite strongly with no apparent negative effect. He indicated he had severe back pain that would eventually necessitate surgery. Oddly enough, as he later explained, he could ride long distances and that riding the bicycle did not hurt his back at all. This is counter indicative from everything I had heard about biking and the back. Riding in a bent over position on a bicycle for extended periods supposedly has negative impact with back issues. In Mike's case it worked totally in the opposite way. If I hadn't seen it I would not have believed it. But, for Mike, it was absolutely true; when he got off his bike he immediately began walking with a cane!

Chapter 7

CHAMPAIGN TO CRAWSFORDVILLE, IN

Our departure from Champaign was quite unique. We started our ride to Crawfordsville IN and looked like a group of escaped refugees from a Barnum and Bailey circus. Prior to our departure, we were supposed to decorate ourselves and our bikes as ridiculously as possible. Many of the cyclists purchased decorating materials that, I suspect, exceeded even their own expectations. Since my time to shop for bizarre paraphernalia was limited, and I am quite capable of looking foolish without much effort, I placed a single U.S flag in my helmet; one of the least decorative of the lot. So this modest display ensured that no one could ridicule me or criticize me least they be exposed as one of those commie anti-patriots. If prizes were given out for the most outlandish, Harry and Nancy would have tied for first place. Both looked ridiculous, as was the objective and those who observed them biking along the roads would stare in wonderment and amazement. "Those damn crazy bikers" thoughts would permeate their thinking processes. And, they would have been entirely accurate!

Group with Crazy Riding gear…Harry front left

"Gosh darn "or words to that effect, were muttered by me as we began our trek from Champaign to Crawfordsville, IN. Tracy had my complete trust when it came to routing us across the country. But, I had a bit of doubt as we started on this particular morning. It was a Monday which meant workers do the rush hour traffic thingy. Of all the roads leaving Champaign heading east from the hotel, the route we were taking would have been my absolute last choice. We were going to leave by the two busiest streets in Champaign/ Urbana. I should know, I lived there, grew up there and had driven my car on those streets for 30 years.

Leaving the hotel, we traveled south on Prospect Ave. Not only is it one of the busiest in the twin cities, it had no bike path and was not particularly wide as most four lane roads tend to be. Arriving at University

Ave. we turned east. At this time of day, it is easily the busiest avenue of all the streets in the area. And here we were a group of crazily dressed bikers on a busy four lane road with no shoulder or bike path in the midst of rush hour.

Wow! I couldn't believe I was riding my bicycle on a road I was quite familiar with as cars buzzed by barely missing us in the process. If ever one of the bikers were going to get hit, this would be it. I was certainly relieved as we finally got to "Five Points," in Urbana. That was a 6-7 mile journey from the hotel and is located close to the eastern edge of Urbana. After that point, traffic slacked and Route 150 would lead us to Danville our first SAG of the day. Tracy has since used a less traveled exit from Champaign.

I should note here the irony of the road from Champaign to Danville, along route 150, did not escape my attention. In the 1950's, as a child, there were no interstate highway systems in the U.S. This particular road was the main artery between those two cities. Relatives, (aunts, uncles, grandparents) on my mother's side lived in Danville. My mother grew up there so virtually every Sunday we traveled this route to visit them. Pedaling along this road with our group, I recalled those trips and it seemed like the road and buildings alongside it had not changed much, quite nostalgic as I recall.

While Sue originally started with our little group, it was clear she was determined to show the rest of the riders her biking capabilities. She stayed with us at the beginning of the day but would leave us in her wake when she so desired. By the time we reached the first SAG stop in Danville, she was well ahead of us and her riding style stayed consistent all the way to Boston.

It should be pointed out, at this time, that the terrain from Illinois to the eastern part of the Appalachian Mountains fit well with my riding style. Training for years on these types of land forms, I had no trouble keeping up with the "racehorses." Karen noted as much in one of her blog posts referring to me as a "strong" rider and noted it was due to my preparation in topography of this nature. Obviously, the posse had no intent of letting me out on a string, then reeling me back in. In this region it wasn't going to happen but if the thought occurred to them, being "caught" would have only been accomplished if I allowed it to happen. Until the mountains, which loomed further to the East appeared; the posse was satisfied with riding along with the urgency of pursuit eliminated from their behavior. I suspect they enjoyed it more anyway.

One of the youngest and possibly fastest of the racehorses, Chris, decided to ride most of the way from Champaign to Crawfordsville with our newly formed group. During this stretch Hank, Tom, Bob, Sue and I began riding as a unit and continued, for the most part, to the end of the journey. While I still preferred the "lone eagle" approach, it was fun and created a diversion riding with these folks.

By this time I had mastered the pace line protocol used by experienced bikers. Leaders pointed out obstructions by shouting expressions such as HOLE! GLASS, WATER, and other debris that might be invisible to the rider in the rear. Rotating leaders was an important part of the pace line process although Sue and her recumbent presented problems so she seldom took the lead, which was okay with her. None of the men in our group tried to push the limit and display "macho" riding speeds so we developed an excellent comradery.

It was during this grouping that I finally identified Hank's riding preference. He would begin in the morning with a good night's rest, (he was in the sack on most nights by 8:00 PM) and liked to begin the day's ride like a "bat out of hell". But, as the day progressed, he eventually slowed to a more leisurely pace and by the end of the ride actually conserved energy so the end wouldn't be as tiring.

Entering Indiana

Riding to Crawfordsville, a distance of about 85 miles, was relatively uneventful. Crops, in the many fields we passed, were just emerging from the soil. It was early June and the farmers got a late start to their planting season due to the vast amounts of rain received earlier in the spring. From my experience as a Midwesterner, who knows something about the farming process, I couldn't remember a planting season as late as this year. Crops at this time should have been much higher. The old saying about corn "four foot high by the fourth of July" (used to be knee high by the fourth of July but has since been upgraded) would indicate a poor crop. Discussing this with our group, I was amazed at how little many of them knew about farming. One of my first indications of these phenomena was when I asked them if they could tell me the difference between corn, beans, or wheat by looking at them in the fields. Quizzing Chris, as we rode side by side, became quite interesting. I would point out a field with the leaves having barely emerged from the soil and ask him to name the particular plant. He guessed and was correct about 30% of the time. That is the same as closing one's eyes and guessing. I had quite a bit of fun with this ploy. As I came to realize, this is no different than me being goo-goo eyed as we crossed the mountains of the Southwest. Living in these regions tends to breed familiarity that may not be particularly interesting to anyone living there but is quite intriguing for those who do not.

Inspecting the fields of grain

Being a Midwesterner, I was not particularly impressed with a tractor coming down the highway. Fact is, I spent most of the fall and spring time dodging them on the back roads around Washington. Not impressed at all. But, the excitement of those in my group from the east and west coast was displayed by them exiting their bike and taking photos when a tractor rolled down the road. That is exactly the behavior I exhibited undulating through the mountains in the Southwest. While most continued riding, I would stop often and photograph the mountains. Upon reflection, this was another interesting sociological aspect of this trip.

Two memorable experiences occurred on the way to the Crawfordsville destination. First, our route took us along narrow Indiana county roads so we passed through many small, iconic Midwestern towns. These are areas located at some distance from the interstate highways so that each town had its own unique identity and personality. One of these communities in particular impressed upon me this uniqueness. Upon arriving at the small community of Hillsboro, Indiana the townspeople erected a welcome sign that stated "Welcome to Hillsboro Indiana-the Home of 600 Happy People and a few old Soreheads"

Love it!!

All of the bikers that passed the sign stopped to photograph it. Looking back, that was one of my favorite signs of the entire trip. After taking a picture, I encountered a worker exiting an "out" building near the sign. He was a maintenance worker, Josh, and I inquired about the sign. Who was responsible? What inspired the village to post such a grand sign?

My questions were answered and he continued supplying additional trivial information. He told me that he, in fact, was responsible for the sign. The motivation was to distinguish this small berg from the many other small towns that dot the Indiana countryside, a stroke of good luck on my part. Fortuitous indeed, running into the person who actually was responsible.

Another experience from this section reflected, as mentioned earlier, one of the major goals of riding across the United States was meeting interesting people and, at times, not so interesting but relevant nevertheless. Interacting with the locals provided a wealth of satisfaction that negated many of the obstacles encountered along the way. Veedersburg Indiana, another one of these small Indiana villages, hosts a small but busy restaurant on the main road through the village. At the Bus Stop Restaurant many of us stopped to get a quick bite of lunch. Walking into the eatery in our biking gear, we obviously appeared to be quite a site. Many of the diners stopped their meals to gawk at us as we entered. As they became more comfortable with our presence and realized we were not a bicycle gang intent on terrorizing their town, many struck up conversations. Once again, after hearing about our journey and the distance we had already ridden they were in utter amazement. After finishing their lunches, many sauntered outside to observe and comment on our bikes.

Since the restaurant had sold most of their pies, which was the only reason I stopped, I adjourned outside to engage the locals. One lady in particular, Marge, stated she and her husband, Roy, were serious bikers and often rode the hills around Veedersburg. I suggested they would be candidates for a cross country bike trip. Tracy got another endorsement from me and I encouraged them to peruse the CrossRoads Cycling web page for more information. They seemed genuinely interested and I would be fascinated to see if they actually followed through. Talk the Talk, Walk the Walk. It was, all in all, a very pleasant encounter to add to the positive nature of the adventure.

I should note here that while many think of the Midwest as a flat straight plain, they only need to ride the areas of eastern Indiana to dissuade that notion. Not to be confused with the mountains of the west or east, the rolling hills in this part of the country provide a measure of challenge heretofore totally unexpected. While I wouldn't compare the state of Indiana with any of the other states that presented riding difficulties like those in Arizona, New Mexico and later the mountains of the east the ride through Indiana was intriguing.

After arriving in Crawfordsville, the routine of showering, resting, eating, and blogging continued. It was here that we became keenly aware that the adventure would soon be finished.

Chapter 8

CRAWSFORDSVILLE TO INDIANAPOLIS, IN

Indianapolis was the destination for the next part of the trip. Being a relatively short 64 mile event, our group looked forward to what could be referred to as a ride with a rest. As was the case for most of the remainder of the journey, the wind would be coming from an easterly direction which was quite uncommon for that time of the year in this particular region of the country. In addition, to confirm our suspicions, after careful checking various sources, it was confirmed that the spring of '09 was one of the rainiest/wettest springs in quite some time. Perhaps that was why the wind was predominately from the east but I can't speak to that as a fact since I do not have a degree in meteorology. In fact, after speaking with the local farmers, they were at least a month behind in their planting. Headwinds and rain would be the weather for most of the remainder of our way to Boston.

Hank, Sue and I began the ride to Indianapolis in a tandem pace line. Having Hank lead our little group was obviously a major mistake we made at the time and, by this time, should have known better. We let Hank lead the group assuming he could read a route sheet. Ha! Fat chance! Along the way we rode past the turn described in the instructions and biked about two miles beyond where we should have made the turn. Entering a small town not mentioned on the map we soon realized we were lost. It wasn't the first time, of course, and wouldn't be the last. Hank was immediately relegated to follower and was summarily dismissed as Navigator. Asking for directions at the local gas station in the town we inadvertently strayed into, an attendant informed us our turn was two miles in the opposite direction. Yes, that is correct, we actually asked for directions. I know that is unheard of for a guy to do this but it is what it is.

Incidentally, it should be noted that because Sue was with us maybe it wasn't such an oddity. The strange thing about this is that if we had made a left turn at the road in town where we asked directions, it would have taken us to back to our original route. Going back to the original path took us on a meandering escapade through the country roads which eventually intersected the state route in town.

Now for the good news/bad news. Missing the turn meant we would have missed a SAG stop at a local farmers house. The reason this is important is because, as had been alluded to many times previously, that was the method allowing Tracy to keep track of her herd. And, by not checking in, she would have to wander around with a search party and try to find us. That would be the bad news. The good news is that I had a great conservation with Bob, the dairy farmer, who showed his hospitality by allowing us to use his front yard as the SAG stop.

Our group at Bob the farmer's front porch

189

After arriving at the SAG doing the ritual washing of hands, signing in and devouring food, I engaged in a dialog with Bob. Shade trees and a huge front porch welcomed us and encouraged us to take our time and enjoy the place; even though we had ridden an extra five miles due to our inability to read a route sheet. Listening to other riders who engaged in conversation with Farmer Bob, I was somewhat amazed at their lack of knowledge about farming methods in general and farmers in particular.

In my mind the questions asked seemed quite elementary. Now, to be sure, I am not a farmer by any stretch of the imagination, but, one cannot live in the most fertile farm land on earth without gaining a rudimentary knowledge of how the system functions.

"Why are the crops so low?" "Can you eat dairy cattle?" "What do you do between planting season; do you have a regular job?" These were just a few of the inane questions asked by my biking friends. While I may seem a bit arrogant, I just assumed people had a more basic knowledge of farming than was being exhibited. And, I must admit, I can guarantee you that I am as ignorant in many areas where some might question my intelligence. Nevertheless, Farmer Bob was very accommodating, did not ridicule any of the inquiries and did his best to provide informational answers.

Growing up in the Midwest and having an uncle who owned a farm, which we frequented often during the summers of my youth, I was relatively familiar with farming procedures. My questions concerned current farming practices and the government's increasingly intrusive role. Farmer Bob was very enlightening when I explored the "till versus no till" aspect of modern day farming. Knowing the advantages of no till or conservation till farming, I was surprised that many farmers today still practice full-till methods.

(I suppose I should inform the reader, ignorant of the difference between these two farming procedures, what each entails.) Full till farming happens when the soil in the field is plowed over and over until it has enveloped the crop remnants and remains an empty black dirt tract of land. No-till or conservation till involves leaving the previous crop residue on top of the soil and not plowing it under until the spring. It saves money, fuel, and time and results in a crop that yields just as many bushels per acre as full-till. In addition, full till fields get their topsoil blown into the rivers and streams as the winds and rains of spring do their damage).

Farmer Bob concurred that all farmers should practice no-till but many still do not. He uses this method and indicated he had been doing so for at least the last ten years. Farmer Bob went on to state that many of the older farmers still full till and the only way they justify it is they become impatient and that's the way they have always farmed. They won't change.

At some level I can understand their attitude but the only thing that is constant is change. (Yes, you can quote me on that!) And, many people, not just farmers, have a difficult time adapting to change. This then begs the question. Should government step in to regulate farming methods detrimental to the environment? They have done so in many other industries. It's a tough question to answer. Farmer Bob didn't think so and he's probably correct. Once the government becomes involved, who knows what will happen. That doesn't mean government should not be involved to some degree with farm subsidies, crop insurance and other programs designed to help the farmer in times of need, but perhaps Bob has a point. He thinks better methods of educating the modern farmer is the answer. All in all I would probably agree with that assessment. After pictures on his front porch and a restful SAG experience, we were off to Indy.

So, what is the point in detailing this feature of the ride? It illustrates two things. First, and has been stated before, engaging the people we meet along the way in meaningful discourse really enhanced the experience. Secondly, it shows the difference in depth of knowledge of the riders depended on the region of the country they were from. I found this intriguing.

Chapter 9

INDIANAPOLIS

The Indy 500, one of the most famous open wheel car races in the world, the Indiana Colts football team, nice restaurants, along with other amenities are reasons Indianapolis is one of my favorite cities. With Chicago to the north, St. Louis to the southwest and Indy to the east, my hometown sits equidistant to each of these cultural centers. So it is with great anticipation that I looked forward to Indianapolis as the destination for this part of the trip.

Our route into Indy from Crawfordsville was a very meandering path, not very direct. I suspect Tracy did this to give us a tour of the areas around the city and avoid many of the busy streets. However, because the distance was supposed to be relatively short, it seemed it took us a long time to navigate the distance between the cities. And yet, I was duly impressed with the neighborhoods we biked through. Expensive, luxurious homes and bounding lush, green golf courses directed our way to the night's destination.

In addition to all the other facilities previously mentioned, Indy is the home to a velodrome, or bicycle racing venue. Many of our group made plans to attend the evening's races, but, by this time I had developed a semi-flexible routine after the days ride. While it was not set in stone, I decided after all the biking we had done since starting in LA, watching bike races had no attraction, at least not enough to alter my routine.

By this time, after arriving at the predestined hotel, I would immediately shower and begin icing my knee. Also, I continued putting ice on the injured quad, so while I engaged in this rehabilitating process I would take time to do my writing. Fresh in my memory and with the opportunity to assume this task I was able to keep a fairly accurate account of the day's events. Placing this information in my blog, along with a picture or two, I often did not take enough time to properly edit my blog entries. Because I had about 400 hits on the blog daily, it was not unusual for my more literate followers to remind me of my ignorance of syntax, spelling, sentence structure and other writing fax paux. Understand, my only intention was to relate the day's events and not make it a scholarly endeavor but I had critics nevertheless. I found them mildly amusing but it did not deter me from continuing this type of correspondence. Given the level of fatigue after each days ride I felt fortunate I was able to write in any coherent manner at all.

After the trip and reading what I had written, I, too, was amazed at the grammatical errors. I certainly am no Hemingway, but have written and graded written material for many years. I should have known better. But, again, I will blame it on fatigue. My story, sticking to it!!

Icing would precede the daily route rap to review the next day's route. That would be followed by dinner then an evening of relaxation. Many would go to the local bar, (Harry) play pool, and in my case, if there was a whirlpool, I would avail myself of its soothing, aquatic, muscle relaxing benefits. Usually by 9:00 PM. I was ready to "hit the sack" and get a reasonable amount of sleep to ensure enough energy for the next day's ride. Therefore, my time in Indy was devoted mostly to the area around the hotel and I did not avail myself of any of the features for which the city is known. Yet, I was not dismayed because I had been there many times and had no desire to visit any of the other sites at this time.

Chapter 10

INDY TO RICHMOND, IN

Richmond, IN. was the next day's destination. It was an 84 mile jaunt, which at this time was the "norm." Again, the wind came from the east but by this time it was expected. We were used to it so it had no negative impact on the day's ride. The impressive thing about riding the country roads between Indy and Richmond was the many small towns we came across and the local folks we met. Hendrik, New Castle, Hagersburg, Hillsboro, and Centerville were but a few of the many small villages that were quite vibrant even though they are not close to an interstate highway. I happened to mention in my blog, and still am firmly convinced, more travelers should get off the interstate highway system to see the real America. These towns exemplify this ideal.

Stopping at an ice cream parlor (local, not a Dairy Queen) in the small burg of Centerville, riding with Hank and friends, we engaged in conversation with two of the local residents, Susan and Barbara. They were teenagers, baby sitting for a lad about seven or eight years old. He rode a "kid" bike and allowed Hank and myself the opportunity to have our picture taken on it. It turned out to be quite amusing and a sight to behold.

Borrowing seven year olds bike…thinking about trading for mine

Our dialogue with the babysitters turned out to be quite informative. Both agreed they lived in a "hick" town but each worked in Indianapolis. They declared they looked forward to the day they could "move out of that place". We found it notable these young women would give up the tranquility and simplicity of a town this size to the hustle and bustle of a large city like Indy. From our perspective, they didn't realize how good they had it, but they won't realize it until they had gone through the process. We ate our treats, took our photos, wished them well and continued on our way to Richmond.

Unfortunately, Richmond, Indiana was another one of those rather ordinary towns which hold no particular item of interest, at least compared to other cities we had already passed through. The routine previously described was initiated. Since the next few days of riding were going to be long demanding trips, it was a good time and place to get to bed early and rest for the coming days.

Chapter 11

RICHMOND TO MARYSVILLE, OH

Entering Ohio....strange weed growing beside sign

Marysville, Ohio was our destination the following day. We would leave Indiana and cross another state line. A good 104 miles on the bike and with our usual 7:30 start, off we went. By this time our little group, Sue, Hank, Bob, Tom, and I rode together and we engaged in small talk along the way. It made the ride seem to be less drudgery, and good, solid friendships were forged.

Several first impressions of Ohio come to mind as we crossed the state line. First, riding the back roads and county roads through Ohio were determined to be, without question, the worst we had ridden since we left LA. Bumpy, not well maintained, and crumbling gravel in many sections awaited our little group. While doing a ride of the magnitude we were attempting, these conditions were not welcomed by our bodies, our bikes, or our psyche. No offense Ohio but let's get those damn back roads back to respectability.

The next impression was the pride in which the property owners had in maintaining their homes. This pride in ownership was exhibited in well-groomed lawns even though the roads were sub-par. We passed at least 15 people engaged in mowing, trimming and maintaining their properties. Hank, who stated time and again that mowing ones yard was a waste of valuable time, energy and resources, would often make fun of those engaged in such activities. "Grow it, don't Mow it" was his mantra. Yet I was mightily impressed because auto traffic was relatively sparse and the folks who lived in those places had no need to impress anyone. It reflected the attitude which people in this part of the country had towards their property and by extension, I surmised, their lives in general. Too bad their road taxes didn't do much to improve the roads.

One of Hank's favorite signs

Delisle-Foreman and Arcanum-Bearsmill were names that left an impression and caught my attention in this part of the country. These were names of the county roads as we continued our ride thru this part of Ohio. This type of nomenclature became more common as they replaced the regular numbered or lettered byways. Throughout our journey we never come across such bizarre names for roads and I thought that was very interesting. As a historian, I should look into why and how these names replaced numbered routes. I suspect it would be quite interesting.

Oddly enough, the ride to Marysville included a foretelling of the type of weather we would encounter for most of the rest of the ride. Traveling in a southeasterly direction, a severe storm was directly in our path and loomed menacingly on the horizon. At the time I was riding with Tom and Hank. Tom's riding companion Bob was somewhere behind us. As we headed into the storm, we had some decisions to make. First, if we stayed on the current course and the storm didn't change its path, we were going to get very wet! As the storm approached, I stopped and covered my bike computer with a plastic bag to, hopefully, keep it dry. Previously, when we rode in the rain, that procedure seemed to work. As I looked for my wet weather gear, I stopped, realizing our weather guru, Jim, assured us we would not encounter any precipitation on this particular day. Okay, who was I going to believe the nasty, threatening clouds in the distance or Jim's prediction? Ha! I believed Jim and chose to not include rain gear on my bike. So, I had no rain gear and anticipated getting drenched.

As the storm moved in, Tom suggested we reconnoiter in a local grocery store until the storm passed. But, as often happened on the ride, we decided to press on. Just as we could feel the first cold drops of moisture, our route took a hard left, turning us in an easterly direction. Our mission now was to outrun the approaching storm and, as luck would have it, we succeeded. Except for a few sprinkles, we avoided the brunt of the squall. Well, at least for a while. Feeling relieved, we pulled into Marysville OH. grateful for having avoided the trials and tribulations of fighting through the shower.

Impending storm in our path....happy to have avoided it

Not looking for adventure at this juncture, the stay in Marysville was uneventful as we continued our evening routines established earlier.

Chapter 12

MARYSVILLE TO WOOSTER, OH

Marysville to Wooster, OH, a ride of 97 miles with another headwind of 10-15 mph, added an element to the ride that is obvious but often ignored. All riders are cognizant of the inherit dangers in an undertaking we were currently engaged. I have often stated that riding a bicycle in general and more specifically across the United States was the most danger fraught experience I had encountered up to that point in my life. That may speak to my existence being somewhat mundane, but I rather doubt that, given my history of "riding the edge." Poor roads, dangerous cross winds, railroad tracks that can catch a wheel, drainage ditches with the grate running parallel to the road, inattention to the surrounding conditions due to fatigue, are among many of the dangers of the ride. But, without a doubt, the absolute most dangerous obstacles are the trucks and automobiles that we bikers must interact with on the roads and highways. For the most part, auto traffic is very courteous and forgiving. Ninety-nine percent of those who encounter bicycle riders on the roads give the biker the benefit of the doubt. Experienced bikers are always aware of their surroundings and take particular care to watch the behavior of traffic.

That being said, the resulting 1% engage in dangerous, reckless and in some cases threatening behavior toward any biker in their path. And yes, I am willing to admit that often the bicyclist engages in idiotic behavior angering motorists resulting in the motorist acting out against such actions. With that as a background, an episode occurred in Delaware OH, which illustrates this point.

After leaving Marysville, Hank and I were spinning along the road together. He lost his desire to head out with the racehorses by this time. Hank was still nursing a "personal injury" which limited the distance he could comfortably ride. However, he was able to ride at the beginning of the day and, when the comfort level became unbearable; he would SAG into the day's destination.

Entering Delaware OH, the traffic was quite heavy. It was the morning rush hour and folks were on their way to their work places. Avoiding the many autos was the focus of our ride as we began. No bike trails were available for us to circumvent all this traffic. In the midst of all the havoc we noticed a nice little respite, a small park. It looked to be an excellent place to stop for a photo opportunity. Located in the middle of the park was a vintage Civil War cannon. What better location to take a break from the hustle and bustle of rush hour and add to the photo journal aspect of our ride.

Civil War cannon at park in Delaware OH

After pictures were finished, we heard the sound of an emergency vehicle and observed it as it rushed by. Having heard these many times on our ride, it was of no particular concern. As we mounted our steel steeds and merged onto the main street of Delaware, the siren seemed to be getting closer, not fading as would have been the normal circumstance. Suddenly, I got a sense that one of our riders was somehow involved. If so, it would NOT be a positive event. Ahead of us we could see traffic gridlock and we were able to ride to the right of the stopped cars. It became apparent there was an accident ahead.

Approaching the scene of the incident with a certain amount of trepidation we observed Tracy and the support team at the spot of the accident alongside an ambulance. "Move along, keep going" Tracy said as Hank and I offered our assistance, even though at that time we were unaware of what had happened. "There is nothing you can do, we'll handle everything. See you at the SAG stop" she continued. I could tell she was stressed and our continue presence would only add to it, so Hank and I kept riding.

Passing the scene, we witnessed a body lying motionless on the pavement. There was absolutely no movement from the person lying prone on the street. It was not long before we realized it was Bob, Tom's riding buddy from New Jersey, who often rode with our group. The situation looked grim but Hank and I continued. As usual, relying on our sense of direction and again misreading the route map, we took a wrong turn. Before long, after a two mile detour, we realized we had missed the correct turn. I'll blame Hank again, but I must admit I think it was my mistake! Our only option was to ride back the same two miles to where we took the wrong road.

On the return trip, we heard a helicopter overhead. It was landing on a nearby school yard playground and was met by an ambulance. Our first inclination was there was an emergency at the school. How odd! In fact, the helicopter was there to life flight Bob from the scene of his mishap to Columbus OH. We found out later that was indeed the case. Bob needed to be flown from the scene to save his life.

So I will reiterate, biking can be a very dangerous undertaking. Charlie was gone, for all intent and purposes I should not have continued riding until my leg was healed and now Bob was definitely not finishing the ride.

As it turned out, Bob and Sue were riding together and about to make a left turn. (The same turn I missed) According to my best information, Bob viewed his rear view mirror to check for automobiles or other four wheel vehicles. Seeing none in his site of vision, he proceeded to turn into the left turn lane. Unseen in his mirror was a motorcycle. The motorcycle hit Bob and his bike causing both to lose control. The motorcyclist must have been very experienced in emergency handling of his vehicle. I imagined this was not the first time he engaged in an incident of this type. His response to Bob's turning tactic was to lay down his bike and slide rather that hitting Bob full on. This maneuver helped the cyclist avoid ugly injury and possibly saved Bob's life. I'm not an expert on this matter but given the seriousness of the situation it could have been much worse. And, I suspect, it was because of the actions of the motorcyclist.

Bob's body had several broken bones (he would be the one to describe exactly which ones) and was taken to the Columbus hospital to save his life. Months after the accident Bob was still recovering. The good news is that he did, in fact, recover fully and is riding again. He even joined us in 2011 as a group of cyclists rode from Maine to Florida. I couldn't recognize any difference in his riding ability since being injured in the Ohio accident. So good news in the end.

Leaving the accident site, correcting for our wrong turn, Hank and I headed to Wooster. While biking etiquette dictates that any ride over 96 miles is a "century" many of us don't buy it, especially the posse. To them a century is what it says….100 miles. So, since the ride was supposed to be 97 miles they would be sure to bike the extra three to make it an actual century. And with our "detour" it was an official century for us.

The unique aspect of the day's journey and continuing for most of the eastern part of Ohio is that it became surprisingly hilly. Who would have imagined that? While it is not part of the Appalachian mountain range it had sections with grades reaching 10-12%. eastern Ohio along with western Pennsylvania is quite hilly even though they are not considered mountains.

After the first SAG, Hank decided to ride the rest of the way in the van. With no other riding companions I decided to take time for a "lone eagle" ride. I was cruising along without my traveling companions for the first time in many days.

The heat was becoming a factor and I knew I needed to shed some layers of riding gear in order to not overheat and also to eliminate extra weight. Layered to keep warm during the 58 degree temperatures that greeted us as the day began, it was time to adjust to the heat. At the final SAG of the day, a distance of approximately 25 miles from Wooster, I shed my rain gear with only my shirt warmer between my skin and potential road rash.

Mack, who was manning the SAG, indicated there would be some climbing the last 25 miles and, as it turned out, he was entirely accurate. Skeptical at first because of some earlier misinformation (recall the Wittenberg, AZ. section) I took what Mack said with a grain of doubt and trepidation. (yea, I know mixing metaphors again) So, when Mack mentioned there would be tough climbs ahead, I had to believe they would be extra difficult.

The first climb I engaged in was quite doable and I imagined Mack had, once again, overestimated the severity of the hills. Exhibiting a "this isn't so bad" attitude, I came around a particularly sharp turn in the road and met an incline that reminded me of "the wall" in New Mexico. While it wasn't as difficult as the mountains in Arizona or the "rollers" of Missouri, they, nevertheless, presented a challenge. Since these were primarily county roads, those constructing these minor venues had no interest in leveling the grade for heavy traffic. I surmised they figured since these were not high traffic passages, they would just pour the asphalt to conform to the existing topography of the land. While that might be okay for auto or truck traffic, for bicyclists in general and me particularly, it presented problems. But, really, were they interested in the least if these roads had bicyclist on them? I think not. Thankfully, there were only about 5 or 6 severe climbs and I was quite relieved when the last one was in my rear view mirror.

One other interesting feature of this part of the United States is the increase in horse and buggy traffic on the highways and byways. Even though we have some of these south of Champaign, near Sullivan, Arcola and Tuscola, I was still captivated with this sight. Amish country, to be sure, was approaching. Even though I had knowledge of their aversion to being photographed, I knew I had to have one to complete my photo journal. I actually understand why they wouldn't want to be photographed like some freak show. Even so, seeing a horse and buggy approaching in the distance, I stopped, removed my camera from my front pack and stood at the ready awaiting the perfect time to capture their image on film (wow another antiquated term… film, yea right). When they were about twenty yards from my position, I took the picture. As they passed I could tell they were not pleased with my behavior. From the driver, as well as the passenger sitting next to him, a middle finger was extended toward me indicating they were not thrilled. Not very Christian now is it? But, I guess I can suffer that rude reaction in order to accomplish my photographic goals. The paparazzi have nothing on me. Ansel (Champ) Adams at work. Or something like that. Probably not!

Amish horse and buggy in Ohio

I should reiterate that since we had crossed the Mississippi River, we have had no tailwinds to speak of. Mystifying to me was my unfailing belief that prevailing winds across the U.S. are from west to east. But, in our case, east to west winds were now an everyday thing so complaining about it didn't change it. Regardless of the weather our ride would continue.

Chapter 13

Radio Interview

As previously stated, a routine was established, not uncommon in the animal kingdom, at the finish of the ride each day. Knowing the importance of keeping a journal, I made the correct decision to bring a laptop computer. Part of my daily routine would be to check my e-mail. While checking my correspondence on the ride before Wooster, I was contacted by a radio station in Milwaukee, WI. They heard about my ride and the fact I was raising money for the Central Illinois Alzheimer's Assn. Inquiring as to my availability for an on air interview, I gave them my schedule and described when it would be convenient do so. I was curious who and how they knew me or anything to do with the ride but I was glad to accommodate them.

A few days prior to the interview, I had a chance to talk to the producers with reference to what we would cover during the actual on air conversation in a pre-interview format. No surprises, no sneaky questions, nothing nefarious. Preliminary questions were ones I had answered many times prior to and during earlier parts of the trip.

"Why did you decide to ride across the country?" "What problems did you encounter?" "What are some of the highlights?" and a myriad of questions similar to ones asked by people I met throughout the journey. Knowing I had taught History in the public school system for 35 years, the interview took a very interesting detour. Arnie Duncan, the new Secretary of Education in the U.S., had just declared how he was going to introduce new policies and procedures to promote and improve the lowly education given to the American children by public school teachers. The radio station personalities asked my opinion his statement. Knowing the focus was to have been about the cross country bike experience, they threw me the proverbial "soft pitch." They had just entered a world of pain. I have shared my views on this subject many times in a variety of venues.

Basically my position is and has always been clear on this matter. And, I think I may have some expertise in the area. With the material teachers have to work with, both resources and students, they do a remarkable job in an attempt to educate ALL the children in this country regardless of their (the child's) talent or desire to become educated. In fact, I informed them, we are the only country on the planet with a public education system that attempts to educate everyone from age 6 to 17-18 years old regardless of their abilities. Other countries, to which we are often compared, require students to test into higher levels to continue their education. Those who do not pass the requirements for the next level, are directed into other programs, usually vocational, that meet their abilities and interests. Numerous studies into this matter have shown time and again that it is counterproductive to attempt to educate the masses beyond basic reading and math. (Read those for details) Yet, the general public and inept politicians insist on comparing our education system to those countries who strive to educate only the elite. And, when our assessment scores are not up to the same level as these countries, our system is ridiculed. Government then intrudes with absolutely ridiculous policies that attempt to increase assessment scores for the public school children. No Child Left Behind is the primary example of government injection of ignorance into the public school system. It was a program that doesn't work, changes the manner of teaching to the lowest level of thinking skills with old recall/regurgitation techniques, eliminates higher level thinking, and puts public education into total disarray. (In fact in the national election in 2012 one of the public policy platforms for the Republican Party in Nebraska stated "higher level thinking will be eliminated in their school districts. I suspect it was thrown out but can't be sure)

The producers of the radio station were enthralled, and stated they had no knowledge of how other countries differ in their public education system compared to the United States. They asked if it would be possible to include this information during the on air interview. I agreed to the request.

Upon my arrival in Wooster, OH, I knew the call was coming but unfortunately my cell phone battery was very low. I felt I still had enough to do a 10-15 minute live radio interview and sure enough the call came through. As luck would have it they called earlier than we planned so I had no time to charge the battery.

To ensure privacy, I moved from my hotel room to the foyer. It afforded a measure of seclusion and had clearer phone reception. The interview began and it lasted at least 20 minutes as I related the same information I gave the producers earlier that week. However, I could hear the beeping in my cell phone warning me of a low battery. The good news was that the station needed to go to commercial and asked if I would be available after the break. I surprised them with a "No, sorry I'm very busy and tired at this time but thanks for the opportunity to talk about Alzheimer's and my views on the plight of public education in America."

I then added, that those who wanted to debate or be critical of my position, contact the radio station, not me. If I would ever agree with the "haters," we would both be wrong! So there! The on air personalities were amused and thanked me for sparing time from my busy schedule to talk to them.

A few days later, one of the producers from the radio station called to inform me the longer the interview lasted, more people began listening to this kook (me) on the radio. Listeners called friends and neighbors, and the stations ratings increased substantially. Well, they just came into my ballpark where I have a decidedly pro-public education stance and an anti-government interference attitude. Welcome to my world. I should have charged an appearance fee!

Finishing my evening routine I was off to bed looking forward to tomorrow's ride to Niles, OH.

Chapter 14

Wooster To Niles, OH

Wooster to Niles OH. turned out to be one of the most bizarre rides of the entire trip for me in terms of equipment malfunction, road conditions and other general bad luck episodes. It was a 91 mile trek with the wind assuredly blowing from the east-northeast at 5-15 mph. Upon awaking and checking my bike, lo and behold, I had a flat tire. The "flat fairy" paid me a visit during the night. Now, one would assume after riding three fourths of the way across the country, I would have the sense to check my tires during the ride at SAG stops and, especially, at the end of the day. In fact, after each day's ride I would clean my chain and generally clean the bike but often failed to do the "finger" check over the outside of the tire. I would usually do that before the ride began the following morning. So, the first thing I had to do was change the flat.

Since purchasing new tires from Rich during our stop in Albuquerque, complete with a Kevlar coating know as armadillo tires, my puncture rate had diminished drastically. From earlier in the ride, crossing the Mojave Desert, my tires flattened eight times, so a puncture at this stage of the ride, for me at least, was rare. However, on this particular day the tire was as flat as the pancakes I wolfed down at breakfast. Morning flats are not uncommon but they are quite annoying nonetheless. The day's ride began on a real downer.

A two mile uphill climb awaited us as we set out. What else could go wrong? Huh, it was just beginning. Changing gears on the climb, the chain slipped off the front sprocket and locked up the bike. I dismounted, informed the rest of the group with whom I was riding to continue and I would catch up at some point. After replacing the chain onto the proper socket gears I set off. This particular section of Ohio had our group making many turns so I needed to pay careful attention to the route sheet since I would be navigating solo.

I should mention at this point that while the chain came off the bike, my Cannondale Synapse did an amazing job holding up over the course of the journey. Most of the other bikers had numerous malfunctions so, aside from the flat tires, I was fortunate. A simple mishap of the chain slipping off was probably a function of human error. That is, I was not shifting properly on the uphill grade and had nothing to do with the condition of the bike.

From this depressing beginning things would start to get real interesting. Generally speaking, I am not particularly superstitious. But as the events of this day unfolded, it certainly warrants mentioning that a black cat ran across the road in front of me after I reattached my chain.

All of a sudden, for no apparent reason, my bike computer quit functioning. I have owned this particular computer since I purchased my first bicycle and have changed the battery many times. It could have not been the battery so my only other option was to check the contact points where the battery meets the computer "pick-ups". Cleaning the points, especially if excessive moisture had accumulated, was a normal maintenance procedure I performed many times. Apparently they needed a quick swab. Again, I had to stop. My riding partners were getting further ahead which meant I would have to continue relying on my own abilities to follow the route sheet. If my computer would have become totally non-functional, following route directions would have been particularly difficult. Therefore, I disconnected the computer from its attachment on the handle bar post, wiped down the contact points thoroughly, said a little prayer, and placed the computer back into position with the hope it would function correctly. Guess what? It actually worked! Miracle of miracles, I was back in business even though I had gotten so far behind my group they were not within eyesight. Aha! The lone eagle rides again.

Deciding my problems were behind me, I proceeded to follow the directions to the best of my ability that were displayed on the route sheet. However, on this particular day, the route would serpentine around in every direction possible. And, of course, I would make an incorrect turn, find my error, get back on track, miss another turn, and so it went on for most of the morning. I got lost so often that by the end of the day, I had added an extra three miles over quite hilly terrain that I normally would not have had to do. As it turned out, the ride was another "century."

Aha! That is not the end of the story. Ohio county roads, I reiterate, are, in my humble opinion, possibly the worst roads we had ridden in the entire 2,500 miles of traveling on the bike. I mean, they were terrible. It reminded me of constantly riding over miles and miles of railroad tracks. I am not exaggerating this fact. It was borne out when Rick, our mechanic, at route rap that evening, inquired if any of us needed to have our wheels "trued." That is a process of taking the "wiggle" out of the tire due to the pot holes and rough surfaces we traversed.

Flat tire, chain malfunction, computer failure, errors following map instructions resulting in lost time, extra miles ridden, and horrible road conditions would in and of itself have been a very eventful day. But, wait, there is more.

With ten miles to the destination for the day's journey, I had another puncture, number ten and the second of the day. The good news is that the posse, whom I was determined to not let catch me again, arrived as I was in the process of changing my tire. Never ones to leave a member of our troop in despair, they all stopped and immediately went to work helping replace my tube. Alec and Harry are particularly adept in flat tire changing and soon I was back and ready to finish the day's ride. In fact, I rode the rest of the way into Niles with the posse and we all stopped at the first DQ we saw. All in all, a positive end to a very eventful day.

Entering Niles after event filled day

As I have stated previously, and this day exhibited once again, what is often described as an apparent negative experience is almost always countered with a few bright spots to lighten the dim ones. Even after all the mishaps of the morning ride, eventually, I caught up with my peeps at a little off road place called the Sugar Shack near Alliance OH. (One of three we encountered with that name and they are not a chain, rather privately owned).

Among other positives on this day included biking through wonderful wooded scenery, the views of the lovely serene lakes and at the end of the day a Jacuzzi, that I jumped into soon after my arrival, to massage away my aches and pains. After another filling meal and pleasant conversation with the other riders I was off to snooze-ville to R and R for tomorrow's test.

Chapter 15

THE RAINS

At this time in our cross country journey, since it would become quite relevant, I will explain the rain situation. Later, I will examine the overall weather conditions of the trip. Suffice it to say that the wind was mostly unfavorable the entire 3000 plus miles. This was in contrast to what one would believe to be the general wind pattern across the United States. One could reasonably expect some days with winds from the east but to experience a vast majority of them from that direction was certainly unexpected. But as stated earlier, it was what it was. From this knowledge about wind direction, or lack of, I concluded that most riders across America do so from a west to east direction for that stated purpose, winds would be behind them. Yet in our experience it was not the case. Because of these unusual wind events, intrigue was added to the adventure.

Now for the rain situation. Spring rains in the Midwest as previously mentioned were heavy and frequent. Since we were now in early June the expectation was that while rain could be likely it would not be an everyday event. For most of our trip up to entering the eastern section of the country, we endured precipitation only a couple of times to the extent we needed to don rain gear. Knowing that a day of rain was eminent, I used my knowledge acquired during the cross country experience to address these weather events. Using the old trick of placing newspapers between my skin and my rain jersey provided a measure of relative comfort. Newspapers not only kept me warm but absorbed the perspiration that oozed from my hairy, porous skin due to the nonporous nature of my rain jacket. The only downside was at the end of the day my entire torso was blackened from newspaper ink leaching into my skin. While it looked quite disgusting, a little soap and water easily removed it. This trick was used quite often during the eastern portion of the ride.

On one of the rainy days in central Ohio, our group stopped at a small restaurant in Selover. Once again our riding group had not properly prepared for the amount of rain we were getting and the situation was becoming very uncomfortable. After placing our order, Hank asked the waitress of the establishment for some latex gloves so he would keep warm. I, too, asked for a pair and proceeded to remove my shoes and socks and place the gloves on my feet. Lo and behold it worked! Another trick learned from experience. (recall the ride to Madrid) Latex against the skin provided another layer of insulation. By the end of the day, my shoes and socks were completely soaked but my feet were relatively dry, another example of biker ingenuity to resolve a predicament. From that point on, I made certain I had a pair of latex gloves in my bags to counter the moisture build-up in my shoes from soaking my feet.

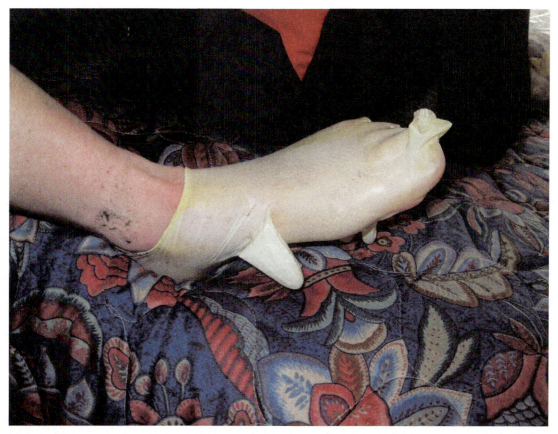

Keeping feet dry….it works

Interjecting the rain scenario at this point previews the coming days riding through Pennsylvania and New York. Incessant rain finally caught up to us. It became the wettest bicycle riding of my relatively brief distance biking career. In fact, the next few days involved the absolute wettest I have ever been in my entire life. I'm even including those days in my youth where I spent countless hours at the local swimming holes, bathing on a daily basic and other generally wet weather situations.

Taking respite from rain

216

The East

Chapter 1

NILES TO ERIE, PA

Sandpaper!! That's the closest approximation of what my hands felt like after riding in an all-day rain from Niles Ohio to Erie Pennsylvania. It was supposed to be a relatively routine trek but as usual, the wind was in our face at between 15-20 mph. That is a little stronger than we like but, once again, we were growing accustomed to it.

At the start of the day's journey, our resident weather guru, Jim, indicated there would be a light drizzle in the morning followed by clear skies the rest of the day. Wrong again Jimbo! I don't know what weather service he was using but his prediction could not have been further from what actually happened. To say I got wet was a cruel understatement. Fish in the ocean could not have been any wetter than my poor wrinkled body on this particular day.

Indeed, the first part of the prediction was accurate. A light drizzle greeted us as we began the day. It then became a steady rain until it reached a torrential downpour of biblical proportions. Hyperbole intended! Our group at this time had morphed into Hank, Tom, Sue and I. Tom, who began having bike problems days earlier, was the first to jump into the SAG wagon. Hank with his relentless health "issues" made riding in the rain very uncomfortable so he too boarded the SAG wagon. As the heavy rain continued, Sue on her recumbent, determined it was too dangerous for her to continue, so at the first SAG stop she was done for the day. That left me "lone eagle" once again. I suspect it was just as dangerous for me but I was still EFI and not about to lose it to wet weather.

Sheets of rain persisted to the extent I had to remove the camera from my front carrier and give it to one of the support staff at the first SAG. Upon reflection, I felt a need to revisit the definition of "waterproof." My carriers were supposed to be waterproof. Thinking I knew what waterproof meant suggested to me my camera was protected, therefore, I wasn't too concerned. However, after stopping to take a photo, (yes even during a driving downpour) I discovered, after opening my front carrier, much to my surprise and dismay, there was a least two inches of water in it. Fortunately, I had my camera wrapped in a "baggie" so the water had not penetrated it thereby ruining my equipment.

Nevertheless, I wasn't about to take a chance by keeping it in my carrier so I proceeded to give it to Mac for safe keeping. Unfortunately, that meant I would not be able to photograph those sites I deemed objects of interest. There would be a huge gap in my picture sequence on the ride to Erie. Since that was another of my objectives of this trip, it would have to be forestalled until the following day and I missed many photo opportunities as a result. Fortunately, Willie was recording this part of the journey with a cell phone camera and was able to share with me those pictures I felt were vital to make a complete photo journal of the experience.

Taking pictures while crossing state lines was essential. Every state line I crossed had a sign that informed all riders of the state they would be entering. Each of these state markers was photographed since we left California and I wasn't about to miss the one that marked the entrance to Pennsylvania. So, as I came to the state line, Willie was waiting there and he was able to get a picture of me at the crossing. I am forever grateful to him.

Now, at this point one might ask what was Willie, one of the racehorses, doing so far back in the pack that he was anywhere near me to take a picture? As it turns out, some friends of his were joining us for the ride from Niles to Erie. They were not as fast as Willie so he stayed back with them. Bad news for them is that it was one of the few all day rains of the trip and they had the misfortune of having to ride through it. The good news for me is that I could still continue my photo journal. Positive Karma again!!

Entering Pennsylvania thanks to Willie for pic

Nearing the final SAG of the day, about 25 miles from Erie, I was not paying attention to much more than the fact I was wet, cold, and generally miserable resulting in nearly missing the stop. My route sheet was quite wet so I didn't pay much attention to it either. The SAG was located on a curve at an open air root beer stand. Because of the cold, rainy weather, the stand was enclosed in a huge tarp with space heaters inside to warm up the clientele. Speeding through the city street, I thought I heard a whistle. It got my attention. I looked in the direction of the sound and was surprised to see Mac waving toward me. Inside the tarped enclosure were other riders enjoying a Coney Dog and root beer. If he had not seen me and realized I was not aware of the SAG stop, I would have completely blown it off and the support crew would have been concerned. To reiterate, ensuring the safety of the riders, we were required to stop at the SAGs and sign in. It is exactly the right thing to do. While required to stop, we could take as little or as much time as we needed before continuing for the day. Miserable weather conditions aside I welcomed the respite.

Fortunately, just as I pulled into the parking area where the SAG wagon was stationed, the rain had diminished to a sprinkle but it was still quite chilly. Removing my drenched carcass from the saddle, I immediately checked my rear tire. One of the conditions of riding a bike as far as we had is that you get a "feel" of the condition of the bike. If something is askew, you can feel it. My sense was that I was losing air in my rear tire. Not giving it much attention initially, I felt the low air pressure was because I recently filled my tire tube with CO_2. The problem using CO_2 in tires is that it has a tendency to "bleed" out through the valve stem, unlike regular O_2. I was hoping this was the case. Due to the weather conditions and my self-imposed discouraged state of mind, I told Mack "If this tire goes flat, I am hopping into the SAG wagon and riding into Erie."

His response was somewhat startling. "No you're not. I won't let you into the van!" Needless to say I was quite taken aback. Mac continued as he noticed the quizzical look on my face. "You're EFI. There is only about a week and a half to the end of the ride. I'm not letting you give it up at this point. If I need to, I will fix your flat." A knowing grin spread across his face letting me know he was serious but in an ambivalent sort of way. That again drove home the point of how important it was at this stage to not give up EFI, and complete the journey across America as I had intended, not giving up regardless of the situation.

Of course, all of my fellow riding companions knew that after 2,000 miles, crossing three deserts, climbing two mountain ranges, nearly killing myself crashing my bike, and an assortment of other nuisances, I was just feeling sorry for myself. Everyone knew at that point, under those conditions, even though I was complaining like a wussy crying in my beer, I would have never taken a SAG. It was a given so I might as well just "shut the hell up."

After a brief stop at the Root Beer Stand, gorging down a chili slathered hot dog, filling my tires with 02 and warming my frosted cadaver by the heaters, I was off again. While the conditions improved somewhat after the SAG, I was surprised I was able to enjoy the wooded areas and observe the many wineries located in this part of the country. As it turns out, eastern Ohio and western Pennsylvania are the second largest wine producing areas in the U.S. Who would have guessed? Maybe it wouldn't be a day with never ending rain. Ha! Not so fast Nemo breath!!

After I left the SAG with Willie and his group in my "dust" well at least in a small puddle, I waited for them as I entered Erie. Both of my route maps were totally waterlogged and unreadable except for the very bottom half of each. These maps were essential in order for me to find my way to the hotel. So, I was hopeful that one of Willie's friends had a legible map. Therefore, I waited for them and sure enough one of his buddies had a useable map. That was the good news, now the bad news. Making our way through Erie's streets, one of Willie's friends had a puncture. And, the rain began picking up again. Everyone stopped to help but I figured I needed to continue to avoid more drenching. I knew the name of the hotel where we were staying but unfortunately the street signs around the town square were very confusing and I ended up about four blocks past the turn crucial to finding the place. Not a bit unusual, I was lost again!

Getting smarter by the minute, I actually asked a pedestrian if he could direct me to the hotel. He indicated it was about two blocks behind me and another two blocks to the east. Making a turnaround, my worst fears were realized. A downpour of rain began, another biblical water fest.

Finally arriving at the hotel, I was completely drenched and paraded my bike with the squish, squish, sound of my shoes echoing across the atrium. After signing in and getting directions from the desk clerk I proceeded to my room.

Sandpaper! That was the feeling in my hands upon removing my biking gloves. For the first time in my life I experienced a sensation totally unfamiliar to me. Rubbing my hands together, the sensation felt like two pieces of sandpaper were being raked across my palms. My hope was that this was only a temporary situation but I couldn't be sure since it had never happened to me prior to this time. An all-day soaking was foreign to my being. Fortunately, after drying out and warming up, the sensation slowly left my hands. Yet, it would not be the last time I experienced this feeling before the end of the trip.

Erie, PA was one of the scheduled rest days. It was a week ago in Champaign we enjoyed our last day of leisure. As was the case from the start, these days were a sorely needed respite from mile after mile of pedaling our machines.

My first impression of Erie was not exactly a positive one. It had nothing to do with the rain that welcomed me upon entering the city. I'm sure it has many redeeming qualities but my time spent there did not impress me. First, the streets are quite confusing as I traversed the town center. From a historical perspective, Erie has the distinction of being an important stop on the early canal system in this country. At least it has that going for it. That aside, it had an aura of a rusty old city needing a major renovation of the downtown area. It exemplified the "rust belt" image the upper Midwest had acquired by this time. A poster boy, if you will, of how older cities had not kept pace with the times.

Malls on the outskirts of Erie reflected the evolution as to how major cities in the U.S. transformed from a vibrant center to its edges. But unlike many cities whose downtowns had regressed into a useless vestige of what they once were, and were later transformed into viable entities, it appears to me the city planners made no attempt to upgrade, update, and rebuild Erie's downtown. Knowing the historical importance of this city, making these improvements would ensure Erie a more useful, relevant place which would preserve their rich tradition with its contributions to the history of America. After discussing my impressions with fellow riders, many of them concurred with this criticism and observation.

Our hotel in Erie was an old historical tenement called the Grand Hotel not to be confused with the beautiful Grand Hotel on Mackinaw Island situated in northern Michigan. Located in the middle of old downtown Erie it provided a source for fulfilling many of the needs of the long distance traveler. Eating establishments, drinking establishments, laundry establishments etc. were all within walking distance making it a great place to rest the bones before the final days of the ride.

As stated earlier, a routine for rest days had been well defined by this time. A thorough cleaning of my bike, oiling the chain, checking the tires for debris that would eventually lead to punctures, and preparing it for the days to follow had become part of my normal routine. Thinking back, I wish I would have started this routine before the ride began. Perhaps it would have led to fewer flat tires. But, regardless of the care one takes with their equipment, flat tires are inevitable. Like the horses of the old west, never ride them hard and put them away wet; same with a bicycle. Take care of it and it will take care of you. The result will almost certainly be positive. In a way, I have anthropomorphized a tangled piece of metal. It had attained a somewhat human element. Okay, not really, but I digress.

Dancing aficionados and drinking citizens met our group as we wandered about the streets the evening following our arrival in Erie. Adding to our excitement on this particular day it was having a downtown festival. After closing off the main "drag" merchandise vendor's tents were set up, a band stand was erected and people congregated in the street to revel in the festive atmosphere that was created. As it turned out, it was a highlight of our stay in Erie. Harry, Alec Ira, Karen (the posse) and I joined the festivities and party atmosphere.

I found it somewhat ironic that the "city of rust" tried to promote a positive event in the downtown area in an attempt to impress its residents so they could, indeed, become a cultural center. A beer tent had been erected and they even had what, in that part of the country, was referred to as a "corn hole" tournament. Most tailgaters at other festival events now refer to it as "bags" but Erie referred to the game thusly. How crude!

As the evening wore on, the music which I really enjoy, blues/jazz evolved into noise I find repulsive, i.e., rap and the ultra-loud New Age nonsense. It was quite clear when they started playing that drivel, it was time to retire to the hotel. "If it's too loud, you're too old" does not apply. More aptly, my motto is "if it's too loud…turn it down!" I guess the positive aspect was that since we had to continue our adventure the next day it was good our group left relatively early and did not consume vast quantities of "beverages"

Since most of my gear was soaked upon my arrival in Erie, many drying procedures had to be employed to make them available for the next leg of the trip. While it was easy to put the wet clothes in a dryer, the hardest item to dry were my shoes. However, a technique I developed and used prior to Erie was to put newspapers into the shoes and allow the papers to draw the moisture into them. It works. After letting them set overnight they would be dry enough to wear without the discomfort of having the socks and ultimately the feet wet for the entire day's ride. So, by the time we left Erie, even though my clothes and shoes were drenched when I arrived, they were perfectly dry and comfortable. Aha! That condition was quickly short lived. All in all, I was somewhat disappointed in the town of Erie. I was expecting a city with more of a historical presence and found none. Hopefully, at some point, the citizens will revisit the impact the city has had on the history of this country and revive the traditions that make it relevant.

Karen, Sue, Ira, Willie, and Magic Mike enjoying Erie PA

As a side note, while resting in Erie, I concocted a plan to wrangle an invitation to the Obama White House to perhaps spend a night in the Lincoln bedroom. Many rooms in the White House are, historically, set aside for visitors. Most users of these accommodations are political contributors who give vast sums of money to the election campaigns of whoever occupies the domicile. Since I do not have vast sums of money to give away I figured I would qualify as a poster boy for the greatness of America. Having ridden across the entire continent I, hopefully, assumed my logic would prevail and Obama's people would send me an invitation. Here are the reasons I listed on my blog with the hope a follower would pass it on President and he would feel obliged to invite me to the White House.

1. Riding across this great nation from LA to Boston, I have observed firsthand the positive nature of the people of this country in one of the deepest recessions since the Great Depressions of the 1930's. I could have been a spokesman representing the positive attitude of what was commonly perceived as "bad times"

2. As a retired teacher who has taught the history of America for 35 years, it would have been an honor to stay in the Lincoln bedroom from a historical perspective, befitting my profession as an extension of history.

3. I attended Obama's rally in Springfield, IL when he introduced Joe Biden as his vice presidential candidate.

4. Secretary of Transportation, Ray LaHood, is from my home district. So, my expectation was that Mr. LaHood should put in a good word.

5. Caterpillar is one of the most productive factories on the planet. It is located in the district. When the president visited Peoria IL to promote his recession recovery programs at the CAT plant, all local politicians greeted him.

6. And last, he was elected from Illinois and all us Illinois boys have to stick together.

As of the writing of this book I still have not heard from President Obama but I'm still waiting with baited breath and fingers crossed!!

Chapter 2

ERIE TO HAMBURG, NY

Our stay in Pennsylvania was short lived. Leaving Erie the next portion of the trip took us on a relatively easy 78 mile jaunt to Hamburg, New York. Although the wind was from the east, it was only 5-10 mph so for all intent and purpose it was a non-factor. For the first time in over a week we didn't have to contend with rain. Because rain was not a factor, the ride to Hamburg was very uneventful in terms of drama and turned out to be a pleasant experience. It was one of the better rides of the trip and I learned quite a deal about an area that was previously unbeknownst to me.

My first impression of the New York highways was extremely positive. The first sign that caught my attention after entering the state and the only one similar to it the entire trip said to "Share the Road."

Entering New York….very wide shoulders

As I found out later, new highway construction in this state required a minimum 6 foot shoulder. This is in contrast to Pennsylvania where the shoulder would often be no more than 8 inches across. A more relaxing ride was anticipated at this time and it would provide more opportunity to observe and photograph unique items we would come upon.

First of Share the Road signs entering New York…very welcomed

After leaving the corn, wheat and bean fields of the Midwest, western Pennsylvania and eastern New York are prolific with wineries. There are over 20 of these vineyards that permeate this region of the country. My experience involving wineries has been quite limited. Small ones can be found on the western side of Illinois near Nauvoo and other small ones in and around the Greater Peoria Area. Touring Napa Valley California in the seventies, I assumed it was the premier region of wine production in the United States. However, the area I was currently biking could compete favorably with any wine producing area in the United States. I may be showing my ignorance of the subject matter, but I consider these areas one of the big secrets to which most Americans are not privy, another discovery on my bike trip.

While the scenery couldn't compete with the mountains and desert of the Southwest, the ride to Hamburg, in addition to the wineries, was a mixture of woods and on occasion a glimpse of Lake Erie visible through the distant trees. I state this with the knowledge that judging scenery is very subjective and suggest this aspect of the ride is relative. Flat farm country followed by wooded areas intermingled with wineries can be a scenic wonder for those who do not commonly observe these phenomena.

Large vineyard in New York. Odd it's located near Walker Road!

Another familiar element to this area is that the environment is conducive to the production of honey and syrup. A second Sugar Shack on our route across America illustrated this point. Riding with Hank, we were made aware of a detour from our main trail by the staff prior to the beginning of the day. The owner was a delightful lady who was determined to make our stop memorable. In addition to letting Hank and I lift her in our arms for a picture near her business Smart Car, as the proprietor of the establishment, she provided us special prices on the honey, syrup and souvenirs in her shop.

Two macho men lifting owner of Sugar Shack

Again, because of the limitations of weight and space allowed in our travel bags, I was not able to purchase many items. However, I couldn't resist buying a jar of maple syrup as a gift to my wife, the lovely Veronica. At the end of the day, it was a most pleasant ride and still one of my favorites. I should have known it would be short-lived as the Yin/Yang of the universe must prevail!

As I recall events pertaining to riding a bicycle in rainy conditions I need to relate the persistent problems inherit to such an undertaking. First, for some reason, the amount of flat tires increases dramatically during wet weathe. I suppose it has something to do with the malleability of the rubber that softens and allows all type of debris to permeate the tire and puncture the tube. Even the Kevlar coated tires are subject to these phenomena.

The second major concern associated with riding in the rain involves the dangers associated with visibility, both by bicyclist and motorist. One of the most important responsibilities a biker must adhere to is to ensure uncompromising visibility. A constant visual identification of everything surrounding the rider is vital for safety. In addition, the rider must be seen, which requires a blinking red light behind the saddle. Yet, rain decreases the entire visual field for both biker and motorist.

Attempting to read a route map is difficult in the best of times but is especially problematic in a steady rain reflecting the third major problem associated with riding in precipitation. I discovered it prudent to have at least two direction sheets ensuring that the one not being used remains viable making it vital to successfully completing the day's ride. When rain was imminent I usually put one of the maps under the leg of my biking shorts. That seemed to solve the problem.

Other difficulties from riding in rain include, but certainly not limited to, less traction between the road and tires, complications regarding weather gear and deciding which eye protection to wear. The reader may wonder why I include this dissertation at this point. Due to all the complaining and bitching from earlier rides in the rain, none compared to the trek from Hamburg to Canandaigua, NY.

Chapter 3

HAMBURG TO CANANDIAGUA, NY

Canandaigua, NY was one of the most memorable of the entire trip due to its unique weather conditions. As I rated the most difficult rides, this 94 mile jaunt from Hamburg was the third most difficult behind Albuquerque to Santa Fe NM and Tucumcari to Dalhart, TX. A constant rain that began at the beginning of the day…. 7:30 AM to the end of the day around 3:00 PM was a situation I had not yet endured. Yes, there were the rainy days I lamented earlier, but none of them were an all-day event. Hard, heavy rains with periods of light rain followed by dry conditions were typical of what I had suffered up to this point. Not on this day. It started with a light drizzle, increased to a steady rain, then, at times, became the proverbial torrential downpour. Where is Noah's ark when you really need it? Floodlights to help increase vision would have been appropriate! (Ha, get it!!)

Riding began with me accompanying Hank and Sue in a light drizzle. About 20 miles later, and shortly before the first SAG, the rain became quite heavy. Visibility at times was limited to a few feet ahead of us. I grew concerned about Sue since she was third in our pace line. We were in relatively heavy automobile traffic and because of her low riding recumbent, the rain water became problematic. She made a very wise decision at the first SAG. It was, indeed, too dangerous for her to continue. Hank also deemed it too hazardous for him to continue. They both took the SAG wagon to the hotel for the evening. Neither was worried about EFI so it was a prudent judgment. It guaranteed they would be able to ride another day.

I, on the other hand, was not about to give up EFI this close to the end of the journey. It now became somewhat of an obsession. Did stupidity over rule common sense? Probably! But I was determined to give it my best shot. Having ridden it these types of conditions earlier, I just knew the rain would cease in intensity before the end of the day. Alas, the weather gods were in testing mode and unbeknownst to me at that time it would be a hard, all day event. Therefore, after the first SAG, I proceeded toward the day's goal by riding alone.

Having stated it many times previously, I enjoy riding "lone eagle" but I had also, by this time, become familiar with group riding protocol and was comfortable doing it. My sense was that riding alone under these conditions was more of a safety concern than riding with a group but it was what it was and I wasn't about to give up. Again, possible a foolish decision because I was determined to continue. EFI..BABY

Having ridden over 2,500 miles at this point, on the same vehicle, I was well attuned to the nuances of my Cannondale. Approximately 10 miles from the second SAG, I could feel my rear wheel was beginning to lose air pressure. Expecting I could make it to the SAG so I wouldn't have to change the tire in the rain, I charged onward. It is difficult enough in the best of conditions and particularly difficult in a heavy rain. Ahead I saw a fast food restaurant so I figured this would be a good place to at least give the tire a look. Maybe I was wrong. Perhaps it was just my imagination due to the constant struggle against the elements. I was hoping so. Approaching the counter at the eatery and perhaps because I looked like a drowned rat, the attendant was not very helpful and, indeed, somewhat rude when I asked to use the rest room facilities. "Yea, it's around the side" stated the hag as a look of disgust emanated from her icy stare. (Hope I'm not being too judgmental here….Ha!)

After checking my tire, it was, to my dismay, losing air. I had three choices. One, change the tube in the rain, two, put some CO2 into it and fill it up or three, continue riding hoping to make the SAG before it flatted entirely. Hoping I would be able to get to the stop in order to change the tire in dry, comfortable conditions out of the never ending wetness was my logical choice. Figuring I could make the SAG in about 40 minutes I decided on that course of action. And, the possibility of adding air with the CO2 may have resulted in a "blow out." High Ho Silver away. I was off.

Each mile seemed like it took forever and I could tell the tire was getting flatter, as the rain continued relentlessly. Finally reaching the town square and seeing the SAG in the distance I knew I had enough air in the tire to make it. The bad news is that if the tire were completely flat and I was riding on the rim before reaching the SAG and I had to walk, I would have to fix it and return to the place it flattened to honorably adhere to EFI. Sure, I could have walked it a few blocks and no one would know but that wasn't about to happen.

As I came around the square my rear tube was utterly flat. It was down to the rim of the wheel but fortunately I made it to the stop with no room to spare. Good fortune, once again, had smiled upon me. Even though the tube was completely flat, it did not ruin the rim, or the tire. Mac, who was very helpful found the rock that had worked its way through the tire causing the puncture. Our rule was it was useless to put in a new tube without finding what caused the puncture. It would flatten within minutes. Mac seemed to have an eagle eye for these things.

The SAG was a welcomed relief from the rain and I had the pleasure of meeting a cross country rider from the 2007 ride. Beverly, who lived in a nearby town, came to the SAG and greeted the 09 cyclists. She was a very sweet, charming young lady and oddly enough I would ride the East Coast with her two years later. She made it a yearly tradition to bring treats to the riders since her 07 journey, a welcomed respite from the rain.

Talking with other riders later, those who actually finished the days ride without SAGGING indicated there were 13 flat tires on this leg of the journey. This, once again, is an illustration of the negative impact wet roads have on bicycle tires.

After the final SAG, the trek to Canandaigua was relatively uneventful but the rain continued to fall. That meant I had no real opportunity to take pictures, enjoy the scenery or have a more relaxed attitude. I still needed to be ever vigilant for possible traffic problems. We had, during this portion of the trip, passed the 3,000 mile mark of the journey. A picture of that event was absolutely necessary and there was reliable Mac to do the honors.

Passing 3,000 mile mark

When I finally arrived at the hotel, once again, I was thoroughly drenched, and again my hands felt like sandpaper. From my previous experience in Erie, I knew this feeling would go away but it was unsettling nonetheless. The main difference between Canandaigua and Erie is that I had to get my gear dry before riding the following day. I looked for a laundry mat at the hotel but there was none to be found. Discovering the nearest one was a mile away at the mall; I packed my gear and started for the drying facility. Foiled again! The rain was still persistent so as I walked along I was getting as wet as when I rode that day. If I continued, my clothes would be as soaked as they were when I went to dry them, so I turned around and headed back to the hotel.

I often pride myself on my ability to find solutions to particular problems. One of my many mottos is "if life gives you lemons, make chicken salad". Okay I realize I am mixing my metaphors but one gets "kookie" after an endurance rain event.

To restate, here are the circumstances I needed to resolve. No laundry with dryers to address the problem of rain saturated clothes. Riding would begin in about 14 hours. Using the heating system in the room was the only viable option at this point. Therefore, I cranked up the heat thermostat in the room as high as it would allow. Strategically placing my wet socks, shorts, shirts and rain gear around the heating vents it looked very much like a Chinese laundry mat. With the door to the room wide open, the room temperature was reduced but it still allowed enough heat to dry my gear.

Seeing the ingenuity of my solution, Hank also placed his wet clothes around the room making it quite a scene. Resourcefulness is the calling card of long distance bikers. To this day, when Tracy recalls events of the 09 adventure, she will always mention this. As she tells it, when she walked down the hallway and looked into our room she had never seen anything like it. Here, Hank and I appeared all bare chest, muscles a blazin' with our biking gear everywhere to be seen. The impression was so dramatic that Tracy always associates me with that event. Good for her.

On a side note, I indicated to Hank that if "it rained tomorrow like it rained today, I would SAG into the next stop at Syracuse NY." There I go whining again and threatening to do something foolish. Hank later mentioned he knew I would ride even though I was disgusted with the weather. I was too close to finishing the ride EFI and it was now becoming a point of pride if not an obsession.

As miserable as the ride proved to be, our evening activities helped defray that negative experience. Hank had a friend, with whom he worked in the past, meet us at the hotel. Hank was kind enough to invite Tom and myself to an evening of fine dining thus avoiding the regular meal at one of the TGIF's. Not that that was a bad thing but variety is always a good thing. Being in the Five Finger lakes region in this part of New York, his friend was going to take us on a boat ride around the lakes. However, the inclement weather prohibited that from taking place so he gave us a brief tour of the city of Canandaigua and we proceeded to dine at a local Italian restaurant.

Again, it met our criteria of avoiding "chain" eateries whenever possible and, as we found out later, it was a place known to the locals as one of the best Italian restaurants in the area. Adding to the upbeat finish to the day, his friend picked up the check; against our minor protestations. Better news was we rode in his friend's car as opposed to walking to our destination; which was the norm for our trip.

After an enjoyable dinner and pleasant conversation with Hank and his friends, the end of the day turned out to be quite pleasurable. Hank's friend drove us back to the hotel and we proceeded to begin the process of resolving the conflict of preparing for bed while still keeping our biking gear in "drying" mode. Hank cleared his bed and was ready to retire. As was his usual method, he would hit the sack early knowing we would have to be up at first light the following morning.

By this time, our evening routine was pretty well established. Hank would turn in around seven or eight o'clock p.m. Starting the day's ride at usually no later than 7:30 AM we were always up by 5:50 AM. I still had not gotten used to a bed time that early so I would usually spend time with the other riders doing various activities. To avoid the misery and discomfort of the heated room I wondered around and found a place to purchase some "beverages." It wasn't long before Willie and Magic Mike joined me in the hotel lounge to finish the evening with festive conversation and drink. By the time I was ready to return to our room, most of my gear was dry enough for me to use the following morning. The yin and yang of the universe prevails.

As usual, Hank was in dreamland and I made every attempt to not disturb his slumber. Hank and I enjoyed a very symbiotic relationship based on respect and common interests. Oddly enough, neither Hank nor I ever needed to be awakened by an alarm clock or other devise of that nature. Both of us had an efficient internal clock that by 5:20 AM. we would both be wide awake anticipating the upcoming days ride.

Chapter 4

CANANDAIGUA TO SYRACUSE, NY

Five thirty, the morning following the Canandaigua ride, I looked out and sure enough there was a steady rainfall. I was somewhat disheartened but hoped it would end by the time we started the day's journey. After the usual established routine of bathroom, breakfast, bathroom, packing our bags, carrying bags to the foyer of the hotel and finally moving our bikes to the starting area, the rain had been reduced to a light drizzle. While I remained not especially pleased, at least it wasn't a downpour and the forecast indicated the rain would stop shortly. That was a relief because I had focused my mental attitude to riding another day in rainy conditions. The threat to SAG to the end of the day was, of course, just the normal bitching one does in the melancholy of the moment. But after the previous night's events, with my biking gear relatively dry, I had gotten my mojo back and was ready to take on whatever Mother Nature had in store for me.

After leaving Canandaigua, in route to Syracuse, NY, a mere 68 miles but with another headwind of 10-15 mph, as was Hank's usual practice, he and his friend from the previous night, headed out at a speed I deemed too swift for my comfort. Knowing this was his established pattern, I figured I would eventually catch up with him along the way as he usually slowed down toward the end of the day. So, once again I was lone eagle.

Cruising along at a leisurely pace, I saw Nancy with her bike resting along the side of the road. One of the worst things that can happen is a punctured tire at the beginning of the day's ride. That can be a real bummer, been there and done that. Stopping to lend assistance a bit of good fortune occurred. Tracy, in the company van, was passing and stopped to lend a hand. That made my support effort irrelevant. Tracy could change a tire in her sleep, and blindfolded, twice as fast I could giving my best effort. Plus, she had all the equipment Nancy would need to repair her bike in the van. Being the kind soul, I waited to see if they needed any further assistance.

Unfortunately, in her haste to get Nancy on the road, Tracy punctured the inner tube she had just installed so she had to redo the entire procedure. Now, I haven't seen Tracy really "pissed" very often, but I could tell she was not a "happy camper." Because of the difficulty of the situation I decided to hang around in case my aid was needed. Aha, coming up fast from behind was the posse. Having developed the habit of leaving last in the morning, taking their time to enjoy the remainder of the ride, they quickly arrived on the scene. Each member of the posse was quite capable of changing a flat so I decided my expertise was not needed and I headed down the road. By this time, Hank and his friend were well off into the distance so I reverted back to my old routine, lone eagle.

Northeastern United States is rife with historical features inherit to that region of the country. As opposed to most of the other areas I had ridden, a day doesn't pass in the Northeast without running into a fascinating part of American history. Like a kid in a candy store, I couldn't wait to actually ride my bicycle through this portion of the United States and looked forward to it even before the adventure had begun.

My first encounter on the way to Syracuse was a tour of Waterloo, NY. It had been established that the first Memorial Day celebration was started in this small village. Most people are unaware of this fact but the local folk are proud enough of it to put it on a sign as one enters the village.

Seneca Falls, NY, was the next historically significant town on my way to Syracuse. I often taught about the importance of this particular town during my tenure as a high school history teacher. In July of 1848 the first women's rights convention in the United States was convened here. Most impressive of the women who organized this event were Elizabeth Cady Stanton, Lucretia Mott, and, of course, Amelia Bloomer among others.

While I will not attempt to turn this into a historical review, it is worth mentioning these towns and villages in an attempt to illustrate the relevance these locations had to me as they relate to a retired history teacher. Teaching for 35 years on the subject of the events in and around this region of the country, and having never taken time to visit it, I was in awe of its historical significance.

Of course, the Seneca Falls convention was one of the major teaching points in the movement toward equal rights for women that culminated in the attempted passage of a women's rights amendment to the constitution. While it ultimately failed, women through various legislative procedures, and against the wishes of many of the male gender, have gotten and are still obtaining the equality they fully deserve. My stance was and still is that women should be given EQUAL RIGHTS not SPECIAL RIGHTS. This is often viewed as being "anti-women" but it certainly is not. In fact, when my students came to the realization of what equal rights meant, most concurred, especially, the females. But again I digress.

Because of time and logistic limitations I was not able to tour the Convention Museum but have put that into a list of places I need to return to at some future date.

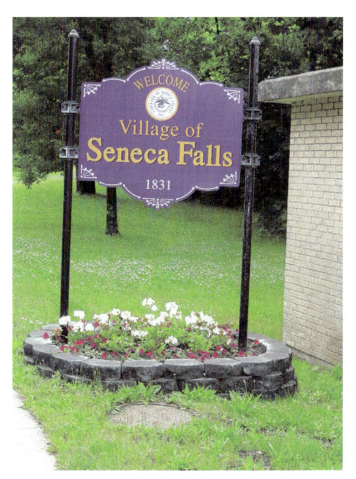

An homage to the woman's rights convention in Seneca Falls

The Erie Canal was the next special location along the route to Syracuse. It was under construction from 1817 to 1825 and opened as a link between the industrial East Coast states with the agricultural Midwest. Flowing from Albany NY to Buffalo NY., it provided a crucial link for transportation of goods between these two locations. In order to advance the cultural and economic development in the U.S. at this time, the Erie Canal was essential.

Most of the canal today is in disarray from negligence since a larger canal system using a lock and dam is currently being used. This newer system allows larger vessels to transport goods on the canals making the original system obsolete. But historical societies from communities bordering the area are making a valiant attempt to preserve what they can of the original canal. It lay directly on our route to Syracuse.

Because of the juxtaposition of the canals to our biking route I came across a station that offered a ride on the original Erie Canal. Of course, I was eager to ride in a boat along the original channel. As I mentioned earlier, I was riding alone at this time and when I came upon the park where the canal was situated, I decided to take the boat trip through history. Entering the pavilion where the boat ride originated, who should be there but Willie and George. They also stopped and we all decided to take the mile boat trek up the canal. While the vessel was not an original barge, it was a replica of the actual boats that were pulled by mules along tow paths.

During the ride, a member of the historical society gave a running oral history lesson of the canal past and present, as well as the renovation project designed to preserve it for future generations. At the southern end of the ride, we were allowed to de-board the craft and engage in a "walk about." Hiking along the tow path, I imagined what it was like during the heyday of the canal period of American history. Allowing us enough time to enjoy the sense of history and the aura of past endeavors we were encouraged to board the boat and return to the starting point. All in all, a delightful side trip of significance to add to the adventure of biking across America.

Original Erie Canal as it looks today

Visible in the picture, one can see the line of the tow path used by mules as they pulled the barges up and down these canals. Imagine the hustle and bustle of workers as they managed to transport goods along this waterway as well as keeping the mules on the paths. These channels exhibit a progressive engineering feat which added to the advancement of American society.

Also impressive, at least to me, is that I imagined the canals to be much wider than they actually are. Having seen many pictures in history text books, somehow they appeared more massive. Yet, in person they are not as they appear in the books. In any event, my experience suggests pictures never do justice to actually being there and seeing these places first hand.

"Mule" pulling boat on Erie Canal

Following the Erie Canal boat ride and refreshed from the time off the bike, Willie, George and I continued together on our way to Syracuse. Just before entering the city, we passed a small park with a lake and hundreds of people in attendance. It became obvious this was some sort of festive celebration, so once again we took a detour to discover its importance. Sure enough, on the small lake, hydroplane boat races were being held. In my neck of the woods, around the Peoria area on the upper and lower lakes of the Illinois River, there have been races of this type on occasion so it wasn't especially unique to me. However, Willie suggested he had never seen races of this type and was intrigued. We rode our bikes toward the water avoiding the human and auto traffic to the best of our abilities in order that Willie could take pictures of the event. Nearing the waterfront, we looked around and what to our surprise; George was nowhere to be seen.

It should be noted on the trek from the Erie Canal boat ride to the park on the outskirts of Syracuse, George suffered a flat tire. Instead of waiting for him to repair the puncture by locating the hole in the tube and applying a patch, as was George's way of fixing his flats, Willie gave him one of his spare tubes and we continued on our way.

After carefully scanning the crowd we couldn't find George. We figured he got lost in the multitude but he was a big boy and could find his way to the evenings stop. After Willie and I had viewed the races to our satisfaction we headed back to the main road. George was still nowhere to be found. However, as we approached the entrance to the park, there he was. He had gotten his second puncture of the day and was attempting to repair it.

What I found amusing about the whole situation was that poor George was once again trying to repair his inner tube the old fashion way. After removing the tube, in order to find where it was punctured, George was using a water puddle by a small tree to see where air bubbles emanated from the tube. Now, to be honest, I haven't used that method since I was a child. And, I certainly never used a water puddle in the middle of the road. As previously described, most of our group just replaces the tube and tosses the old ones away when we reach the hotel. Hopefully, the hotels did not send them to a landfill, rather, use one of the many recycling options available. Another of our riders, Ira, was the only other member of the group who would repair his own tubes but I was unaware that George did as well. Of course, their procedure was considerably cheaper and conserved resources, but it was far more expedient to just put in a new tube.

Upon viewing the situation, Willie and I were in total disbelief and somewhat amazed. We assumed George had been repairing his flat tires using this method the entire trip. Honestly, that is truly amazing on many levels not the least of which is that the modern patches for tubes are not very effective. In my experience, patching tubes with the new repair apparatus has never been as effective as just installing a new tube.

As we got nearer to the scene, an "old timer" gentleman was giving George advice on how to properly affix a patch to a hole in the tube. He told George he needed to "vulcanize" the rubber before adhering the patch. That idea comes from long, long ago when one would apply glue to the patches prior to placing it to the tube. Subsequent to placing the patch to the rubber, one would light the glue afire with a match to slightly melt the rubber and the patch would stick to the rubber more efficiently. While that was indeed the best way to fix a hole in the tube, it took considerably longer. I vividly remember doing this as a kid and because the newer repair kits no longer use glue, sticky patches are used to get the job done. Both Willie and I chuckled as we got closer to the scene and realized what was happening.

In order to save time and get back on the road, Willie offered George another of his spares. George was grateful for Willie's generosity and accepted his gift. Having replaced the old tube, we were once again on our way to the day's destination at a local hotel. Despite all of our distractions and stops, we arrived at the hotel around 3:00 pm leaving us plenty of time to relax and recuperate. While Syracuse is one of the bigger cities along the way on our crossing of America, it was rather unremarkable with no real adventure, drama, or other excitement worth mentioning.

Chapter 5

SYRACUSE TO LITTLE FALLS, NY

After an uneventful evening in Syracuse, we were up and ready to ride the next day to Little Falls NY. On this particular day, the weather was not an issue. The wind, while still in our face, was irrelevant and the company was enjoyable. A somewhat short 78 mile distance to the day's destination, I rode most of the time with Hank, Tom and Sue. As we were on the county roads it gave us a visual indication of how rural New Yorkers lived. Two observable images impressed me the most. First, similar to folks living on the back roads in Ohio, the pride which the homeowners had in their properties was evident by the way their lawns were attended. Nicely mowed, trimmed and tidied reflected this pride in ownership.

One thing that amused me to no end was when Hank would yell at those mowing their properties. Just like his attitude toward their Ohio brethren, who eschewed push mowers and its physical benefit, most used riding mowers and Hank would shout toward them "Hey! Your grass looks really great!" While the mowers were not aware of the mocking tone in his voice and gestures, they would always smile back and wave in a very friendly manner. What they were not aware of is that Hank considers mowing a waste of time, waste of resources and adds to the pollution problem of the planet. There's that California attitude rearing its head again. I cracked up every time he did this.

Another favorable impression of our ride into Little Falls was the magnificent homes built in these rural areas. Large metropolitan areas were a considerable distance from here and yet, even in this "backwoods" locale, people spent quite a sum of money on their houses. But, as a negative aspect to these fine homes, (yin/yang working again) the proximity of shacks that looked like they had been trucked in from the back hills of

Appalachia were evident. These dwellings were so downtrodden that the roofs were made of dirt and it was not uncommon to observe vegetation growing from them. The contrast was stark and immediate.

Biking through this area and observing the beautiful, well-kept homes sitting next to ramshackle properties, I couldn't help but ponder whether or not there were zoning ordinances. Houses with sod roofs could only draw down the value of the more expensive complexes. I concluded there couldn't have been any building restrictions and surmised it was because of the relative isolation of being a rural community that made zoning virtually nonexistent.

Our route into Little Falls followed the Mohawk River. Following along its path, the adjacent road was not difficult, no hill climbing or rough surface. Because it was located in a valley, it followed the confluence of the river making it a very easy ride. Weather and road conditions here were a welcomed relief to the severity of rides earlier in the week so it was quite a welcomed respite before the climbs through the mountains of the east that loomed in the distance.

Another one of the more notable observations on this ride was the many small towns we passed through established soon after the American Revolution. Along with its name, each of these small venues would put the date they were settled on the signs that greeted visitors. This would be the case as we continued into Massachusetts and Boston in particular.

After another rather unexceptional ride without the danger, adventure and drama of the previous two weeks, our arrival into Little Falls was a welcomed divergence from the large cities we visited in Ohio and New York. As a reminder of the early history of this area, Little Falls was, at one time, a hub of industry and commerce. Valuable rocks and minerals ingrained in the hills surrounding the city were mined and used to make it a commercial success. As a viable destination and because the Erie Canal had become antiquated and dysfunctional, the U.S. government built the largest, highest lock in the world in this location. It remains a functional instrument of travel by boat as it follows the Mohawk River. Several of our riding group took the time to tour this modern replacement piece of Americana.

Highest lift lock

After touring the lock many of us discovered a very unique, iconic antique shop. Perusing many of the items in the store, and to my utter horror, it occurred to me that what they were calling "antiques" were, in fact, artifacts that were common elements in the days of my youth! How discouraging. Toys I played with as a child were now "antiques."

Examples of these "antiques" included an eight ounce Coke bottle, metal noise makers that one would spin around to celebrate a special occasion, posters of my favorite movie stars, and, a personal favorite….. a poster of who would hopefully, one day, be my girlfriend; Rachel Welch. Okay, so there was never any chance she would be my girlfriend (actually I didn't do so badly anyway!) For one thing, even at that early age, she was too old for me and for another, yea! As if I would have a chance. But, a young boy could still dream!!

Anyway, it occurred to me as I was looking at the "old' objects, perhaps I too had become an antique since I could easily relate to these items as a bout of nostalgia set in. Oddly enough, my definition of an antique would be something from the 20's, 30s, and anything older, so I was somewhat aghast that items from the 60's and 70's now fit that definition.

Spending an enjoyable hour or so "shopping" without buying anything and enjoying a double decker ice cream from an old time scoop, I left content but saddened somewhat by the idea that I had become antiquated!

Since our ride to Little Falls, was so short, easy and uneventful we arrived in plenty of time to take in those sites previously mentioned. After our evening meal, I convinced Hank to take a walk up a small hill to the "downtown" section for a couple of beers before calling it a night. I was somewhat surprised because Hank was usually looking forward to his usual 8:00 bedtime but tonight he decided to humor me. As it turned out it was probably a big mistake.

Also, it should be mentioned at this point, the state of New York, like so many other states, had recently passed a no smoking ordinance in public spaces. That particular law had a dramatic affect on local businesses, especially taverns and bars, where smoking was the norm.

Hank and I along with a couple of the other riders, Willie and Chris, spied a local saloon and decided it was where we would waste some time. Sitting on an old fashioned bar stool and talking to the bar owner, Spike, we received incredible insight into how the no smoking ban affected the local pub business. As the owner, he informed us he would never have had to bartend himself prior to the smoking ban. Miners in the area, who made up the majority of his business, smoked. Since they couldn't smoke in these venues they had no reason to go to the bars. In fact, he had to lay off two of his workers because business had dropped off so dramatically. His cook and one of the waitresses were out of work because of the business decline. Cooking, waiting tables and working the bar fell on him. He informed us the only time he brought in a waitress was on the weekend. And, even with those reductions, he indicated, financially, he was barely able to stay open. Several other taverns in the area closed due to lack of business.

We concluded it was the "perfect storm" of the business downturn during this period of history. With the deep recession of 2008 continuing into 09 combined with the no smoking ban, the unintended consequences were that if people couldn't smoke, especially after losing their jobs, it had a huge negative impact on the tavern industry. That was true in the small community of Little Falls NY and establishments of that type across the entire country. Communicating and interacting with the locals, stated many times, as one of the primary objectives of this trip, was once again appreciated.

Yin and Yang, balance in the universe would once again prevail as the positives of our group's foray into downtown Little Falls was balanced with a negative of that visit. Still unable to discern its origin, either the food service at the hotel or our visit to the local drinking establishment, whatever the case, Hank and another of other riders incurred a very virulent case of food poisoning. The morning following our evening adventures, Hank was in such bad shape he was unable to ride and sagged to our next destination, Albany, NY. Actually, it affected him the rest of the trip. He was never up to the same energy level he exhibited before the food poisoning incident. We never really discovered the source of the bad food but it certainly had a negative impact on Hank and as we discovered later, Alec.

Chapter 6

LITTLE FALLS TO ALBANY, NY

Little Falls to Albany, NY was another of the more enjoyable rides of the trip. While it was a mere 69 miles and the wind was irrelevant in terms of direction and speed, the sense that the journey was soon to end began to permeate our thinking. With only three long rides ahead I decided to be sure to enjoy what remained of the experience. Route 5 was the designated road we followed to Albany. Riding beside the Mohawk River, the scenery changed from the gentle swishing of rushing water emanating from our right in combination with heavily wooded areas to our left into the green rolling hills of eastern New York. My mind's eye conjured up memories of the scenery from the movie "Sound of Music". "The Hills are Alive with the Sound of Music" LaLaLaLa............Ahhh I can still hear it now! Again I digress and this time into song mode!!

Becoming the norm which followed for most of the rest of our experience, especially in the historically significant eastern U.S., one highlight of this region was a stop at the National Kateri Shrine and Indian Museum. This particular museum exemplified how the European settlers were befriended by the natives of this area. After Christianizing the local Indian population, the Europeans eventually massacred them, and absconded with their land. But, isn't that pretty much the story of the Conflict of Cultures between white settlers and the indigenous population in this country. That is not necessarily a value judgment, rather an observation of what happens when two divergent cultures collide. This particular stop was another example of it.

Statue at National Kateri Shrine and Indian Museum

Portrayed as the smallest church in America, just outside Albany, I came across another of the places of interest during this section of the journey. Located in the middle of a small scum covered pond, this church claimed to be the smallest active church in America. Couples can still use this religious establishment to get married. My guess is that attendance was limited to just members of the actual wedding party. Non wedding party participants who wanted to be present at the actual ceremony would find it particularly difficult to find a seat and I'm sure ushers would have a hard time seating attendees according to the side, bride or groom, of preference. Throwing of rice and/or other debris at the bride and groom as they left the church would have also been problematic. Yet, couples overcome these difficulties to get married here. (It should be noted that the smallest church in America is, in fact, located in Georgia but I suspect the difference is the Georgia church does not have functionality in terms of participation. It's more of a showcase than one where actual religious ceremonies are preformed)

World's smallest church

Our stay in Albany was without any particular drama. Yet, somehow, members of the posse decided to take a trip to Niagara Falls. Harry rented an automobile and several of them made a day trip to one of the most popular tourist attractions in this part of the country. Hummm, I wonder why I wasn't invited. Perhaps they forgot. I, indeed, did inquire and they explained they didn't think I would be interested. In reconsideration, I probably would have declined but I doubt it. I can honestly say it really didn't bother me a bit that I was left out. Well, okay that was a lie. Going to see the Niagara Falls would have been icing on the cake for this particular day. Maybe someday I will get over it. Alright I'm over it!

Green Mountain range, White Mountain range, and the Hampshire mountains lie ahead as the last geological obstacles before the end of our transcontinental journey. In retrospect, those mountain ranges mirrored the first week of the ride crossing the Rocky Mountains in the Southwest. How appropriate that we will terminate the cross country adventure with two days of traversing mountains bordering the northern edge of the Appalachian Mountain range that divides eastern U.S. from the Ohio valley region. Why not finish the ride with a challenge?

Chapter 7

ALBANY TO BRATTLEBORO, VT

Gentle rolling hills faced us as the ride from Albany NY to Brattleboro Vermont began. Another irrelevant head wind (irrelevant in terms of its negative impact on us) and an array of weather conditions awaited this 86 mile jaunt. These foothills were the precursor to the mountains that awaited us. Since this was the first time I had ever been in this part of the country, especially Vermont, I was mightily impressed. I keep reminding people that the Northeast is the best kept secret as a place to visit or vacation in the entire country. I also remind them to not bother visiting these areas in the hope it will not be as overpopulated as many of the other touristy parts of the country. Let's keep it relatively pristine….. so stay away!

Scenery for the ride to Brattleboro was as magnificent as the Southwest except the mountains here were covered with greenery, and not as high. The ascents and descents were as steep and, at times, as long as those on the west coast, but it seemed much easier than Mingus or Yarnell. Of course, one could argue as riders we were in better shape physically which made the climbs seem easier. I guess I would agree with that but, nevertheless, it was as enjoyable an experience as any of the earlier rides. From the rolling foothills the landscape evolved into two major climbs. Once again I rode basically lone eagle as Hank was still not up to his usual energy level. Tom and Sue had already gotten an early start and I looked forward to riding alone.

After a couple of weeks of relatively flat ground the first major hurdle was a seven mile upward crawl that forced me into "granny gear" lasting at least three of the seven miles. Even at this late stage in the journey, and with considerable improvement in my ability to climb, the smallest gear was still needed to comfortably ascend degrees of this magnitude. Not to be forgotten, Mother Nature (sorry for the sexist remark, perhaps People Nature) let me know she can still be a formidable force. Trudging up the first severe grade, I was greeted with a rigorous headwind as a test of my resolve. It should be clear at this point that there would not be any obstacle, physical, mental or otherwise that would prevent me from finishing the ride into Boston EFI, so as the weather conditions worsened it only made me more determined to do so.

Reaching the pinnacle of the seven mile climb and looking forward to the downhill descent, a bucketing rain began to fall. At this time I was well aware that common sense trumped stupidity. Therefore, I knew I had to limit my speed to what was a safe descent rate. My normal "hell bent for leather" approach was immediately abandoned coming down the east side of the mountain. I felt from the beginning and continue to restate, the punishment of the climb should be rewarded by a fast, careless descent, but not on this day. Too close to the end to crash and burn. Therefore, I began to "feather" the brakes and ride in a safer, sane manner, much to my chagrin. Racing toward the base of the hill, I knew another climb awaited me.

Hogback Mountain was the second major climb of the ride to Brattleboro. Another 12-13 percent grade nearly five miles long was rewarded with a view from the summit that was utterly breathtaking. A relatively flat top with a rest area awaited my arrival. The rain had stopped, at least temporarily, revealing a magnificent panoramic view of Vermont as it blended into New Hampshire. One could see for more than a 100 miles from the small restaurant and lookout patio at the top.

View from the top of Hogback Mountain

Most of the ride through this part of the mountains followed a flowing stream about 20-30 feet wide. While the gently flowing creek might have had a name, I was unaware of it and felt no need to identify one. Feeling energetic, listening to the gurgling water racing past, riding on smooth road and totally enjoying the experience, I told myself I should stop and "frolic" in the stream. However, I decided against doing so because my mindset, at this time, was to finish the ride and rest for the following day. It soon dawned on me to eliminate this mindset, especially during the final days. I knew I would not regret it. Whatever I wanted to do during these final days was only going to enhance the experience.

Another impact of the ride was the knowledge that I was riding through the Green Mountains. As I rode, once again my mind reverted to historic images. Visualizing Ethan Allen and the Green Mountain boys planning for and staging their attack on Fort Ticonderoga during the American Revolution made the experience fascinating. I was keenly aware of this history and as I traversed Hogback Mountain I could only imagine the amount of expertise the little band of soldiers needed to be successful in their capture of this British fort. I was, indeed, mightily impressed. (Parenthetically, from a historical account, the fort was not particularly well guarded using only old British soldiers as well as those convalescing from earlier injuries to protect the weapons inside the fort. However, let's not diminish Allen and his boys' efforts and continue to image it as a battle of great importance.)

Peaking the top of Hogback Mountain, after what I considered a ride that was not as difficult as I had imagined it would be, two of our riders were awaiting my arrival. Willie and Sue greeted me and we enjoyed a short-lived breather before deciding to descend together. Unfortunately, as luck would have it, rain began as we took off. As usual, it started as a slight drizzle but the foreboding clouds coming over the top of the nearby peaks indicated we were in for another downpour. Remember, Sue rode the recumbent and usually sagged in these types of weather conditions. She was the first to leave the mountain top as the conditions worsened. Willie was on my wheel and I figured we would easily pass her. Yet, as the rain began to amplify, I reverted back to my "safe mode" style of descending. Because of her previous encounters with wet weather I determined Sue would easily be caught and passed. Ha! That was not going to happen.

After we began our descent, it wasn't until we were at the bottom of the mountain and the rain had subsided that we caught Sue. "Amazing, remarkable, surprising were the words that came to mind when we convened at the base. How she was able to maintain such a high speed in those adverse conditions on her recumbent stunned even me. I was thoroughly impressed. Thankfully, she didn't lose her balance on the slippery, dangerous road especially when I thought I might lose mine at any time.

Hank, who was still recovering from food poisoning, did not ride that day. Two other riders also lost EFI on this section of the ride. Chris, one of whom I referred to as a race horse, had developed a condition in his shin that did not permit him to ride the rest of the way to Boston. After discussing his condition at dinner that evening he indicated his shin had sustained a stress fracture. He had a difficult time putting pressure on his leg, sought medical attention, and was advised to discontinue riding to avoid permanent complications. Chris didn't ride the last two days but, at least, he was able to do the ceremonial 15 mile ride to Revere Beach on the last day.

Entering Vermont

When I finally arrived in Brattleboro, Hank was asleep in our room. He had made arrangements to have dinner with one of his former associates. This particular associate was going to ride with Hank the following day. I could tell Hank was really hurting because he hadn't gotten out of bed since his arrival earlier that afternoon. He certainly was in no position to join his friend for dinner or any other activities. I finally prodded Hank to at least go into the lobby and meet with his friend. After their conversation, he indicated he would not be riding the following day and asked if I would accompany the young man. I consented and informed him he could join me for any or all of the following days travel. Riding fast and hard was not my style. Knowing those parameters, if he chose to join me, he was welcomed. His friend was relieved because he had driven a long way, brought his bike and looked forward to the experience.

As we got to know each other, I discovered the young man, before going into sales, was a professional trainer with the Boston College sports programs. He, actually, was the individual who initially looked at

Chris' injury and made the determination he shouldn't continue riding. Wrapping Chris's leg allowed him to put minimum pressure on it without further injury but not to the extent he would be able to ride. No use risking further injury which may become permanent.

After a voluminous meal at a smorgasbord and enjoyable conversation with fellow riders, I returned to the hotel. Figuring I would see my family the following day and not wanting to burden them or have them wait for me while I washed my biking gear, I decided to launder my riding jerseys. What a good boy am I, I thought. Placing them in the closet I wanted them to be good and dry as I packed them for the final ride of the adventure. I was so proud of myself.

Chapter 8

BRATTLEBORO TO BOSTON, MA

Day 50-The final day of riding across the United States of America. Actually after viewing the map Tracy placed in the hotel lobby each evening, we hadn't ridden ACROSS the continent, rather we DIAGIONALIZED it. I'm not sure that is a word but that was, in fact, what we did. Like most of the rest of the riders, my reaction on the last day of riding a bicycle across the United States was one of mixed emotions. The excitement that permeated our group, as it would be the last long ride of the trip, was tempered with a bit of melancholy.

Packed and ready to go we set out for Burlington, MA a suburb of Boston. Greeted with a headwind of 10-15 mph, but at this point who's counting, and looking forward to the 91 mile jaunt, I began with Hank's friend in tow. Karma certainly was not going to allow us a languishing, casual stroll into Boston, rather it turned out be the most difficult since the rollers of Missouri. The first 50 miles rambled through the steep, hilly sections of the Hampshire Mountains. Then, as the terrain leveled out, the automobile traffic became problematic. Reiterating earlier statements concerning riding in traffic, I must again point out that auto traffic was the biggest issue for riding the roads for most of the cross country experience. In fact, I would suggest it was the biggest danger, regardless of the many days of inclement weather, mountainous climbs with no guard rails, harrowing descents, trash on the roads etc. Automobile and truck traffic were the most dangerous obstacles of all of the others combined.

Tom and I entering New Hampshire

Enduring ninety-one miles of hilly, mountainous riding through Vermont and New Hampshire the scenery was once again as awesome as any other on the trip. Trekking through the mountains, many at a 12-13% grade, can get very tiring, especially after biking over three thousand miles. Because the same stream I followed the prior morning was still flowing beside our pathway, I decided to stop and frolic in the stream.

Sue, Willie and Hank's friend, Mike, started the day riding with me but when I decided to stop and wade in the stream, only Sue had the courage to join this mini-adventure. To this day, if I hadn't have made this minor detour, I would still be regretting it.

Removing our shoes and leaving our bikes alongside the road, which was probably not a particularly good idea because of possible theft, off we went. As we followed the stream away from the road, we were rewarded with the discovery of a small waterfall. It made the stop even more worthwhile. Sloshing through the water brought back childhood memories. Good friend and neighbor Fred, whose family owned a cabin on the Vermillion River near St. Joseph in Illinois, would often invite me to join in their festivities. In addition to fishing, eating and general mischievous behavior we would remove our shoes to wade and "frolic" in the river. I can still feel the mud gushing through my toes. Given the dangers associated with this in terms of stepping on various objects that could do considerable damage to the feet, nevertheless, we had a great time. The good news is that I never injured my feet or got infections from any vermin present in the river.

With that memory vivid in my mind Sue and I enjoyed the wading and hiking along the stream. It remains as one of my favorite memories of the adventure.

"Frolicking in the stream on road to Burlington

After the short breather, we were back on the road to Burlington. Traversing the Hampshire Mountains we entered Massachusetts. From that point until the end of the journey, I was keenly aware of the historical importance of this section of the country.

Looking forward to, and knowing it was a short ride ahead, the towns of Lexington and Concord awaited with all their historical significance and charm. Approaching the outskirts of Lexington, an idea developed in my peculiar little brain. Riding around the square in Lexington, recalling Paul Revere's ride, and knowing it would be somewhat unseemly, I couldn't help but yell loud enough so that the tourists walking in the area could hear me "THE BRITISH ARE COMING, THE BRITISH ARE COMING." Many of the sightseers who heard the roar looked at me with a gaze of amusement and I suspect thought I was some kind of "wacko." Mostly true, but I had another motive. While it surely was a goofy thing to do, I made people aware that biking behind me were, in fact, three Brits. Magic Mike, Crazy Harry, and Mac, one of the support staff, are all of the British persuasion who were following me and would be in the area shortly. So, indeed, the British were coming! Now, I should note here, that my warning did not mean they needed to go to their cars, hotel rooms or homes and arm themselves. It was just a reenactment. No hostile action needed.

Bell tower on the famous Concord Square

Coming into the final SAG stop of the trip eagerly awaiting my arrival, were Hank and poor Alec. Alec, one of the posse, who up to this time was EFI, had curled up in the SAG wagon unable to do any physical activity. Our guess was food poisoning from the Little Falls stop finally got to him on the last day of the long ride. I spent extra time at the SAG taking pictures of one of my favorite staff personnel, Margaret, and conversing with many of the other riders who, like me, were in no hurry to arrive at the day's destination.

After the leisurely, extended stay, I finally began the last 30 miles of the trip. My thoughts were with Hank and Alec since I knew both, especially Alec would have done anything to be able to ride the last few miles into the day's destination in Brattleboro. Without any question in my mind, if Alec were remotely able to ride he would have done so but seeing him curled on the seat in the SAG wagon I knew he was not going to ride. And, because he lost EFI this late in the ride, his disappointment manifested itself on the last day as reflected in his attitude toward riding the final leg of the journey.

"Okay Champ, did you remove your gloves and wash your hands?"

Another one of the historical highlights of this part of the journey was the monument and statue of General Brattleboro for whom the road and town are named. This memorial was a tribute not only to the Revolutionary War veterans but also recognition of all who served in the U.S. Armed Forces. It was impressive and quite a tribute to that group of Americans.

The rest of the day's ride was relatively uneventful with no significant climbing or impressive headwinds to impede the last 30 miles. As Burlington came into view I was overwhelmed with the emotion that the end of an enormously significant accomplishment was coming to an end. When I arrived at the hotel, I was met by my family, Veronica, Christopher and Eric. We never forget the wonderful families who blessed our lives, but seeing them together as I approached the hotel...... well you can just imagine. I was at a loss for words.

Revere Beach was an eighteen mile jaunt from the hotel to the Atlantic Ocean. It would be much like the parade of bikers that started seven long weeks ago in Manhattan Beach. Thus our 3,415 mile adventure would finally end.

On the night of our arrival in Burlington, Tracy and the support staff provided a huge banquet to celebrate our accomplishment. All the families of the riders attended and it was a wonderful way to end 50 days of being a family of bicyclist enduring the positive and negative aspects of the journey. Tracy did an excellent job of sharing a story for each of the bicyclists. Her favorite memory of me was my response to the wet conditions following the ride from Hamburg to Canandaigua, NY which I described earlier. To this day that picture has burned itself into her memory so when I see her, that is the first thing she relates recalling our time together.

Another feature of the banquet was awarding various display items from the quest. Those items include the U.S. map showing our route across the country and signs showing the partial increments at the 1000, 2000 and 3000 mile marks.

The most coveted item was the U.S. map displayed each day in the hotel lobbies showing the distance we covered on that particular day. I still remember when we first saw it. Observing it in the lobby in LA it had no real significance or importance. Seeing it in the lobby in Riverside, CA we began to realize why it would eventually become a coveted item. It showed the "short" distance we covered on a particular day and as the journey continued the black line kept getting longer and longer. It was a reminder of where we began and where we ended each day but it also showed the great distance we had to cover to reach the Atlantic Ocean. Knowing these items were to be given to members of the group, we all wondered what criteria would be used to bequeath these items.

As the award presentation began, I knew I had accomplished nothing that would warrant one of the posters. I was sure others overcame more or accomplished more than me. My only thoughts were that whoever was given one these would be very grateful and treasure it forever.

As Tracy began commenting on the first poster to be awarded, she described an individual who had an accident, which included many of the group, was taken to the hospital in an ambulance bloodied and beaten, also several members of the group, and returned to the route rap session looking like a "refugee from a mash unit." She continued that that individual had no chance of riding the next day and what a pathetic picture this person portrayed coming into the hotel that night. Tracy continued "This individual was up at 6:00 AM the next morning testing his bike and his physical condition in the hotel parking lot." "The support crew who watched in disbelief was utterly dumbfounded. Other members of the group were also skeptical as to this individual's purpose and certainly his sanity."

All of a sudden, I realized she was referring to my accident in St. Joseph MO. Tracy continued to explain that this individual had shown "a lot of courage" and it was "inspirational" to the rest of the group. Calling me to the front of the banquet hall to award me the poster, I was, indeed, honored and still relish the memento. I had all the members of the group sign it and it has become one of my favorite vestiges of the ride. And yet, I have related the episode to many people on many occasions and concluded I do not necessarily view it as an inspirational feat, rather, a tribute to STUPIDITY! For all intent and purpose, I should have adhered to the doctor's prescription and taken time to let the injury heal. But, as I have stated quite often since the journey, I was still EFI at the time, and I was going to do my best to accomplish this objective.

I also remind inquirers, truth is told, if I were physically unable to ride after the accident, I would not have done so. That's why I was testing the leg the next morning. If the pain were intolerable I would have sagged until I could ride without pain. And, yes, I know the possibility of another accident and the risk of further injury, but…..well like I said….stupidity probably overruled reason.

269

"Inspirational" award given to me by Tracy

Day fifty began as a beautiful sunny, clear Boston morning. At last, a cloudless sky with a tailwind! Yes, by this time the superstition of not using the word "tailwind" because it might cause unfavorable winds was totally irrelevant. And, as it turned out it made no difference, as one could ascertain from earlier submissions, because the wind was mostly in our face during the crossing. But to keep with the Yin/Yang of the universe, there had to be a negative. Wearing our CrossRoads jerseys was suggested by Tracy as we traversed the final eighteen miles toward the Atlantic Ocean. Great idea. Getting prepared, I invoked my usual pre ride routine. Looking for my jersey, that I normally meticulously pack the morning after each ride, somehow I couldn't find the ones I had diligently laundered in Burlington, 90 miles in the opposite direction. Low and behold, I realized I left them in the hotel room closet to dry and had not packed them. Panicked, I figured I would wear my white, long sleeved cooling jersey. I wore it on most days under my regular jersey anyway. We called the hotel in Burlington and yes, they had found three jerseys in one of the rooms. Drats! There was no way I could drive back and get them so I had to have them mail the jerseys to my home in Washington.

Again, the pre ride routine continued as I filled my tires with air, checked for obstructions and got ready to ride. While engaged in this routine, I noticed that Alec was wearing his street clothes. I inquired as to why he wasn't suited up for the last leg of the trip. He explained he was still pissed he couldn't finish EFI so the last few miles were irrelevant. Making a serious attempt to persuade him to join the group, I finally realized he had his mind made up and would meet us at Revere Beach. What a bummer. Then I had an epiphany. If Alec were not going to ride, perhaps I could borrow his CrossRoads riding jersey. He not only encouraged me to wear it but also stated I could keep it if I wanted to do so. I could tell he was extremely "bummed" and on some level, I couldn't blame him.

Upon reflection there is no doubt I would have done the same thing. Obviously, I could not keep Alec's jersey because after the disappointment of not finishing EFI waned, he would realize it was still quite an accomplishment and would have regretted letting the jersey go. As a result, I was able to finish the ride with the rest of the group wearing a matching jersey.

On this last day, riding was a mirror of day one in Los Angles where we rode in a ceremonial two by two peloton to Huntington Beach and dipped our rear tire in the Pacific Ocean. Eighteen miles from the Atlantic Ocean marked the last stretch of the journey. The first fifteen miles we were to ride at our own leisure and meet at a predestined point, a church parking lot, about three miles from the ocean. Oddly enough, the entire group, racehorses, plows horses and Clydesdales, rode pretty much as one with no particular pre assigned order. In retrospect, I should have known that was going to happen as we had bonded into a very cohesive group and no one was eager to be the first to the ocean. Remember, it wasn't a race!

Arriving at the rendezvous point in a church parking lot, the entire support team had arranged to escort us to Revere Beach using the SAG vans and Tracy's rental van. While waiting for things to get organized, it was evident that we were anxious to finish the adventure. Giddy and eager, Ira "mooned" the entire group, a rather disgusting sight if truth be told. Tracy told us to pair up and we would be led by the two oldest members of the group, Hank and Nancy. After those two, the order was random so George and I paired up. Knowing it was the final day, final ride and last time we would see most of the group, a sense of elation was evident, yet with a hint of sadness realizing the end was near.

When we had reached Revere Beach, we all removed our shoes, carried our bicycles toward the ocean waters and dipped our front tires in the Atlantic Ocean.

Dipping front tire in Atlantic Ocean after 3,415 mile bike ride

What a feeling of accomplishment. Seven weeks ago, as eager "rookies," we dipped our rear tire into the Pacific Ocean and now as veteran long distance bikers, the journey ends. Many photographs were taken of ourselves, our comrades, and families as no one was quite ready to let the moment go.

Group at end of ride

Christopher, me and Eric on Beach

After long goodbyes, emotional reminiscences and promises to keep in touch, we all went our separate ways. My plans were to tour Boston historical sites with my family. What a wonderful end to an extraordinary experience. Los Angeles to Boston riding a bicycle Every Foot and Inch-EFI had been accomplished!

Chapter 9

THE RIDE SUMMARY

EFI BABY! Those two words were mentioned often by Harry who joined the five of us that were able to accomplish that feat.

Many objectives and goals were identified, as stated earlier and reiterated many times, prior to and during the trip. First and foremost was completing the entire ride across the country. If that meant sagging, taking a few days off, whatever, I was determined that this would be the number one priority.

Second was to experience the many historical sites I knew would be in my path. Museums, famous cities, iconic paths and trails, etc. awaited my arrival and I was eager to experience them.

Thirdly, was to engage people along the ride, locals, to get a sense of the attitude and personalities inherit to different sections of this great nation.

Other not so essential goals were established along the way to stay motivated. Not letting the posse catch me, improve my climbing ability, and learning proper group riding protocol are a few examples.

And, finally to do the entire ride EFI, Every Foot and Inch! Every Fantastic Inch

Realizing these goals, I knew would be difficult. As a microcosm of one's life journey, I recognized the means were more important than the end. That is, it was imperative to experience the adventure, embrace the positives and negatives and when all was said and done, enjoy a sense of triumph regardless of how many goals were or were not accomplished. And, what is most important is how one defines success. Success means more than just accomplishing one's goals. If, when all is said and done, a particular objective was not achieved, looking through the process and establishing that everything possible was attempted then, that in and of itself, defines success. I use the example that everyone cannot be number one in the class but if through the effort to achieve it the individual has done his best then that is a measure of success. All the people I had the pleasure of sharing the cross country biking experience accomplished their goal, biking across America.

As an added element to riding a bicycle across the United States of America many friends and family inquired numerous times about the experience. A theme developed from these queries. Questions about the difficulties of attempting a feat of this magnitude were numerous. Presentations to various groups around Illinois have evolved from an overview of a ride across the continent to a motivational presentation that encourages one to set goals, attempt to do one's best to accomplish them, know there will be obstacles along the way and understand that doing ones best is the ultimate measure of success. Therefore, I will address these inquiries in what I would consider most to least difficult.

Injuries. One of the most common questions pertained to what injuries were common to a 3,400 mile bicycle ride. From my observation, 100% of the bikers had some type of injury. My injuries will be addressed first. At the age of 61, it is evident that the body tends to break down faster and takes longer to recover than it did in my youth. That may come as a surprise to some but I really doubt it. Keenly aware of that fact, I will endeavor to describe the various physical ailments I overcame. Many have already been mentioned so, at this point I will recap.

Cramping was the first ailment I needed to address. Thinking I had trained and ridden sufficient miles in my pre-ride preparation, by the end of the first days ride to Riverside my calves experienced severe cramping. Many of the other riders had the same problem. Two solutions were presented to alleviate this malady. First, we began using a product known as Second Legs. This was to be taken the day before riding long distances. It was to help prevent the buildup of lactic acid in the muscles that leads to the cramping condition.

The second "cure" for cramping was magnesium sulfate as suggested by one of the more knowledgeable riders who had a chemistry background. However, I suspect the continued acclimation process to the prevailing conditions helped more than anything. In addition, riders needed to take an electrolyte supplement to ensure depletion of that chemical was minimal. Adverse effects of electrolyte depletion would lead to dehydration, cramping and a myriad of other woes which could possibly limit success in completing the trip.

Also, it was important to NOT take an excess of these supplements as this could lead to other negative reactions. Balancing these dietary additives was paramount to ensuring an equilibrium, not too few, not to many. Oddly enough it didn't take long to figure out how much the body needed.

My next injury came as I was carrying my bike down a set of steps at the hotel in Riverside, CA on the second day of the ride. Since I didn't use clips, my pedals have a "spikey" surface to reduce slipping and foot movement. After stepping down from the last step, the "spikey" pedal dug into the back of my calf near the Achilles tendon. It punctured the skin and began bleeding. Of course, I doctored it myself but it began swelling and stayed in that condition for the next several days. In addition to the pain involved, I was careful to not place it into a hot tub as the chemicals and bacteria prevalent in those structures could lead to infection. And, I wanted to be sure none of the other riders became infected. The bad news was I couldn't take advantage of the healing effects of the smoothing waters the hot tub provided which we all looked forward to after a particularly day of riding.

Probably the most common affliction besetting the group was seat rash. Even though we all trained prior to the ride and had our saddles broken in, the "keester" is not accustomed to continued riding day after day for 5-8 hours or longer. Virtually all the members who completed the entire journey were affected by it.

As for me, seat rash is one of the afflictions that I did not have to deal with. Thoroughly applying generous amounts of chamois butter prior to beginning the day and applying it at various times during the day helped me avoid the seat rash problem. My technique involved putting the butter on both skin and biking shorts. At each SAG stop, I would give another lavish application. As the ride progressed, I began wearing two pair of spandex biking shorts. This not only cushioned the saddle but ensured proper friction reduction.

Another possibility that kept me from the seat rash problem, and I suspect it was the most important factor at least in my case, was I ride a specialized saddle known as an Air Bunz. It is a weird looking device that adjusts to the riders "seat" bones in the pelvic region and has no elongated extension. While it looks funny and even ridiculous to some, after getting adjusted to its feel, it is the most comfortable saddle I have ever ridden.

Having an episode of what I commonly refer to as "numb nuts" many years ago, I decided I needed to make a choice. Find a saddle that eliminated this problem or give up biking. My neighbor, a pediatrician, would constantly remind me of the negative effects of riding a bicycle over long periods of time on the "private area."

Having read of this dilemma I began my research on the internet. Finding a saddle addressing the problem of constricting the perennial vein which adversely affects distance bikers was paramount. There appeared to be many products that address this particular condition on the market but the one that seemed to address the issue best was a product called the Air Bunz. I ordered one. The first generation consisted of two air filled bladders on either side of a metal bar constituting the seat area. Before each ride I needed to inflate the bladders to my own comfort level. I loved the seat but after a few years the support bar broke which made it useless. So, I looked to replace it but, unfortunately, the original Air Bunz Company no longer made ones with the fillable air bladders. Perhaps, the reason was because the bladders failed too often and were too expensive to replace on a regular basis. Whatever the problem, there were none to be found.

Perusing the Air Bunz webpage, the newer models incorporated the same physiological features without the bladders. I ordered one and after adjusting it to my personal seat dimensions I began the breaking in process. At first it felt really strange but after several adjustments I began getting used to it. The more I rode, the more comfortable it became and the seat addressed all my concerns regarding the potential for permanent impotence. Because of that particular seat, I feel it contributed to me being one of the few that did not encounter seat rash as we traversed the country.

Air Bunz seat….looks really weird

The severity of the seat rash problem effected many riders to the extent they needed to use medicated pads for several days in order to be able to ride in a relatively pain free mode. Other than complete rest, this was the only alternative for those afflicted with this condition.

Another common physical ailment involved the pain and numbness in the hands and fingers. Riding with weight forward on the handlebars, extreme pressure was exerted on our hands. Many attempts to minimize this problem were introduced. First, a cushioned tape wrap was applied to the handlebars. Secondly, seat heights were adjusted to relieve the angle of the down force on the handlebars and thirdly, adjusting one's hands often on the bars were used.

Another option used by a couple of the riders was aero-bars that allow one to rest on their forearms. In my situation it was not an option since both shoulders have suffered significant trauma through the years and aero-bars place substantial pressure on them. Yet, in my case as well as many of the other riders, Al and Alec especially, these precautions did not prevent the numbing effects we inevitably incurred.

After the first day and for almost two weeks afterward, by the end of the day, I could barely use my left hand and fingers. In fact, the second finger on my left hand next to the "pinkie" was totally useless. As I tried to type my blog, that finger would not function at all. My hope was it was a temporary condition and would clear up after the trip. But, I couldn't be certain. Nevertheless, it wasn't going to dissuade me from completing the adventure. In fact, it was several weeks after the journey was completed that it returned to full functionality. In retrospect, I'm confident that it would have become permanent at some time if I continued that particular activity.

My right hand suffered another "pressure" overuse condition. A small blood blister developed deep on the tendon or on the nerve under the meaty part of my hand near the thumb. It would get so painful that I had to adjust my hand position quite frequently. Even that wasn't enough. I needed a solution. And, as stated previously, that is one of the positive events about an undertaking such as this. Problems occurred and solutions were always available. My solution was to wear two pair of gloves. While this helped to some degree, I finally resolved to obtain a sponge, cut it in half and put both pieces under the hand portion of the glove nearest the skin. All of this cushioning allowed me to finish the ride albeit with some discomfort in the hands. I figured I would have to live with that affliction but after a few months it too disappeared.

On a side note, because it took so long to take off the gloves and sponges inserted to help alleviate the hand injury, I violated a major rule of the support staff at the SAG stops. They insisted, and properly so, that all riders remove gloves and wash hands with anti-septic soap before handling any of the snacks or drink items around the SAG area. Avoiding the transmission of bacteria or sickness to other riders was the reason for that rule. Great idea! But, later in the ride, I would often NOT follow this procedure.

One amusing incident illustrating the importance of adhering to the glove removal policy involved Magic Mike, probably the least offensive and non-violent individual on the trip (aside from me, of course! Ha!) His demeanor reflected an intelligent, passive personality. As stated earlier, basically due to laziness, removing the multi-layered hand protection would involve taking extra time, perhaps a minute or two. After arriving at one particular SAG stop in Ohio and engaging in the ritual signing of the roster, I took a piece of fruit from a bowl without following protocol. Standing beside me was Mike. Reacting instinctively, he smacked the fruit from my hand after noticing my gloves were still intact. His intent was not to hit me, rather, swat and miss, then indicate I should remove my glove as per instructions. He was as startled as I and immediately began to apologize profusely. From that point on I was sure to remove my gloves. Not because Mike smacked me, but I realized it was very arrogant on my part and particularly lazy to not follow a simple rule that ensured the health of the rest of the riders. My compromise was to remove the sponge and gloves from my right hand and wash it thoroughly before handling food. That seemed to placate everyone especially the support staff. Lesson learned!

Another rider afflicted with the hand numbing phenomena was Al. After reaching Flagstaff, AZ he took his bike into a local shop and had them adjust the height of the seat and the handlebars. This seemed to help somewhat but the hand numbing remained a problem the rest of the trip.

Alec, recall from the stomach flu incident, had three fingers on his left hand go numb and on the last day of the trip indicated his hope was that feeling would eventually come back into his hand. Like me, it took several months for Alec's fingers to get back their normal feeling. Thankfully we all regained the use of body parts negatively affected by a 3,400 mile bicycle ride. Even today, I still ride with two pairs of gloves and two pair of riding shorts.

In terms of additional injuries, personally, I have already described the accident in St Joseph, Mo. I was one of the fortunate ones to not have any other serious maladies. This could not be said for many in the group.

Dehydration was another of the physical problems encountered by many of the group. While this occurred early in the trip, especially crossing the Mojave Desert, incidents of this particular woe were vastly reduced by the end of the trip. We had all become acutely aware of the liquid needs of our own bodies. As a supported ride, none of the participants should have had a problem with dehydration but it wasn't until three of our people were taken to the emergency room following our traverse across the Mojave Desert that we no longer reached that stage. If you are thirsty, dehydration is the next stage. Drink plenty of liquids prior to getting thirsty and that alleviates the situation.

Hemorrhoids! It shouldn't come as a surprise that this would be a condition associated with long distance biking. Sitting normally for hours at a time in a chair can cause this. Now, try sitting on a bicycle saddle for hours at a time for days at a time. The surprising aspect is that it did not affect more riders than it did. But as related earlier, one rider in particular developed a severe case of hemorrhoids. Unnamed at this point to avoid embarrassing him, so, again, let's just call him Sid. But you know who you are! Sid's hemorrhoid condition became so severe that at one point he was taken to an emergency room in Pennsylvania to see if anything could be done. The ER doctor explained to Sid that if he removed the "roid" his riding would be over for the duration of the distance to Boston. Stating that the hemorrhoid could not be damaged any more than it already was, if he could tolerate the pain, he could continue to ride. And, that is exactly what he did. At the beginning of each day, he would push the extended section of the protruding intestine back into its proper position and begin the days ride. You talk about "crazy bikers".

"MOTHERFUCKER!" Now, as it turned out the person afflicted with this predicament, Sid, would become involved in an incident that everyone involved found highly humorous except, of course, Sid. On this particular day, I was riding with Tom and Sid. Protocol, when riding in a group, calls for the lead rider to invoke proper hand and verbal signals to ensure the safety of everyone in the pack. Whoever is in the lead position needs to warn those behind of obstructions and obstacles in the road. For example, if there were glass in the road the leader of the pack would yell "GLASS" and point to where the glass lay. This enabled trailing riders the opportunity to avoid running over the glass and possibly incurring a puncture. Another example; if there were a pot hole or crack in the pavement the leader shouted "HOLE"! and immediately point out the obstruction to warn trailing riders of this danger. It just so happened that "hemorrhoid Guy" Sid was leading our small three man pace line. All of a sudden, Sid did not see a pothole and thumped it square on. The shock of hitting it sent shivers of pain through his hemorrhoids emanating to every pain cell in his body. Following protocol, even in his painful state he shouted, (now I assume the only reason he shouted this was to warn us) MOTHERFUCKER!! Bob and I burst into uncontrolled laughter; to the extent I almost wrecked my bike. Our utter amusement was not because SID hit a pothole but his reaction was absolutely hilarious. He had broken protocol or perhaps established a new designation. From that point on, whenever we came near a pothole in the road, instead of yelling "HOLE", we shouted "MOTHERFUCKER" and pointed to the obstruction to warn trailing riders of the impending danger.

At first Sid was pissed at us for finding amusement in his painful condition but he soon realized it was nothing more than a gleeful reaction to his use of the term. Our intent was not to mock his condition, rather, nothing more than an instant reaction to his statement. He was quick to see our point of view and began to join us in our jocularity. Just another day traversing the United States of America on a bicycle. Parents, warn your innocent children to avoid the previous insert due to its foul language.

Nancy, one of our female riders, incurred a slightly sprained shoulder and road rash. Passing through town of Seneca Falls, NY, she had a run-in with the curb throwing her off her bike and causing the injury. Taken to the emergency room, after being treated and released, she took a few days off and began riding again toward the end of the journey. My reason for noting this is because, at the time, I was surprised there were not more incidents of this type. With all the obstacles on the roadways it seemed to me that hitting these bits and pieces would bring about more injuries like the one suffered by Nancy.

Potentially, the most serious of the injuries, excluding Tom's accident, was Chris' affliction. As one of the premier riders whom I identified as one of the racehorse group, given to riding hard and fast for miles at a time, he developed what would be diagnosed as a pressure fracture in the lower part of his leg. Because of the tremendous pressure he exerted on the leg day after day for over six weeks, his condition was such that he could barely walk on it let alone ride a bicycle. It was decided that if he continued biking, even backing off his usual style, it could have become a permanent condition. Chris had to forego any further riding for the duration of the trip and he expressed deep disappointment at this. But, as has been stated many times among our group, "Don't let stupidity override common sense." It isn't worth it.

Peter, another one of the racehorses complained of knee pain. He indicated that as often as he biked he had never encountered such pain. With my limited knowledge of sport injuries and having observed Peter's riding style I identified what I believed to be the cause of his injury. Following behind him for several miles I observed that when he rode without exceptional stress his leg motion was the traditional up and down with a symmetrical appearance. But, when he began to climb or increase his speed, his left knee would continue the up and down motion and his right knee, the one with the pain, developed a whipping motion.

That is, on the up stroke, he would toe out slightly in his clips. As it reached the apex he would whip it back into place with considerable pressure on the down stroke. Because the knee pointed away from the bike then suddenly whipped straight down as he finished the stroke, it put incredible pressure on the medial ligaments of the knee. That is where he indicated he had the issue. Obviously this was his normal riding style but after 6 weeks of that kind of constant pressure with all the riding we endured, it finally became problematic. Following the ride, I suspect, his knee was not permanently affected and he is back to his normal riding pattern.

These are most of the injuries that our group endured on the cross country ride. I'm sure I didn't cover many of the smaller difficulties such as short term colds, extreme hangovers, or even constant fatigue but those previously presented were the major ones.

Chapter 10

THE EXPERIENCE

Since I covered some of the negatives involved riding a bicycle 3,400 miles, I will now examine what was one of the truly outstanding features involved riding across the United States. In terms of accomplishing goals established at the beginning of the adventure, without question, it was important to engage in and interact with the many wonderful people I encountered along the way. This list of people not only included the riders, those of our group, but those interesting people we met as we crossed this great nation. I cannot remember anyone who acted derisively, auto occupants excluded, toward our group, especially when they found out what we were trying to accomplish.

Riverside, CA our first stop along the way, was where I met the first individual that stood out as memorable. After many of our group finished placing our wet riding gear around the pool area at the hotel to be dried by the sun, a male, Steve, in his late 20's to early 30's emerged from his room and began looking at all the biking clothes with a puzzled look on his face. Wandering around the area, he finally approached one of our riders and inquired "So, what is with all this biking gear?" After informing him we had just left LA and were going to ride to Boston his expression changed to one of respect. For the first of many times I would hear this expression during the journey, he continued "Wow, that's amazing. I would love to do that sometime. I think I could do it." This statement followed his observation that many of the bikers were somewhat older than one would expect to be engaging in such a grueling undertaking.

Upon further observation, I was somewhat amused by his statement considering he made it after blowing a stream of smoke from his lungs following a long inhale of the cigarette he was holding in his hand. Trust me, I know there are many people who ride a bike and smoke. Many have done and continue to do so, but any distance biker knows they need as much lung capacity as possible and, of course, smoking diminishes that ability. I couldn't help but think…. good for him that he thinks he can and would like to do it at some point. Perhaps we were the inspiration he needed to discontinue that nasty, filthy habit called smoking. And yes, that is, indeed, being judgmental.

The next memorable encounter that comes to mind is the couple I met in the middle of the Mojave Desert in New Mexico. Our SAG stop was basically in the middle of nowhere on Route 66. Nearby, where the staff and van were stationed, was a picnic table under a canopy. However, our stopping point was in the sun about 100 yards from the table. While refreshing my quickly dehydrating body with fluids and energy bars, I could see a group of motorcyclists in the distance. There appeared to be about 9 or 10 of them. As they approached, it was obvious they were a group of Mexican bikers and they looked like trouble. Sleeveless shirts with massively, tattooed arms bulging from them, bandannas instead of helmets covering their cabezas and a surly scowl on their faces was the picture they presented as they stopped at the picnic table. Indeed, they looked menacing. Gang colors and their headwear reflected the stereotypical "gang" impression….. to be avoided at all costs. There was a good possibility our adventure would be over before it really started.

True to my nature, always inquisitive and maybe somewhat naïve, I decided to approach them and engage in civil conversation. I mean, here were are in the middle of the Mojave Desert with nothing around except miles and miles of desolate sand and what were we engaged in?…riding bicycles. I'm sure they were quite curious as to why we were doing this in such an inhospitable environment. We almost certainly looked as strange to them as they did to us.

Closing the distance between our two groups, I could tell even though they appeared rough and surly, they had women riding in the "bitch seat" who were of the more mature nature. The closer I got to them, the less intimidating they appeared. Arriving at the picnic table with my bike in tow, I approached who I determined was the leader of this group. I asked "Hey, I will trade my bicycle even up for your Harley." That cracked him up and also cracked the ice. He, his woman and the rest of the bikers broke out in laughter and we soon became quick and fast friends. Inquiring as to what I was doing in this God forsaken area riding a bicycle, they were mightily impressed with the response. "We left LA two weeks ago and are on our way to Boston." They appeared dumbfounded with looks of delight and admiration.

"You mean you rode your fuckin' bikes all the way from Los Angles? That's California, right?" "Man, now that's what I call crazy." (That's the second most common reaction when people learn of our trip.)

Following this exchange, they introduced themselves and insisted on taking pictures. Obviously I wasn't about to refuse! Ben and Delha, became my new best friends. After the pictures were finished we had a pleasant conversation and soon thereafter I indicated I needed to get moving. It should be mentioned that none of the others in our biking group joined us. I suspect I know the reason but nothing ventured, nothing gained. The lesson here became quite clear.

Judgment of others shouldn't ever occur because of appearances and stereotypes. While I'm not opposed to judging someone based on attitude and actions, I need to apply a better criterion. Another lesson learned.

The following picture of me and my new "besties" was taken by another of their biking crew. This individual obviously had no knowledge of lighting as it applies to a photograph. It wasn't until later that day when I realized the light in the background shaded their faces but that was the best picture I could get. However, that in no way diminished the fun I had meeting and talking with those folks.

Me with new friends Ben and Delha

Guymon, Ok was the shortest ride of the experience, 37 miles. Because of its short duration we all rode at a relatively leisurely pace. Arriving in Guymon around noon, a group of us stopped for lunch at a quickie hamburger joint, the Burger Barn. As the five of us entered the restaurant, we stood out like sore thumbs. After placing our order, the owner, Stan noticed our unusual clothes, biking spandex, jerseys, gloves, etc. and inquired into our business. After informing him we were in the process of biking across the United States, he insisted we have a photo taken with him. His objective was to place the picture in his establishment along with other famous people who had visited this place. It was an honor to oblige him and to this day our picture still remains on the wall at the Burger Barn restaurant in Guymon, Oklahoma. So, in the world famous Burger Barn in Guymon is a picture of our gang hanging on the wall. Thankfully it's not on the local Post Office wanted wall!

Hooker OK. As described earlier the "Hookers" at the souvenir shop remain as one of my favorite memories of people of a particular area. Their ability to have fun with the village name and a willingness to share their stories and history was reflected throughout the entire experience.

Without question, the absolute highlight of my interaction with locals occurred in the town of Maysville, MO. Recall this was on the day following my accident in St. Joseph.

Many people come to mind as I traversed the country, as mentioned previously, and there were many others who were memorable. Nameless people who helped direct us when we were lost, servers in the numerous eating establishments, and casual acquaintances with whom we exchanged pleasantries, added to the positive nature of the trip as well as fulfilling one of my primary objectives.

Chapter 11

OBSERVATIONS

The learning experience. From a philosophical perspective, I had never entertained the idea the journey was an epiphany invoking experience in terms of an introspective life changing event. That is, from my view, it was one of the many life experiences that are part of my being. As a microcosm of how living is played out in this existence, I increased my understanding of how life skills are reflected in our character. In some cases, this experience reinforced my knowledge base. Establishing a set of goals and achieving them was important. Along with this, knowing there would be obstacles to impede me from achieving these goals would be part of the effort. Reiterating a very important point; success would not always be measured by meeting various objectives, rather, doing ones best to do so. No excuses for quitting, only reasons after all avenues have been exhausted, would be accepted.

Why was this important? As a teacher/coach for 35 years that is the one point I stressed to over 10,000 young people I had the privilege of tutoring. Do your best, work to your potential, never quit, and strive for success. These were more than just empty epitaphs, rather, a path for success in life in general. Since I had more than 400 people follow my blog each day, if, at any time, I did not strive to accomplish my goals, all those years of emphasizing these values would have been irrelevant. I was not about to let that happen. Talk the talk, walk the walk.

One of the first instances of self-discovery was that even though I felt I had trained sufficiently for the ride across the country, it became apparent, early on, I had not. Riding in relatively flat terrain on my training outings, even though I put in thousands of miles, became my biggest liability.

Assuming the mountains would present a problem was, indeed, a fact. With my pre-trip venture into the mountains of Arizona I knew I would be able to navigate them but because of the number and degree of incline, they were a struggle. While they were not intimidating to the extent it would stop me from completing my journey, especially early on, they were enough of a challenge to the degree it reduced the fun factor. If I ever attempted this a second time, I would be sure to use the existing hills and valleys in the Tazewell county area. Although their length does not compare to the mountains of the west or east, a daily ride up the steepest slopes in the area would have particularly helpful. On occasion I rode up the McCluggage Bridge hill and the Route 116 hill heading into Germantown Hills and Metamora, both a 10% incline. It would have prepared me better if I used these routes more often.

In addition, looking back, a good test would have been the curvaceous road leading up the hillside across the river, Grand View Drive. Its distance is less than a mile but it does recreate the switchback drives similar to Mt. Mingus and others along the Rocky Mountain range or the eastern mountains. Even riding in southern Illinois along route 51 south of Carbondale provided many hills of some length, but none compared to the mountains.

Another important factor I learned from this experience about myself, even though my life experience dictated I had already faced it, was I did have the intestinal fortitude to do something as hard as riding a bike across the United States. Were there times I wanted to quit? Of course. Were there days I complained about conditions? Obviously. I certainly do not begrudge those who would take days off and they were for all legitimate reasons. It didn't take long for me to realize that complaining never changed one thing. Even if I had not accomplished EFI, the quest would still have been successful.

Sociological aspect of the journey. Fascinating to me was the way groups formed during this event. I had seen this over time in many social situations and during the cross country ride this phenomenon developed rapidly. The formation of groups was based on various criteria. I have always been one to try to avoid being associated with one particular group. Rubbing elbows with "highbrows" as well as having friends "in low places" was my standard operating procedure. For our riders, the first groups formed based on riding abilities. Later, other groups formed from a common interest in other life experiences. For example, Hank and I got along famously because he had a very high interest in history. While his background was in the business community, history was always important to him, but everyone can't be a history teacher. Or maybe so!! Plow horses, racehorses and Clydesdales have been mentioned previously as examples of the Sociology of the group. These types of behavior have always intrigued me.

Food consumption-Many people have inquired about what I ate, how many calories I consumed and if I lost weight. I tried to consume between 4,000 and 5,000 calories per day. Even at that rate I still managed to lose 10 pounds with the expectation I would lose none. I would start the day with a big breakfast. It would usually consist of a waffle or pancakes, cereal, a muffin, fruit, eggs and bacon or sausage. On the rides at SAG stops I would consume energy gel, bars, fruit and an assortment of goodies Margaret and Mac provided. I seldom ate big meals while riding. Several of the riders were able to do so. Recovery foods at the end of the ride included chocolate milk and occasionally a stop at a Dairy Queen.

Dinner consisted of eating anything and everything. Pasta was a favorite in addition to other high carb foods and plenty of them. After the ride if I continued that amount of calories consumption I would soon look like Jabba the Hut. Fortunately soon after the ride I cut back to my regular eating habits.

Other observations- Trying to not offend anyone's religiosity I pontificated from time and to time on the concept of balance in the universe that affects the human condition. This philosophy has been identified in various cultures throughout human history. Ancient Sumerian religions especially Zoroastrianism, Egyptian Maat, and many Eastern religious beliefs have expounded extensively on this subject. I am now and have been a firm believer in this notion. And, I applied it throughout the cross country adventure. With excruciating uphill climbs were exhilarating down hills, rainy overcast days were relieved by beautiful sunny days, self-imposed depression was relieved by joyful anticipation of what was to come and on and on.

As part of this, Karma played an important role. Good deeds were rewarded and inappropriate actions were punished. Adopting these philosophies, in my view, helped me enjoy the experience much more knowing the tough times would not last and to enjoy and look forward to the future. This was the underlying force that contributed to me achieving EFI.

Many would question this attitude in terms of the wind direction which, from the account, was blowing against us for the major part of the ride. Doesn't this negate the balance thing? Not so fast Buddha breath.

The year after the ride I engaged in a biking adventure from Portland Maine to Daytona Beach, Florida with many of the '09 riders. This 1,700 mile trek had a favorable wind almost every day. So there!!

Those viewpoints, of course, are not adverse to Christian philosophy. As bad as things may have appeared, I knew in my soul that God would not present any obstacle I would not be able to overcome. Those who do not believe in guardian angels need to explain how I was able to overcome those potential ride ending episodes which presented themselves throughout the journey. For the more pragmatic that would dismiss this assertion with science, logic and reason, this is my story and I'm sticking to it. And yes, I just evolved from historic observations to religious pontification.

Chapter 12

Post Ride

After finishing the cross country adventure I was asked by the director of the public library in Washington, Pam Tomka. to do presentations to various groups about this experience. I had no intention of presenting one but when asked repeatedly by the Children's Librarian (my wife) I consented. My intent was to describe the experience through a power point production in conjunction with photos. While I was concerned with the idea it would be perceived as me wanting to talk about myself I quickly indicated it was not about me.

Two presentations evolved from the original. First was a 45-60 minute display. The second was a short presentation followed by a video that was produced by good friends and photographers, Rich Burk and Kevin May. It was 20-30 minutes combined with video. The major difference, other than the time exception, is my power point had many scenes while the video displays many of the people in our group.

To make my presentation relevant, I adapted it to the various groups requesting the program. Historical societies, retirement groups, Kiwanis Clubs, Boy Scout groups, city council meetings, Sierra Club, and school classrooms are the groups that primarily called for the program.

Without going into much detail, each presentation starts with the three most common statements people make when they discover I have ridden across the country. First, "Wow, that's amazing." I mention I do not disagree with that. Second is "You must be crazy." Again, I do not disagree with that statement but not to the extent I need meds. "Boy, I could never do that!" is the third most common comment. That is the one I take exception to and disagree with vehemently, especially when it comes from young people. Because of the last statement, my classroom presentation has evolved into a motivational presentation. If I could do it, anyone can. From this introduction I delve into the experience and leave at least 10 minutes for questions. Even though I begin the presentation with specific facts about the trip, often questions regarding those same facts still are asked. How long did it take? What kind of bike did you ride? How much did your bike cost? are the most common.

Yet, the difference in the age of the audiences give rise to a question from young people that the more mature groups are too polite to ask. "How old are you?" is always asked by the youngsters. I suspect I know why they make this inquiry. Perhaps they are thinking "How can someone as old as him do something so difficult?" Because of that thinking my tried and true response is "As old as I am, I was able to set goals, strive to accomplish those goals and whatever the outcome know I did my best." My hope is this attitude, from a perceived "geezer," inspires young people to do the same.

Another common query is if I would ever ride across the country again and/or what am I planning for my next big ride. In answer to each inquiry, my first declaration is, "having already ridden the distance, that goal has been accomplished." Yet, if I were ever to do it again, it would be to do it without the group assistance." I would do it alone. The ole "lone eagle" thing again. That would involve a different kind of planning along with more energy, effort and time.

To conclude, at the beginning of the ride at the first meeting with the group, in Huntington Beach, CA Tracy read a quote by Teddy Roosevelt that pretty much sums up the experience of setting goals, knowing accomplishing them will be difficult and doing one's best to do so.

"Far better it is to dare mighty things, win glorious triumphs, though checkered by failure, than to take rank with those poor spirits who neither enjoy much nor suffer much because they live in that gray twilight that knows neither victory nor defeat."

EFI, BABY!!

Prologue

Since finishing the cross country ride I have ridden the East Coast from Portland, Maine to Daytona Beach, Florida. Tracy and the Cross Roads company provided the support for that ride. Nine of the riders from the cross country trip were also on that trip. Seventeen hundred miles was the distance and keeping with the yin/yang concept, as mentioned previously, we had a tailwind virtually the entire distance. Many of the Sociological practices of grouping by riding ability, previous associations and other common interest were evident. I still ride between 5,000 and 6,000 miles per year and just recently rode 10,000 miles in one year. I suspect that will decline the older I get. Riding the Great Alaska Highway is certainly on my radar as a ride and while it may be farfetched, riding the length of Africa is something I find intriguing. Regardless of age, as long as my health is good and I haven't been run over by maniacal motorists, I will continue my biking experiences.

Essential statistics of the ride

1. Total riding distance-3415 miles

2. Average daily ride-85 miles

3. 45 actual riding days-5 rest days=50 total days

4. Shortest ride-38 miles Guymon, Ok - Liberal Kansas

5. Longest ride 115 miles-Blythe, CA to Wittenberg, AZ.

6. Hardest ride (for me at least) Tucumcari, NM to Dalhart, TX.

7. Crossed 15 state lines

8. Crossed 3 deserts-Mohave, Sonora, Painted Desert
9. Mountains traversed-Rockies…Appalachian Range-Green Mountains, White Mountains, New Hampshire

10. Roads Used-Interstate Highways, 25 and 40 (Arizona, New Mexico) State Roads, County Roads

11. Total flat tires (punctures) Me-14 everyone else at least 3

Advice for doing future Cross Country Rides

1. Train, Train, Train…all terrains, all weather conditions.

2. Don't take stuff you don't need. At a minimum, all you really need, in addition to articles you will carry on your bicycle, is: bike shorts (2), jersey (2), bike socks (2 pair), arm coolers, street shorts (2), street shirt (2), windbreaker, sandals or Crocs, a toothbrush and maybe deodorant

3. Take a cell phone that is capable of receiving signals from remote locations

4. Begin a diary or Blog and up-date it daily

5. Take a good digital camera or bike cam.

6. Buy a good quality road bike from a professional bike shop and get a bike fitting from a professional bike shop. Pay special attention to the five points where you come in contact with your bike: bottom, feet, and hands.

7. Rain gear is essential. You will get wet

8. Buy good quality shoes, padded shorts, and padded bike gloves.

9. Use tire liners; gatorskins or armadillo tires won't protect you from getting flats caused by wires on freeway shoulders.

10. A bandana is handy. It keeps the sun off your neck and can be moistened for cooling.

11. Use a "head sweat," or bring a bicycle cap to wear under your helmet. The visor helps keep the sun off your face and the rain off your glasses.

15. Chamois butter is not optional! Use it.

Riders completing the journey

Nancy-good rider-steady-an inspiration to women who do not believe they are
capable of doing this kind of physical activity regardless of age.

Ira-excellent rider rode with the posse, genuinely good guy, talkative
Alec, excellent rider as well as person, posse sweep

Karen- excellent rider, always positive, navigator for the posse, sweet, kind

Harry- excellent rider, wild man, leader of the posse, made the ride fun and
exciting, from Liverpool England and taught me proper spanner use

Peter, excellent rider, taught me that to be annoyed is preferable to being pissed off! Another good guy who sometimes reminded me of the Pope

Al, excellent rider, charger, improved daily, competitive

Jim-Excellent rider, sharp and very knowledgeable-relied on him for weather
information. Sue who rode the recumbent. Excellent bicyclist

George-Good rider but could bike with the those who rode fast if he desired to do so, steady, very patient and positive-rode with a pace that pleased himself

Michael-free spirit, do your own thing, very independent, third cross country trip

Willie-excellent rider, visited fire station at every town to raise money
for his cause, very positive, follow your passion baby!

Bob and Tom

Bob-Tom Both excellent riders, but when they wanted to, they could ride with the best. I was honored to ride with them because of their safety techniques.

Chris, excellent rider, injured near end of ride-impressive cognitive abilities,

Hank, "one speed" not too fast, not too slow, excellent climber, my roommate for 7 weeks, an outstanding individual, an honor to call him friend. A true Superman!

Support Staff

Super Mechanic Rick

Support staff member Mac

Third member of support staff-Margaret picture with knife near end of trip

Tracy-One of the most dedicated, positive, professional, organized people I have
ever had the pleasure of knowing. Awesome lady, you are the Champ

Tom-excellent rider and provided encouragement for the riders, great to have him on the team. Also, it was a pleasure meeting his wife Robin. Two wonderful people.

About the Author

History teacher for 35 years and department chair. Began biking in 1996 following knee surgery. Since beginning my biking experience in June of 1996 I will have ridden 100,000 miles. Following retirement in 2009 I decided to ride across America on a bicycle. From teaching history to visiting those places in person, the ride turned into quite an adventure. From meeting all the great people along the way to the beautiful scenery that can only be experienced from a bike, and visiting historical sites, the ride was an experience of a lifetime.

CPSIA information can be obtained
at www.ICGtesting.com
Printed in the USA
LVOW01s2231310516

490679LV00005B/6/P